Passive House Details

Passive House Details introduces the concepts, principles, and design processes of building ultralow-energy buildings. The objective of this book is to provide design goals, research, analysis, systems, details, and inspiring images of some of the most energy-efficient, carbon-neutral, healthy, and satisfying buildings currently built in the region. Other topics included: heat transfer, moisture management, performance targets, and climatic zones. Illustrated with more than 375 color images, the book is a visual catalog of construction details, materials, and systems drawn from projects contributed from forty firms. Fourteen in-depth case studies demonstrate the most energy-efficient systems for foundations, walls, floors, roofs, windows, doors, and more.

Donald B. Corner is a practicing architect and member of the College of Distinguished Professors of the Association of Collegiate Schools of Architecture. He has been recognized for research and innovative teaching in building construction and detailing. For the past 20 years he has offered an integrated course in the technology and design of the building enclosure.

Jan C. Fillinger is principal of STUDIO-E Architecture, a certified passive house consultant, an educator, and a developer of sustainable projects in Eugene, Oregon, USA. His academic and professional design work focuses on reducing carbon emissions, through socially and environmentally conscious strategies, climate- and site-responsive buildings, and urban high-density projects.

Alison G. Kwok, PhD, is an architect and certified passive house consultant. She teaches design studios, building performance seminars, and environmental technology. Her research includes adaptive and mitigation strategies for climate change, thermal comfort, and building performance case studies. She is co-author of the *Green Studio Handbook* and *Mechanical and Electrical Equipment for Buildings*.

Passive House Details

Solutions for High-Performance Design

Donald B. Corner
Jan C. Fillinger
Alison G. Kwok

Routledge
Taylor & Francis Group

NEW YORK AND LONDON

First published 2018
by Routledge
711 Third Avenue, New York, NY 10017

and by Routledge
2 Park Square, Milton Park, Abingdon, Oxon OX14 4RN

Routledge is an imprint of the Taylor & Francis Group, an informa business

Library of Congress Cataloging-in-Publication Data
A catalog record for this book has been requested

ISBN: 978-1-138-95825-8 (hbk)
ISBN: 978-1-138-95826-5 (pbk)
ISBN: 978-1-315-66128-5 (ebk)

Typeset in Syntax
by Florence Production Ltd, Stoodleigh, Devon, UK

DISCLAIMER
The information in this book has been derived and extracted from a multitude of sources
including building codes, industry codes and standards, manufacturer's literature, reference
works and personal professional experience. It is presented in good faith. Construction details
are the work of architecture or design-build firms. The authors have redrawn the details for
graphic consistency in cooperation with reviews by the designers. Although the authors and
the publisher have made every reasonable effort to make the information presented accurate
and authoritative, they do not warrant, and assume no liability for, its accuracy or complete-
ness or fitness for any specific purpose. The information is intended primarily as a learning
and teaching aid, and not as a final source of information for the design and construction of
building details by design professionals. It is the responsibility of users to apply their professional knowledge in the application of the information presented in this book, and to consult
original sources for current and detailed information as needed, for actual design situations.

Cover photo: Karuna House, Newberg, Oregon. ©JEREMY BITTERMANN PHOTOGRAPHY

Contents

Foreword   ix
Preface   xiii
Acknowledgments   xv

Introduction   **1**

1 Design Process for an Optimized Enclosure   **5**

    Activities   6
    Site and Climate   7
    Performance of the Whole   8
    Selection of the Parts   10
    Design Development Concepts and Methods   14
    References and Resources   18

2 Foundation Systems and Details   **19**

    Pumpkin Ridge Passive House   22
    VOLKsHouse 1.0   24
    Freeman House   26
    Stellar Apartments   28
    Fineline House   30
    Jung Haus   32
    Specht Residence   34

3 Floor Systems   **37**

    Balance Project   40
    Skidmore House   42
    Windy View Passive House   44
    Midorihaus   46
    Karuna House   48
    Orchard Street House   50

4   Wall Systems   **53**

    Skidmore House   56

    Arlington House   58

    Full Plane Residence   60

    Portola Valley Passive House   62

    CH2   64

    MARTak Rest/Work Space   66

    Warren Woods Ecological Field Station   68

5   Roof Systems   **71**

    Midorihaus   74

    Hollis Montessori School   76

    New York Street Passive House   78

    VOLKsHouse 1.0   80

    Lone Fir Residence   82

    Orchard Street House   84

    Pumpkin Ridge Passive House   86

    Project Green Home   88

    Zero Cottage   90

6   Openings for Windows and Doors   **93**

    Stellar Apartments   96

    Lone Fir Residence   98

    Madrona Passive House   100

    Jung Haus   102

    Bayside Anchor   104

    Freeman House   106

    Tighthouse Brownstone   108

    Warren Woods Ecological Field Station   110

7   Openings: Mechanical, Plumbing, and Electrical   **113**

    References and Resources   120

8   Case Studies   **121**

    Ankeny Row Net Zero Community, Portland, Oregon   123

    Cowhorn Vineyard House, Jacksonville, Oregon   137

    Earthship Farmstead, Stuart, Virginia   149

    Empowerhouse, Washington, D.C.   163

    Hayfield House, Bolton, Connecticut   177

    Karuna House, Newberg, Oregon   191

    Louisiana Passive House, Lafayette, Louisiana   205

Madrona Passive House, Seattle, Washington   215
Orchards at Orenco, Hillsboro, Oregon   229
Prescott Passive House, Kansas City, Kansas   243
San Juan Passive House, Shaw Island, Washington   255
Saugerties Residence, Saugerties, New York   267
Uptown Lofts on Fifth, Pittsburgh, Pennsylvania   281
Viridescent Building, Falmouth, Maine   293

Appendix A: Abbreviations and Graphic Symbols Used in Detail Drawings   *306*
Appendix B: Project Information   *308*
Bibliography   *311*
Index   *313*

Foreword

The devil is in the detail. This idiom—a well-known statement with a figurative and/or literal meaning—has been liberally applied to both design and construction efforts. It has, in fact, been attributed (mistakenly, so it seems) to Mies van der Rohe. Whatever its provenance, this particular concept is decidedly more figurative than literal. It is generally taken to mean that "details matter" or that "success lies in the details." Putting a different spin on the idiom, it could be interpreted to mean that details can be devilish (as in difficult, perhaps even diabolical). A counterpart idiom declares that *the good is in the detail*.

All of the idiomatic interpretations suggested above apply without reservation to a passive house (*passiv haus*) project. Details assuredly do matter in such a high-performance building type—and they can be the devil to get right. Considerations, such as thermal bridging, that were simply noise in the system on a low-performance building project (typically among the things lumped together as "other" in a bullet list or pie chart) become a labeled concern on a passive house project. But why?

Passive house is an ultralow-energy design standard. It pushes the envelope, both figuratively and literally, on the design of building enclosure elements. A passive house—not necessarily a house, as larger-scale projects become the norm—will exhibit very low annual energy demands. These demands are constrained by the standard in several ways: as maximum allowable heating demand, maximum cooling demand, and a strict limit on annual primary energy consumption. There is also a limit imposed on infiltration rate.

Passive house is a performance standard that requires the designer and the contractor to collectively meet defined and demanding outcome targets. The design challenge lies in creatively meeting these stringent performance requirements—often in the face of prior office and educational experiences that did not always value design exactitude. The construction challenge lies in understanding what meeting these stringent performance requirements means in light of potentially long-held field practices. Details play a critical role in bridging the design and construction realms for passive house. In fact, many successful passive house projects are done by design–build firms. Whether design–bid–build or design–build, the details play a truly critical role in a successful project.

A look at building design heat loss will help explain the elevation of the effect of details from background noise to discernable note in a passive house project. Design heat loss is solely a function of building enclosure design. Design heat loss also more or less determines maximum building heating demand. Design success in reducing winter heat flows through floors, opaque walls, opaque roofs, and windows/skylights leads to lower heating demand. Designers know how to do this: they add thermal resistance (R-value) to the various assemblies. The exceptions (the non-homogeneous elements) in a typical assembly cross section, however, become more and more critical as R-value is increased. It is not the center-of-glass properties that limit window performance, but the frame and edges. It is not the space between wall studs that causes concern, but rather the area at the wall studs (and the headers and footers and bracing).

The American Society of Heating, Refrigerating and Air-Conditioning Engineers (ASHRAE) defines the thermal performance of a wall or roof with two distinct heat flow paths as: $U_{assembly} = (U_{path1} \times \% \ area_{path1}) + (U_{path2} \times \% \ area_{path2})$. The weak link—let's say it is path 2, where heat flows through wood or metal framing instead of through insulation filling the gaps between the framing—acts as a drag on overall assembly thermal performance and becomes a larger and larger part of the total heat flow as improvement efforts focus on path 1. Path 2, the weak link, is called a thermal bridge. Passive house abhors thermal bridges.

Infiltration (air leakage) is another example of a weak link in the building envelope. Air leaks into (or out of) a building wherever there is nothing to stop the airflow. Essentially, there is a gap in the building enclosure. It turns out to be devilishly difficult to stop infiltration. The gaps are generally not purposeful—they are unintentional. It takes concerted attention to detail in both design and construction to plan for the unintentional. Failure to reduce infiltration, as other heat flow paths are improved through higher-R-value assemblies, results in infiltration becoming an increasingly larger percentage of the building heating demand. Passive house abhors excessive infiltration.

Passive house performance demands reduced heat flows and airflows through the building enclosure. The transitions between assemblies—window to wall, wall to roof, wall to floor—and within assemblies—such as where structure is beefed up for sills, headers, and corners—become the focus for excellent detailing. Such intentional reduction in heat flow and airflow, however, can change the patterns of moisture flow through the permeable enclosure assemblies. This can lead to long-term wetting of components that should not be wet, resulting in material degradation and potential indoor air-quality problems. Design to mitigate moisture accretion requires hygrothermal (water–heat) analysis and the development of hygrothermal-friendly assemblies and details. Passive house abhors moisture damage.

The designer of a passive house project must be able to draw the line—literally. It must be possible to draw an unbroken line that defines the plane of the thermal barrier without hesitation or fudging. The same is true for an unbroken line that defines the plane of the air barrier. And—perhaps—the same is true for a line that defines the plane of the vapor barrier (correctly called a retarder). This last line is, however, negotiable, depending upon project-specific analysis. It is clear that impeding heat and airflow are desirable objectives in a passive house. It is not so clear that impeding vapor flow is always the best approach.

The intended outcome of a passive house project is a building that is highly energy-efficient, substantially durable, thermally comfortable, and aesthetically pleasing, with great indoor air quality. Most of these outcomes are addressed by the design of the building enclosure. Some are addressed by mechanical systems. Attention to detail is critical in both realms. As the rules of the game change, old ways of doing things may no longer be valid. One of the more intriguing examples of this game change involves passive house screw-ups—or, more precisely, screw-outs. Removing screws that missed their mark when finishes were being attached to substrate materials can—without the perforations being repaired—leave the enclosure plane unable to perform as intended. Holes not drawn by the designer or intended by the contractor—who would have thought they mattered?

Some of the details that make a passive house project succeed may be visible to the everyday observer. If so, they should be elegant and aesthetic. The vast majority of performance-enhancing details will, however, be concealed within the bowels of the construction. Even though unseen except during construction, these details should also be elegant. They should represent a simple solution to the problem at hand; they should be easy to construct; and they should be robust, reliable, and resilient. Passive house loves elegant details.

Most energy codes and standards have parallel compliance paths, typically including a prescriptive path, a trade-off path, and a performance path. Building designers tend to chaff at a purely prescriptive path, because of the perceived incursions on design creativity and flexibility that come with being told "do this." Building designers tend to welcome performance-based paths, because they demand creativity. At the same time, the analytical demands of a performance path tend to cause architects to off-load computational responsibility for compliance to consultants. In conventional projects, this leads to the use of engineering or energy consultants. In a passive house project, this leads to collaboration with a certified passive house consultant. In both cases, architects can relinquish only so much design responsibility before their roles change radically. Project architects should control project details, often in conjunction with consultants—but not at the whim of the consultant.

This is a sorely needed book that provides designers and constructors of passive house projects with exceptionally useful examples of proven and well-considered details. The good is in the detail, and this book is full of good (perhaps exceptional) details.

Walter Grondzik, PE
Professor of Architecture
Ball State University

Preface

People engaged in the making of buildings are of necessity optimistic. It takes energy and perseverance to work through the conflicts and compromises that define the process. Design exercises the power of positive thinking. It is striving to make good things happen, reaching beyond the careful avoidance of mistakes. Today, we face environmental challenges that lead us to question if optimism will be enough? In his writing, Dr. Cornell West cautioned, "Optimism is a notion that there is sufficient evidence that would allow us to infer that if we keep doing what we're doing, things will get better." He calls instead for "audacious hope . . . that is something else. Cutting against the grain, against the evidence" (West, 1993).

The buildings in this book are vessels of hope.

The makers of these projects have invested in them a belief that they can overcome the evidence, starting in one place to make the world better. These buildings represent the dramatic human impulse to make a change, to make a difference. The purpose of this book is to expand this investment in change, to promote design responses that cut against climate change, resource depletion, and environmental degradation. Through the generosity of our many contributors, we are able to share their innovative approaches, with certain hope that they will inspire further innovation.

This book presents a visual catalog of construction details, materials, and techniques drawn from recent ultralow energy buildings in North America. The objective is to describe and illustrate a breadth of strategies that will produce high-performance building envelopes. In making this collection, the intent is not that they be adopted out of context, but rather that they be seen in context, as the products of integrated design. These are illustrations of successful outcomes, the details through which environmentally responsive buildings have been realized.

The passive house concept has deep developmental roots on the North American continent with passive solar design and superinsulation techniques in the 1970s, and yet has only recently returned to prominence within the building culture. In the 1990s, European building scientists refined the techniques developed for a central European climate zone. In less than a decade, in North America, there have been hundreds of completed projects characterized by thermal comfort, exceptional indoor air quality, and net zero or even energy positive performance.

We use the term "passive house" as reference to an energy standard and a collective set of design and construction principles. The projects featured in this book follow passive house design principles and have either received or are fully qualified for certification by the Passive House Institute, US (PHIUS) or by the Passivhaus Institut (PHI) in Germany. On a qualitative basis, they have been chosen to demonstrate how high-performance objectives positively influenced the design outcome. The selected projects offer special qualities of living space and a meaningful contribution to the contexts in which they are found.

The organization of this book follows the construction process, from the ground up. Individual chapters cover the foundation, floors, walls, and roof. Following that are the installation of the windows and doors, and then the integration of service systems. The design process is, of course, very different. It moves back and forth between the components, evaluating each of them in terms of their contribution to the whole. The narrative in each chapter compares and contrasts design options for that assembly. The second half of the book contains case studies that compare characteristic details across different cultural contexts, climate zones, and building types.

The goal of this first edition of *Passive House Details* is to provide prospective building owners, contractors, and design professionals with a basic graphic resource, a set of clearly documented construction details that have proven their worth in high performance. We also wish to address the needs of students of architecture and building construction. Curricula in these fields have been overwhelmed by rising expectations of environmental fitness and by the explosion of building science information that must be brought to bear on a successful project. There is rarely enough time in our processes of education to fully explore the design implications of such things as vapor diffusion, or thermal transmission though complex assemblies. It is our sincere hope that the explicit examples catalogued in this volume will help to bring such elusive concepts to life.

REFERENCES AND RESOURCES

Passive House Institute United States (PHIUS): www.passive house.us/ (accessed January 10, 2017).

Passivhaus Institut (PHI): www.passiv.de/ (accessed January 10, 2017).

West, C. 1993. "An Abiding Sense of History," Wesleyan University, Middletown CT, May 30, 1993.

Acknowledgments

Creative projects, of design and building, are always a team effort. Similarly, this book is the product of a special collaboration between authors, colleagues, a committed team of talented students, helpful friends, and supportive families. The many generous and thoughtful design professionals, builders, and owners who have shared their projects are the ones who made it at all possible.

We thank the numerous organizations and individuals involved with the passive house movement and with high-performance building. As committed teachers, we have a sincere appreciation for the educational materials and settings provided through the PHIUS certified passive house consultant training, builder training, conference presentations, and poster sessions that have become a wellspring for the industry. We are indebted to PHIUS founder Katrin Klingenberg and co-director Mike Kernagis for their tireless efforts. Their generosity extends to scholarships that have allowed many young students to prepare themselves for professional roles in this expanding field.

As with the projects themselves, gathering the documents in this book required close cooperation between owners, designers, builders, and consultants. More than thirty-five firms assisted us with drawings, comments, marked-up sketches, and the stream of correspondence needed to bring the parts together as one. Without all of you, this work would not have been possible. The construction images in this book came to us from all of the dedicated members of each project team. We combed through literally thousands of shots looking for the "picture worth a thousand words" that would put each detail in context and begin to describe how the passive house can be constructed. We wish to recognize the wonderful resource that has been created through internet posting of construction histories by owners, builders, and architects. Many professional photographs have been generously provided to support our educational intent. We believe the beauty of these images will inspire new projects of equal quality.

A book such as this one requires attention to tasks large and small over the days, weeks, and months of compilation. Ryan Dirks, a University of Oregon alumnus who is now with STUDIO-E Architecture in Eugene, took the lead on all of the drafting and was invaluable as manager of the student team that contributed so much to the final production. University of Oregon team members included: Spencer Anderson, Alyssa Franco, Logan Goins, Matthew Nyweide,

Eric Schmidt, and Kayla Zander. We cannot say enough about their dedication to this effort, meticulous attention to their tasks, and the collaborative spirit in which they took it on. University of Oregon alumnus Ayush Vaidya, now with Code Unlimited in Portland, brought on board his experience with previous publications. He processed more than 400 images, editing the photos, captions and credits, and editing to produce the final manuscript.

We gratefully acknowledge architect Graham Irwin of Essential Habitat for his expert contributions to the technical sections of Chapter 1 and for his inputs to subsequent chapters. We also acknowledge Professor Walter Grondzik, of Ball State University, for his critical reviews of drafts and for the spirited foreword.

We hope that this book will provide a resource that encourages instructors to create courses, workshops, or project assignments that engage a new generation of professionals in the design and construction of high-performance building envelopes.

Finally, we thank the staff at Routledge for their professional guidance, especially Wendy Fuller, editor; Grace Harrison and Norah Hatch, editorial assistants; Christina O'Brien, production editor; Louise Smith, copy editor.

Introduction

Forward-looking, environmentally conscious buildings must be designed for dramatic reductions in energy use, global warming potential, and carbon footprint. Structures must provide a healthy, supportive environment with consistently high performance levels over the long term. The value of the building must be measured over the full span of its useful life, from initial acquisition costs to ongoing maintenance and final disposition.

There are many comparative metrics for an ecological approach to design:

- Net zero source energy: Each building must generate one unit of energy for every unit it consumes throughout a year. Annual energy consumption includes the on-site usage, plus all of the primary energy needed to extract, generate, transmit, and distribute those units of energy to the site (Torcellini et al., 2006).
- Architecture 2030 Challenge: Climbing through a series of progressive benchmarks, all new buildings and major renovations shall be carbon neutral by 2030. No fossil fuel, greenhouse gas-emitting energy will be used to operate the building. This will be achieved through sustainable design strategies, on-site generation of renewable power, and/or limited purchase (20 percent maximum) of off-site renewable energy (Architecture 2030).
- Net zero emissions: The overall objective is to completely eliminate the effective carbon pollution of the planet. Carbon emissions due to buildings, and all other sources, must be drastically reduced. The remainder must be balanced by natural factors such as forest carbon sinks, and technologies of carbon capture and storage that keep the pollution from entering the atmosphere (The Carbon Reality Project).
- Living Building Challenge: The Living Building Challenge is a green building certification program with comprehensive measures tracking materials, resources, and performance attributes in the built environment. The current version (3.0) includes twenty design imperatives organized in seven performance categories called Petals: Place, Water, Energy, Health & Happiness, Materials, Equity, and Beauty (International Living Future Institute).

These metrics engage processes of our daily lives that extend far beyond the boundaries of a single structure. They ask us to account for all of the energy that is consumed in meeting our demands. We must account for the materials that we use and the by-products that we leave behind. Ultimately, we are held responsible for the water, vegetation, habitat, and all of the natural systems and resources affected on our behalf. Although these advanced measures of health in the environment are broad and inclusive, we understand that buildings alone account for a significant percentage of the demands that we make on our resources. They directly and indirectly account for material consumption and energy use that exceed sustainable levels. The first step along any sustainable path is to reduce those demands.

We use buildings to close the gap between the ambient climate of a given site and the living and working conditions that we consider comfortable. What is left of that gap is bridged by active space conditioning, heating or cooling, and we must do as little of either as possible. As we admit sun to reduce active heating, or block the sun to reduce active cooling, we must reconcile our other needs, such as a sufficient harvest of daylight that we can turn off electric sources. The principal instrument that we use to control all of these variables is the building envelope. To reduce the demands we make on resources, we must look very critically at the envelope in terms of: how it is made, what it is made from, and how it performs.

The building envelope shapes all of our other opportunities. In commercial structures, the high-performance envelope greatly reduces capital expenditures on mechanical systems: tons of cooling, volumes for ducts, diameters of pipes. It reduces operating energy for fans and pumps. As we cross key thresholds, the improved envelope allows us to use radically more efficient means of conditioning, such as radiant heating and cooling of larger structures. Ultimately, our goal is to drive down operating energy demand to a level that can be met with on-site renewable sources. Optimizing the building envelope makes this possible.

In this book, we have adopted passive house building standards as the measure of optimal envelope design. They offer an explicit set of guiding concepts and goals that can be used to attain a significant and measurable level of energy efficiency within a specific, quantifiable comfort zone. A passive building is designed and built in strict response to five building science principles:

1. continuous insulation through the entire envelope, without any thermal bridging;
2. extremely airtight envelope, preventing infiltration of outside air and loss of conditioned air;
3. high-performance windows, typically triple-paned, with high-performance doors;
4. a balanced form of heat and moisture recovery ventilation with a minimal space conditioning system;
5. management of solar gain to exploit it during the heating season and minimize it in cooling seasons.

Striving to meet passive house standards reveals fundamental principles of good envelope design. It imposes a discipline on the detailing of buildings that is critical to ecological architecture. The path to net zero energy in buildings has three distinct phases (Christensen et al., 2005). In the first phase, we adopt conservation measures in the envelope construction that have no net cost. That is, they reduce the utility bills by enough to cover the mortgage increment that is due to the improvements. In the final phase, we have realized everything that the envelope can give us and we direct all of our further investments toward renewable sources that take us to net zero. The greatest design challenges arise in the phase between these two. As we change the envelope to improve performance, further reductions in utility bills become harder and harder to achieve. At this point on the path, there are complex design alternatives to study. We must weigh and balance construction costs, energy savings, and environmental benefits until we are satisfied that the best combinations are in play. As we push the envelope to its practical limits, it is in this realm that passive house design strategies are brought to bear.

Passive house methods set performance standards for the building as a whole, rather than prescriptive standards for the individual parts. The documentation of numerous successful projects in North America and Europe demonstrates the market reach of a performance-based approach, influencing, not only individual designs, but also the available components and systems from which they are built. Passive house standards resonate with environmentally motivated designers and builders because they connect directly to the decisions and actions that members of the project team are asked to make, and able to realize. In concert with the owner, the team: specifies materials and equipment, develops building concepts and configurations, articulates a construction strategy, and attends to the details. The passive house process inspires creative efforts in all of these areas and rigorously inspects the performance outcomes that result.

Beginning in the first chapter, this book will emphasize a process of integrated design that leads to an optimized envelope. The details presented in this volume are not an inventory of ready-made solutions, but a view into a body of work that is always growing and changing. They illustrate a range of design options, marking out a territory, or "solution space," within which further refinements can be made. There are real opportunities for growth, extending the reach of ultralow-energy projects to design contexts in which they have not yet been fully embraced. Across North America, there are significant differences in terms of climate zones, construction practices, and energy economics. Evolving passive house standards establish specific performance metrics that better recognize these contrasts (PHIUS+ 2015). "The goal is a simple but fine-grained performance-based design methodology that guides the designer to identify the most cost-effective path to [net zero energy] with the greatest overall benefits to building owners and society" (U.S. Department of Energy/National Renewable Energy Laboratory, 2015).

As increasing numbers of projects are developed, we anticipate that patterns of preferred practice by region will become more distinct. We will see greater differences in envelope thickness in response to thermal conditions, and variation in the treatment of barriers for moisture control.

Comparing the California and New England examples in this collection only begins to suggest the richness and variety that is possible.

Ultimately, successful projects are those that can be constructed, operated, and maintained within the means of the owners. An effective, cost-efficient building strategy must combine discipline with ingenuity. Both of these must be manifest in the details.

REFERENCES AND RESOURCES

Architecture 2030: http://Architecture2030.org/2030_challenges/2030-challenge (accessed January 10, 2017).

The Carbon Reality Project: www.climaterealityproject.org/blog/idea-whose-time-has-come-why-net-zero-emissions-way-future (accessed January 10, 2017).

Christensen, C., Horowitz, S., Givler, T., Courtney, A., and Barker, G. 2005. "BEopt: Software for Identifying Optimal Building Designs on the Path to Zero Net Energy." Conference Paper, Golden, CO: National Renewable Energy Laboratory, NREL/CP-550–37733. ISES 2005 Solar World Congress, Orlando, FL, August 2005.

International Living Future Institute: http//living-future.org/lbc (accessed January 10, 2017).

PHIUS+ 2015: Passive Building Standard North America; www.phius.org/phius-2015-new-passive-building-standard-summary (accessed January 10, 2017).

Torcellini, P.A., Pless, S., Deru, M., and Crawley, D.B. 2006. "Zero Energy Buildings: A Critical Look at the Definition," ACEEE Summer Study on Energy Efficiency in Buildings, Pacific Grove, CA, August 2006.

U.S. Department of Energy/National Renewable Energy Laboratory. 2015. *Climate-Specific Passive Building Standards*, prepared by G.S. Wright and K. Klingenberg (PHIUS) and Building Science Corporation. NREL: DE-AC36–08GO28308.

CHAPTER 1

Design Process for an Optimized Enclosure

Architectural design is a complex and subtle process. It requires full intellectual engagement and is deeply satisfying when good solutions emerge. Design involves a combination of experience and insight. It is driven by precedent, springing from the accumulated knowledge of architects, owners, and builders in a particular culture or community. Creative insight allows that knowledge to be captured and transformed to serve new purposes.

Many of the best designs are those grounded in the sense of a region. There are characteristic architectures, for example, in New England and in the Pacific Northwest. They each have a set of recurring themes that are based on long-term performance in use and in place. These working traditions are the building blocks for higher-performance designs going forward. Early settlers in New England were challenged by the harsh climate. They responded with tight, concentric plans, carefully chosen openings, and attention to the surface–volume ratio of the building. New England traditions lend themselves directly to successful passive house designs in that region. Buildings in the Pacific Northwest are recognized for significant overhanging roof forms that shelter walls and windows from the rain. Overhangs remain a logical, cost-effective means to extend the longevity of a structure. Northwest houses were once heated with forest by-products, such as sawdust, burning virtually all day. Heat that was allowed to escape through the envelope prevented the accumulation of moisture inside the walls. Contemporary low-energy homes do not waste heat and strive to block airflows that carry water through any gaps in the weather shell. Drying outcomes are greatly improved by overhangs that deflect water away from the walls in the first place.

Good design is of great ecological significance. Buildings that work well, that are loved and cared for, stay in service longer. There is a tremendous amount of energy embodied in a building, locked into the materials and in the work that was done to process and assemble them. The longer a building stays in use, the greater the opportunity to recover that environmental investment. Life cycle cost analysis reflects favorably on sound investments in primary structure, elements that remain undisturbed through extended periods of use. A more critical analysis must be made regarding the weather shell and interior finishes—systems that are frequently replaced, at great expense of energy, because they have either degraded or simply fallen out of fashion. At the residential scale, primary structure, weather shell, and interior finish are largely provided in a single, integrated system. To control the long-term environmental footprint of a residential building requires thoughtful and appropriate investments in a durable, high-performance envelope.

Defining an effective building envelope is an essential part of the design process. The envelope is not a generic treatment wrapped around the building at the end of design, but something that evolves continuously along the way. The building envelope passes through all phases of design investigation. There must be careful analysis of precedent and the identification of performance goals and aesthetic objectives. There is schematic design—balancing solids and voids, attending to the placement and proportion of the openings. There is design development—selecting from alternative materials and systems while integrating them into a smoothly functioning whole. Finally, there are construction documents—the vehicle used to transfer this long, collaborative effort from the design studio to the project site.

The focus of this book is on the details, with recognition that they are specific products of the broad and inclusive process required to make good architecture. In order to provide this focus, this chapter presents a discussion of the design process that is limited to themes that are fundamental to high performance, measured by passive house standards; this is followed by a discussion of design development considerations, technical analyses for the envelope, and useful tools.

The design of a project—whether residential or non-residential—to passive house performance standards involves progressive definition and refinement in four major areas:

1. activity program and organization;
2. site and climate response;
3. performance of the building enclosure as a whole;
4. selection, integration, and refinement of the component parts.

The design process treats these considerations, not sequentially, but interactively, visiting and revisiting each set of issues in turn. Underlying all are considerations of project budget, as well as the materials and skills that are available and appropriate to the location. Passive house standards do not apply just to single-family residences, but the majority of passive house activity in North America to date has involved residential buildings. The majority of the projects featured in this book are also residential. Thus, the following discussion of the design process has a residential focus. This should not be interpreted as a bias toward residential design, but rather as a reflection of the wide diversity of design considerations encountered in non-residential projects.

ACTIVITIES

So that the performance of a passive house project can be optimized, and its costs controlled, the spaces within should accommodate the intended uses as efficiently as possible. Generally, the smaller the building, the smaller its environmental impacts. Accordingly, spaces should be of a size that is truly productive. Activity settings should be rehearsed using comparable furnishings and mapped to reveal what is needed to support the recurring events of daily life. Attention must be given to body measures, proximity, arrangement, clearances, and movement. The dining table, in its size and shape, is inextricably bound to the quality of the experience at a meal. Extra steps, taken repeatedly across an expanse of empty floor between the table and the kitchen, will consume energy on a variety of levels. There must also be adequate space for special occasions. Flexibility must be provided, so that a few everyday things can be moved aside when it is necessary to expand the table for Thanksgiving dinner.

The organization of parts within the whole must also be efficient. Circulation through a dwelling should pass along the edges of an activity setting rather than cutting a swath right through it. This requires careful attention to the relative position of rooms and the location of doors that join them. The shape and position of staircases have a tremendous influence on the efficiency of a plan. Good stairs depart from the social center of the public level and deliver residents to the logistical center of the private one. The gathering of bedrooms logically around this point of arrival eliminates the need for a long corridor. Privacy, in close proximity, can be enhanced by placing storage closets as thickened walls between the rooms.

Within the thermal envelope of a building, priority must be given to activity settings that really will receive year-round use. Expanded living areas that serve a special event or a particular season can be provided in buffer spaces that do not require continuous, active conditioning. Porches or readily accessible decks add to the generosity and spontaneity of a home while reducing the volume that must be fully controlled. Outside the building shell, design considerations for activity must include analysis of the comfort zone and the microclimate produced by adjacent structures.

There are many references that support and inform a human-centered approach to building design. As a framework and a starting point, the best single source remains *A Pattern Language*, by Christopher Alexander and his co-authors, Ishikawa, Silverstein, Jacobson, Fiksdahl-King, and Angel (1977). Liberally illustrated building examples have followed in publications by some of the co-authors, by their academic colleagues, and by the generations of students they have collectively influenced. There is an extensive behavior-based literature for multifamily housing design as well.

SITE AND CLIMATE

One of the first activities in building design is a thorough analysis of the potential site. The attributes of particular importance to a passive house project include:

- climate and microclimate:
  - seasonal temperature and humidity patterns;
  - diurnal temperature ranges;
  - solar incidence on the site;
  - wind patterns;
- physical structure:
  - topography: advantageous but manageable slopes;
  - water flows: surface and subsurface;
  - vegetation: tree canopies;
  - opportunities for access: construction and thereafter;

- regulatory context:
  - property size and boundaries;
  - buildable area: setbacks;
  - height limits;
  - permitted uses: zoning;
- architectural context:
  - adjacent buildings: size and type;
  - characteristic materials: sense of place.

When fortune smiles, a preliminary inventory of desirable characteristics can be used to select the best fit from a number of potential site options. It is clearly advantageous if a site supports the design preferences for a high-performance building. A site that faces south on the private side will allow major rooms to open to the sun and the outdoor space. Access from the north allows garages, car parking, entry vestibules, and service spaces to be clustered on that side. A passive house does not depend on these conditions, but they are frequently present in successful projects. Ultimately, buildings should develop a reciprocal relationship with the site. Site attributes should help to reduce the environmental stress on the building. The building, in turn, should improve the ecology and microclimate of the site.

Larger sites offer the opportunity to focus on the ideal *position* for the building. Can the approach and access be arranged so that the public and private sides of the house face in the preferred directions? Can the house be built above or against a slope? Each degree of tilt toward the sun acts like a change in latitude. Can the house be placed among deciduous trees that will admit sun in the winter and offer shade in the summer? Are there evergreen trees that block the winter winds? If such trees are not available initially, is there room to plant them? Do the principal vistas from the site align with the preferred orientation of the major rooms, or must there be a differentiation of on-site and off-site views?

As sites get smaller, and regulatory limits take effect, the choice of position may be severely limited. The critical question may become one of *orientation*. Is the preferred orientation possible? There are many neighborhoods in which the ends of the houses face the street, so that the longer edges can face the sun and a private garden. Zero-lot-line zoning may help to make this work. Solar access on smaller sites might be shaped by trees or buildings on adjacent parcels and, therefore, be out of the designer's control. A skyline plot of obstacles can help determine if the shadows cast and solar access allowed are helpful or harmful, by season.

Finally, there may be the opportunity to consider the building *configuration*. Passive solar design techniques suggest that buildings be oriented toward the sun and elongated in the east–west direction to maximize solar gain through the illuminated façade. The elongated plan allows glass in the principal rooms to act as a passive collector of the sun's energy. If the building has significant mass, the benefits of that gain can be extended throughout the day. By contrast, the narrow ends of the building receive less of the low sun from the east and the west, which is much more difficult to control. Frank Lloyd Wright's iconic Solar Hemicycle House near Madison, Wisconsin, vividly demonstrates early passive solar design. South-facing windows provide for direct solar gain and daylighting of most activity areas. An earth berm against the curving north wall provides winter protection. The stone in that wall and the concrete floors provide mass for thermal storage. The entire house celebrates access to the sunny terrace surrounded by the signature curve. However, with little insulation in the walls and roof, and without night shutters on the windows, the house gives back much of what it gains from the sun.

A passive house design, as distinguished from a passive solar design, does not imply a house that is heated by the sun. A passive house relies on a high-performance envelope to reduce energy demands for heating and cooling. Guidelines for the shape of the building encourage compact, non-elongated forms with a low surface-to-volume ratio, so that there is less area through which heat losses can occur. These principles extend beyond single-family houses to retail, office, civic, and education buildings. Multifamily apartments in which the units shelter each other offer a particular opportunity for passive house design. Site and orientation still come into play in a passive house, but the building does not rely on

them to deliver a high level of energy harvest. Well-placed windows provide useful gains during the winter, in addition to daylight, views, and a temporal connection to the outdoors. Solar gains cannot be allowed to create a demand for cooling energy. Whether by deciduous trees or adjustable building components, there must be external shading during the overheated periods.

The advice to "insulate before you insolate" applies to both passive solar and passive house design. These principles and practices can work together. The key is to drive down total demand by constructing a well-insulated, airtight envelope in both cases. The principal activities of the interior must be arranged so that as many as possible enjoy a preferred exposure within the limits of a compact form. In climates with a high diurnal temperature range, flushing the building with cool air at night may bring passive cooling. Passive house designers are cautious about the size and location of windows, but, with careful study, it may be possible to shift window positions slightly to take advantage of prevailing breezes for cross ventilation. The building may have a positive influence on the wind patterns, as in the classic case of a screened porch placed in the path of cooling air that accelerates in its journey around the corner of a building.

Elongation of a passive house may apply best to that larger set of activity spaces that are not contained inside the thermally isolated core. Transitional space, shaded terraces, and outdoor rooms can enhance the appreciation of the site. If they are stretched out to the east and the west, they can help to protect the building from overheating and not interfere with winter sun. Seasonal migration to extended living spaces across the site is a valuable alternative to overglazing as a means to connect to nature.

PERFORMANCE OF THE WHOLE

The design of a passive house represents a paradigm shift in architectural design. Previously, the typical process was driven by considerations of human activity, the site, and the formal intentions of the architect. Building technology was folded into the ongoing stream to reach the best available performance in a solution that was derived from largely non-technical considerations. Structural systems were developed to withstand the anticipated loads, and, at the end, the thermal conditions were analyzed, and mechanical systems were sized to meet the resulting heating and cooling requirements. By contrast, passive house design adopts a clearly defined thermal performance target as one of the essential points of beginning, in essence "sizing" the mechanical system in advance. The building program specifies space conditioning limits at the start. All of the design intentions must be evaluated and coordinated with respect to meeting this goal. The passive house standard is a challenge, requiring holistic thinking and fully integrated design.

A passive house design begins with the establishing of performance goals for the building enclosure as a system of interdependent parts. All building shells provide some degree of thermal insulation. To be fully effective, this insulation must be uniform and continuous. In a passive house, the levels of insulation are much higher than in conventional buildings, and great care is taken to balance the targets established for the floors, the walls, and the roof. The equations for heat loss are cruel masters. It is the total that matters, the sum of $(U_1 \times A_1 \times \Delta T) + (U_2 \times A_2 \times \Delta T) + \ldots$ for all of the components. If heat is streaming out through inadequate walls, it is virtually impossible to overcome that by lavishing more attention on the roof. Similarly, within any assembly, there cannot be gaps or discontinuities that allow heat to bypass the insulation through "thermal bridges." Consider the amount of heat that passes through 1 sq. ft. of wall insulation that is 4 in. thick (~R16 = R4/in. x 4 in.). In a steady-state model, that same amount of heat will pass through an embedded steel bolt that is only ⅜ in. in diameter (~R0.012 = R0.003/in. x 4 in.). That same amount of heat will pass through an exposed patch of 8-in. concrete foundation wall no larger than the cross section of a single 2 x 4 (~R0.64 = R0.08/in. x 8 in.). At the center of a wall with 2 x 6 framing on 24-in. spacing, dense-packed with cellulose, 16 percent of the heat loss flows through the studs, although they form only 6 percent of the area. At higher levels of performance, this too is a problem, but orders of magnitude less troublesome than thermal bridges of materials more conductive than wood.

Of equal concern is the elimination of air leaks. Striving for high performance by adding insulation alone is futile if heat is conveyed through the envelope on streams of air. The approach of continuous, thick insulation with an airtight shell is referred to as "super-insulation," a term coined by Wayne Schick at the University of Illinois at Urbana-Champaign, who helped develop the "Lo-Cal" house in 1976, an important precursor to passive houses. Although the actual levels of insulation are climate- and project-specific, super-insulation is fundamental for a passive house.

Passive house building assemblies are also designed to standards of hygrothermal performance: minimum moisture accumulation and ample drying capability. This is a complex topic that will be taken up at the end of this chapter. Lastly, passive house best practice accounts for the environmental impact of the manufacture, installation, and even the eventual disaggregation of the assemblies.

Once the performance standards for each part of the building skin are established, the next step is to experiment with the patterns of solid and void. The size and location of windows have perhaps the greatest single impact on the making of place within a building. Windows provide daylight for activities and views that connect us to surrounding nature and community. They allow the mood of the interior to change over the course of a day, a weather cycle, or a season. In a passive house, windows have an enormous impact on the "energy balance" of a building. They must be deployed and managed with great care.

The best available windows are demonstrably a weak link in the thermal isolation promised by the building skin. Table 1.1 offers a rough comparison of wall performance based on relative window area (percentage of glazing), window quality (R3 versus R8), and the amount of insulation invested in the opaque sections. With moderate quality windows (R3) and a high percentage of glazing (30 percent) the overall wall performance is completely dominated by the windows. The overall equivalent R-value changes very little, despite doubling or tripling the wall insulation. High-performance windows (R8) are essential if the benefits of super-insulation are to be realized. Adding insulated floor and roof areas to

Table 1.1 Comparison of Wall Performance with Glazing Area

20% Glazing			30% Glazing		
Window	Wall	Overall Value	Window	Wall	Overall Value
R3	R20	R9.33	R3	R20	R7.42
R3	R40	R11.53	R3	R40	R8.51
R3	R60	R12.50	R3	R60	R8.96
R8	R20	R15.38	R8	R20	R13.79
R8	R40	R22.22	R8	R40	R18.18
R8	R60	R26.09	R8	R60	R20.34

the equation will dampen these extremes, but the extraordinary influence of window area will not go away.

Like the opaque components of the building shell, windows transfer heat via conduction and convection, but they are capable of admitting far more heat in the form of radiant solar gains. Ideally, the windows of a passive house building make an overall contribution to the heating demand, though it is typically only south-facing windows that make a positive individual contribution in the northern hemisphere. South-facing windows should be sized so that solar gains equal no more than about 30 percent of the heat losses, lest overheating occur during shoulder seasons. North-, east-, and west-facing windows typically lose more heat through conduction than they gain from the sun during the heating season, so they need to be carefully balanced against the need for daylighting, views, and egress (WARM, 2012).

During the cooling season, control of solar gains is critical. A good passive house design requires analysis and quantification of shading, from the building itself, from neighboring buildings, and from the landscape. South-facing windows are typically the easiest to control with fixed overhangs. East- and west-facing windows are more difficult to shade, generally requiring vertical shading elements. In some locations in the northern hemisphere, north-facing windows can admit solar gains, although typically only during the cooling season.

As solar gains are potentially helpful during the heating season, but harmful during the cooling season, in mixed and mild climates, passive house window design involves balancing heating reductions against cooling increases on a yearly basis. This is simple in concept, but complex in execution. Because of their great influence, both thermally and experientially, windows are the major variable in the schematic design process. It must be possible to explore various options and compare them accurately in terms of overall building performance. In practice, this is best done with energy-modeling software capable of processing all of the relevant inputs.

Changes to the solid parts of the building may not be as volatile architecturally as are changes in the voids, but accurate, comprehensive analysis requires specific inputs for both. Starting values for foundations, floors, walls, and the roof must be quickly refined to reflect local conditions: climate, building code, and construction practice. Developing realistic expectations for different components of the building is the fourth area of the design process and is addressed in the next section.

SELECTION OF THE PARTS

Most building projects begin with a budget. The largest component of that budget is the cost of construction. The budget has to be based on a set of assumptions about the materials and methods proposed and whether or not they are reasonable choices in the local building culture. Passive house projects share this point of beginning, but their higher expectations of performance bring a greater urgency to the search for effective systems and assemblies. What is widely accepted as conventional practice will not

Table 1.2 Comparison of Component Surface Areas for a One- and Two-Story Residence

1,200 ft.² (111.5 m²) Residence	One-Story, 30 ft. x 40 ft. (9 x 12 m) Base			Two-Story, 20 ft. x 30 ft. (6 x 9 m) Base		
	ft.²	(m²)	% of Total Surface Area	ft.²	(m²)	% of Total Surface Area
Ground slab area	1,200	(111.5)	32	600	(55.7)	19
Wall area	1,400	(130)	36	2,000	(186)	62
Roof area	1,200	(111.5)	32	600	(55.7)	19
Total surface area	3,800	(353)	100	3,200	(297)	100

meet passive house standards, at least in the near term. Assuming that the budget has limits, it is critically important that each new building configuration be based on sound thinking about material use, constructability, and length of service. The performance gains must be real, and the costs must be reflective of value.

This leg of the process begins with research into the options for each of the building components. Chapter introductions in the body of this book offer a structured tour through the possibilities that are demonstrated in the collected details. After reviewing this resource and others, the next step is to discuss the options with qualified local builders and design consultants to find out which strategies are favored in a particular place, and why. The details in this volume explore the intersections between components: roof–wall, wall–floor, and floor–foundation. These intersections have a great deal to say about the character of the building.

As schematic design options are developed, they should trigger a list of the key details to be researched and developed. Table 1.2 compares surface areas for two versions of a 1,200 sq. ft. (111.5 m²) residence. The one-story scheme suggests that there might be an equal interest in the nature of the ground slab, walls, and roof. By contrast, the two-story scheme is dominated by the walls. If the project is headed in that direction, finding effective strategies for high-performance walls becomes a priority. This example is a vastly simplified measure, but it serves to demonstrate how the design team must recognize the pressure points that are intrinsic to a certain

scheme, and that they must research effective approaches to those conditions.

Typical construction practice is to insert insulation into building assemblies that are sized for structural, not thermal, performance, and that are designed with little or no concern for airtightness. By contrast, passive house details differentiate and explicitly designate structural, thermal, and airtightness functions. This divergence in approach is partly due to differences between a passive house and a building just compliant with code, but also because the forces that determine structural design (gravity, wind, etc.) are far more uniform throughout the world than is climate. Passive houses adopt insulation requirements based on thermal performance, and so the levels of insulation in passive house buildings vary far more with climate than in conventional construction. The difference between what structural dimensions offer as space for insulation and what passive house standards require is most pronounced in walls, as roofs and framed floors usually result in fairly deep structural members.

The structural volume of a passive house building shell is insulated, but a dedicated thermal layer is added, usually to the outside, and often exceeds the insulation in the structural components. Because many structural materials are poor insulators, this additional, continuous insulation layer mitigates thermal bridging that would otherwise occur. A particularly challenging detail in a passive house is the connection of the foundation assembly to framed walls above. As such, passive house detailing often starts at the foundation and works its way upward.

Slab Foundations and Conditioned Basements

Slab-on-grade floors and conditioned basements present challenges for continuous insulation. Concrete is good structurally but poor thermally (~R0.08/in.). Any concrete that penetrates the thermal boundary represents a significant compromise to building performance in the form of a thermal bridge. Such a thermal bridge may also pose the risk of condensation, which affects durability and indoor environmental quality. Effective passive house details, therefore, provide for the necessary structural function of the foundation while allowing for an uninterrupted layer of insulation around the entire building. The foundation must be located either entirely inside, or entirely outside, the thermal envelope.

It is generally simpler, if possible, to locate the entire foundation within the thermal boundary. The concrete then increases the thermal mass within the conditioned envelope, which helps moderate daily temperature swings inside the building. This requires that rigid insulation be installed between the concrete and the earth where the foundation is below grade, and between the concrete and the outdoor air where the foundation is above grade.

If the foundation is located outside the thermal boundary, a continuous layer of insulation must be installed between the foundation and the interior of the building. This arrangement removes the benefit of additional conditioned thermal mass, but may be necessary in extreme structural conditions, such as tall retaining walls, unstable soil, high-seismic areas, etc.

Raised Floors

Although raised floors are not typically recommended for a passive house, there are circumstances that may require them, such as flood zones, steep slopes, and retrofits. The "crawl space" beneath the raised floor may be either sealed and conditioned, or vented and unconditioned. Conditioned crawl spaces can provide space for mechanical equipment and ductwork, but they require that the entire perimeter of the crawl space, including the ground, be insulated. They have the thermal advantage of ground

tempering, but the disadvantage of creating additional building volume that must be conditioned.

Walls

In milder climates, the continuous thermal layer in walls often takes the form of exterior rigid insulation, such as rigid rock wool, foam, or cork. In more extreme climates, where insulation requirements are greater, an exterior insulation cavity with minimal thermal bridging is often constructed. This can lower costs and improve the environmental footprint of the building by allowing the use of less resource-intensive insulating materials, such as cellulose.

Airtightness in walls is often implemented by sealing the structural sheathing, but can also be accomplished with a thin membrane. It is desirable to have the airtight layer protected from damage by occupants, and so it is often located toward the middle of the assembly, rather than near the surface. This approach can provide a "utility chase" in the structural layer, between the interior and the airtight layer, where wiring and plumbing can be run and receptacles and fixtures can be installed, without concern for air leaks through the interior finish. The utility chase is typically insulated, but not relied upon to provide the entire thermal boundary.

Wall Cladding

An additional structural concern for passive house wall assemblies is support for the exterior cladding. Exterior wall insulation layers often cantilever out from the structural system, with limited support capacity for cladding at the outer edge. In practice, wood and fiber-cement siding are easily manageable, but brick, stone, and stucco claddings can present challenges because of their weight. Masonry systems may require a foundation that is located outside the thermal envelope. Lightweight, acrylic stucco systems were developed in Europe for application directly to insulation products that wrap the outside of existing buildings. These products are marketed in North America as EIFS (exterior insulation and finishing system), using EPS (expanded polystyrene) as a base. In Europe, a dual-density rigid rock wool product is available that can have stucco applied directly to it. In areas of high rainfall or when cladding materials that readily absorb water are used, it is also beneficial to use a cavity wall, or "rainscreen" system, to block the movement of moisture toward the interior. Drainage cavities can be developed in a wide range of materials.

Roofs

For any building, the roof is the first line of defense against water, and protection from water is the first priority in building enclosure design. Overhangs at the roof, or at selected places along the walls, deflect water away from the other building components and greatly increase their chance of success. The detailing of a roof overhang is one of the most influential steps in the establishment of the character of a building. The thermal performance of a roof is driven by insulation volume, and that volume is relatively easy to increase. Restrictions on the available volume arise when a portion of the roof form is occupied as living space or as a conditioned service zone. The subtleties of roof edges and occupation are addressed further in Chapter 5.

Passive house roofs are similar to passive house walls, but face additional structural and hygrothermal challenges. Hot air rises, which drives moisture into roof assemblies in winter. Furthermore, roofs are exposed to the night sky, which, when clear, can have a strong radiant cooling effect. The exterior layers of a roof assembly are, therefore, more prone to condensation than those of walls. As the sheathing layer is often at risk from condensation damage, it is common practice to vent the area beneath it to the outside, so that moisture can be removed. Venting of the roof is also helpful for preventing ice dams in areas of high snowfall, as it tends to cool the exterior of the roof assembly. In mixed and cooling-dominated climates, reflective ("cool") roofing can be advantageous in reducing cooling demand, as it rejects much of the sun's heat. Unvented and poorly vented reflective roofs can pose hygrothermal challenges, however, as the drying potential of the sun is greatly reduced.

Windows

The total performance of a passive house design requires that the windows contribute in a meaningful way to the thermal integrity of the shell. Specification of high-quality windows is essential, but not sufficient. The effectiveness of windows also depends on how they are configured and how they are installed.

The glazing in a passive house window usually performs better thermally than does the frame. It is, therefore, an advantage to use fewer, larger units, rather than multiples of smaller units. This minimizes the ratio of frame area to glazing area and, conversely, increases the potential solar gain through a given opening in the wall. The significance of frame area is not intuitively obvious. Assuming a 2-in.- (51-mm-) wide frame, each window unit of 2 ft. (0.61 m) x 4 ft. (1.2 m) is 24 percent frame, whereas a single 4 ft. (1.2 m) x 4 ft (1.2 m) window is only 16 percent frame. Configuration also matters, as 16 sq. ft. of window in a 2 x 8 ratio moves back to 20 percent frame.

Reducing the number of operable units improves the airtightness and thermal performance of a building and reduces project cost. Operable windows should be strategically located in sufficient quantity to facilitate natural ventilation for cooling and allow for egress and connection to the outdoors. Well-designed passive house single-family residences tend to have fewer operable windows than typical constructions, but larger passive house buildings tend to have more.

Passive house design considers the performance impact of the installation of a window in the wall. This is known as "*psi* installation" ($\Psi_{Installation}$) and it is measured as a linear heat flow coefficient around the perimeter of the window frame (Btu/hr. ft. °F or W/mK). Larger window units are also beneficial in this regard, as they minimize $\Psi_{Installation}$ for a given window area. If larger single units are not an option over multiple units, it makes sense to "gang" the windows together so that they share a frame on one or more sides. This reduces $\Psi_{Installation}$ compared with the same units, installed near each other, but each in a separate rough opening. $\Psi_{Installation}$ is also affected by the installation position and details. The best results are typically found with the window located at the thermal center of the wall, with the perimeter of the frame "over-insulated," or covered with insulation. (In projects where solar gains are a critical source of usable heat, setting the window in from the outside can be suboptimal, owing to shading from the window surround.) Passive house window frames usually lack nailing fins and are installed with screws driven through the frame or clips into the rough opening, so that they may be inset into the wall. The frames often also have the exterior cladding held back from the perimeter to accommodate over-insulation. Although $\Psi_{Installation}$ can seem a trivial consideration at first glance, it has been shown that the total perimeter of windows in a typical building is large enough to make this a critical performance consideration.

In the end, design is an iterative process that must bring the pieces together. As the various building assemblies are reviewed and selected, it is important to sketch the junctions where one meets the other. One must be able to trace all of the barriers through the details to affirm their continuity. The water-shedding surfaces should lap continuously downward and outward. The weather-resisting barrier should do the same. The thermal and airtightness boundaries of the building must be explicit and unbroken. The sequence of construction should be rehearsed in the process of drawing to determine if the continuities that are required can be feasibly accomplished. Particularly challenging conditions, such as the corners of a window, must be thought through in three dimensions, although two-dimensional drawings are produced. All of these processes must continue as the details are refined. It is good practice to indicate in the final documents when the airtight layer should be tested.

DESIGN DEVELOPMENT CONCEPTS AND METHODS

This section presents extended considerations, modes of analysis, and quantitative techniques that should be engaged as the project moves from preliminary design into design development and documentation. As described in the previous section, the envelope is optimized through a cyclical process that engages each of these concepts and techniques again and again. They are not presented here in order of priority or importance, but with the understanding that the design team will take each of them up in turn as the refinement of the project continues.

Energy Modeling

An energy model is a critical tool for prediction of the performance of passive house designs and ultimate certification of the projects. A model is a computer simulation of the building operating within its climate. The software applies data regarding exterior temperature and humidity, available solar energy, and internal heat gains to a description of a building and predicts the interior conditions, peak heating and cooling needs, and energy use for a typical year. Software may perform calculations for each of the 8,760 hours in a year, in what is known as an "hourly simulation" or "dynamic calculation." Alternatively, the calculations may be simplified by coarser time segments being used.

Energy modeling has a long history. In the 1920s, engineers used calculation techniques to predict heat flow. By the 1960s, hand calculations to determine cooling and heating loads were in regular use, and, in the early 1970s, computer simulations of building performance were being developed. In the mid-1970s, researchers at the University of Illinois used the U.S. Army Corps of Engineers' "Building Loads Analysis and System Thermodynamics" (BLAST) software to predict how much energy could be saved with high levels of thermal insulation, airtight construction, and heat recovery ventilation during the development of the "Lo-Cal House"—an important precursor to the passive house.

In the early 1990s, European scientists analyzed what was termed "Passivhaus" using a custom energy-modeling computer program called DYNBIL. The software was cumbersome, with more than 2,000 required inputs, in addition to climate data. To make passive house design more accessible to architects, the PHI developed the Passive House Planning Package (PHPP) in 1998. An Excel-based, simplified, monthly static energy model, it was intended to be low cost and easy to learn and use correctly. In 2012, Fraunhofer IBP collaborated with PHIUS and Owens Corning to develop WUFI®Passive, a software program that combines monthly and hourly energy modeling with hygrothermal analysis, with the express purpose of better analyzing climates with high cooling and dehumidification requirements.

Ideally, energy-modeling software can help the design team optimize a building by indicating the performance impacts of design parameters, including insulation values, window areas, shading geometry, ventilation rates and heat recovery efficiency, lighting, appliance, and mechanical system performance, etc. An energy model can also determine whether the building meets certification criteria for both enclosure performance and total energy use. For passive house, certification is a two-step process. During the design stage, the building design and the energy model are reviewed for consistency and compliance with performance criteria. If acceptable, the building is "pre-certified" before construction begins. After construction is complete, the building is tested and commissioned. If as-built results are acceptable, and the building has been constructed according to plan, the building can be "certified" as a passive house.

As computer-aided drafting (CAD) is replaced by building information modeling (BIM), tighter integration between design and energy modeling is possible. A BIM building model will contain sufficient information to populate the required inputs of an energy model. Both WUFI-Passive and PHPP (with the add-on program designPH) can import SketchUp models and extract building geometry. Autodesk's Green Building Studio for Revit facilitates energy modeling directly inside the BIM software for green building certification, but does not yet support passive house calculations. Nemetschek's Vectorworks BIM software now features Energos, which does passive house calculations directly inside the program and responds in real time to design changes. In the future, more real-time energy model options should enable a faster, easier, more informed design process.

Thermal Bridge Analysis

So that a passive house energy model can be simplified, assumptions are made about the nature of the building enclosure. One assumption is that each of the building assemblies has a consistent R-value throughout, and that there is no increase in heat flow where assemblies connect. In essence, each assembly is modeled as a disconnected area of monolithic material. The heat flow through each area is calculated separately, and then the individual flows are summed to give the total heat flow.

As actual building material junctions provide more complex pathways for heat flow than per this assumption, the assemblies in the energy model are deliberately oversized to compensate. Where two assemblies meet, each is measured to its exterior limit, which effectively "double counts" outside corners. For most passive house construction, this adjustment provides adequate compensation. Where it does not, a separate "thermal bridge" calculation must be performed, and the result must be brought in to the energy model as a correction factor, referred to as a "*psi*" (Ψ) value.

The *psi* value is a linear heat flow coefficient, expressed in Btu/hr. ft. °F (W/mK). Although thermal bridging can never be completely eliminated from construction, a junction is said to be "thermal bridge free" if the calculated *psi* value is less than 0.006 Btu/hr. ft. °F (0.01 W/mK). In some cases, the actual heat flow through a junction is less than assumed, because of oversizing. This situation is described as a "negative thermal bridge," and the correction factor would actually lower the heat flow predicted by the energy model. If negative thermal bridges are used in an energy model, it is generally required that the *psi* values for every junction in the building be analyzed and entered, to prevent "cherry picking" of beneficial junctions.

Whereas an energy model analyzes perpendicular heat flow through an assembly, also known as "one-dimensional" (1-D) heat flow, a thermal bridge analysis involves heat flow, not only through, but between, assemblies (2-D heat flow), or even 3-D heat flow, in the case of a "point thermal bridge" (such as a fastener or a building corner where three assemblies meet).

To perform a thermal bridge analysis, a detailed model of the specific condition must be created in software designed to analyze multidimensional heat flow. In some cases, hourly simulations are used to develop dynamic thermal bridge values. The analysis, however, is typically time- and temperature-independent, although a worst-case design temperature can be used to evaluate condensation risk.

Because thermal bridge analysis is so specific and detailed, it is time-consuming. In addition to performance and durability impacts, this is another reason to create thermal-bridge-free details whenever possible. With experience, designing thermal-bridge-free details becomes second nature.

Moisture Management

The Canada Mortgage and Housing Corporation organizes best practice guides for moisture management around the four Ds of enclosure design: deflection, drainage, drying, and durability (Canada Mortgage and Housing Corporation, 2005). Deflection refers to shedding of water using overhangs and projections to push it well away from materials that need not be repeatedly wetted. Drainage refers to a second line of defense that captures water at a weather-resistant barrier and returns it to the exterior. Durability refers to selection of materials that can withstand the moisture they are likely to receive without degradation. Drying is the most complex of the concepts. It refers to the seasonal balance between the accumulation and removal of moisture. Assurance of adequate drying requires a study of all the ways in which heat and moisture move through a building assembly, referred to as *hygrothermal performance.*

During winter conditions, the interior air of the building is typically warmer and moister than outdoor air. Under such conditions, moisture, as well as heat, tends to migrate toward the outside via air leakage and direct transmission through building materials. The moisture migrates until it arrives at one of three potential outcomes: it encounters a barrier (also known as "vapor retarder") that limits further travel, it reaches a surface that is cold enough to cause it to condense, or it escapes to the exterior. The most problematic result is interstitial condensation. The assembly should either have a vapor retarder located to prevent moisture from reaching the dew point, or it should be as vapor-open as possible to promote cycles of drying. During summer conditions in humid climates, the outdoor air is warm and moist compared with the indoor air, and so the heat and moisture flow is from the outside in. Building assemblies in these locations should be designed to resist inward vapor drive. In some challenging climates, there is both extreme winter cold and extreme summer humidity. In these circumstances, assemblies must be designed to cope with vapor drive from both directions.

Accumulated moisture in an assembly may result from vapor drive, from air leaks carrying water droplets, from bulk water leaks, and/or from moisture resident in the building materials at the time of construction. It is considered prudent to design for drying, even if the assembly shows no significant tendency to accumulate moisture from vapor drive.

Some vapor retarders are materials installed specifically for that function. In other cases, building materials chosen for other purposes coincidentally block vapor movement. The location and potential effect of such materials must be carefully considered. If vapor-retarding materials are present in the assembly, it is important not to create a condition where part of the assembly is surrounded by vapor retarders on both the inside and the outside. This is known as a "vapor retarder sandwich" and it prevents accumulated moisture from leaving the assembly, which can lead to mold growth, decay, and/or degradation.

There are specialized materials known as "smart vapor retarders" that are vapor-tight to humidity but vapor-open to liquid water. They are typically applied toward the source of the vapor drive. They block moisture migration from humid air but allow saturated building materials to dry out.

The challenging climates in which the vapor drive may change direction are elegantly addressed in the online publications of the Building Science Corporation (buildingscience.com). Author Joe Lstiburek recommends an assembly that he refers to as the "perfect wall" (Lstiburek, 2010). In a perfect wall, all of the barriers (air, vapor, and water) are developed in one plane, at the center of the assembly. The surrounding materials are free to dry either to the inside or the outside, thus avoiding a "vapor sandwich." If there are vulnerable materials (wood studs) on the inside, there must be sufficient moisture-resistant insulation on the outside (such as mineral wool) to prevent the barrier plane from cooling to the point of condensation (dew point). This type of assembly is readily applicable to passive house construction, where the air barrier is frequently developed at the sheathing plane near the center of the wall. Insulation commonly added to the exterior can prevent that plane from reaching the dew point. The concept of the perfect wall is also applicable to a "perfect roof."

An extreme vapor drive condition can result from the use of assemblies that include cladding that absorbs water, such as masonry. When such claddings are wetted by rain and then dried by the sun, the "solar drive" can push moisture toward the interior of the building assembly. It is generally a good idea to provide a vented air space between the cladding and the water resistive barrier (WRB). In the case of masonry cladding on walls, this feature can be critical. A wall assembly in which the cladding is freely ventilated on the back side is referred to as a "rain screen cladding system." Even when the cladding does not store much water, rain screen systems are beneficial for durability, particularly in areas with high annual rainfall (~60 in. or more per year).

Solar drive is typically helpful for the hygrothermal performance of roofs, as it promotes inward drying of the entire assembly. Most roofing materials are sufficiently ventilated that solar-driven moisture from outside isn't a problem, but it can be for unvented asphalt shingle roofs in hot and humid climates. Unvented roofs can also face a hygrothermal performance challenge from reduced solar drive, when the roofing is reflective and/or covered with solar panels or other shading devices, thereby reducing inward drying. The challenge is to balance hygrothermal requirements with cooling reductions and other benefits.

Hygrothermal Analysis

Designing for good hygrothermal performance is a mixture of experience, intuition, and numerical analysis. A variety of numerical techniques can be performed, with a spreadsheet or hand calculator—as well as more sophisticated hygrothermal computer models that provide for in-depth and time-dependent analysis. The appropriate approach depends on the circumstances.

In passive house design, this type of analysis is used to evaluate moisture flow, accumulation, and removal in building assemblies. Materials that are vulnerable to moisture damage must remain below a critical moisture threshold. To avoid mold and mildew growth in vulnerable materials, humidity and temperature must be kept within safe limits.

Hygrothermal analysis was originally done with hand calculations and/or solved graphically with the dew point, the Glaser, or the Kieper methods (TenWolde and Bomberg, 2009). These are steady-state (time-independent) approaches and assume worst-case outdoor temperature and relative humidity for the building location. These methods only evaluate the movement of moisture by diffusion through the materials. Air or water leaks are not considered, nor are the effects of (a) moisture storage in the materials, (b) solar gains, or (c) daily and seasonal variations. These methods are, at best, a general guide to what may occur in an assembly. On the other hand, such analyses are relatively simple to perform and interpret and can be a good starting point for more in-depth analysis.

Climate-specific, dynamic (hourly) hygrothermal analysis with computer models is now readily available. WUFI (Wärme und Feuchte Instationär), developed by the Fraunhofer Institute for Building Physics and Oak Ridge National Lab, is one such model. WUFI addresses most of the hygrothermal aspects overlooked by earlier methods, although some (such as air leakage) are entered empirically, rather than modeled.

Although a dynamic hygrothermal analysis can generate quite accurate results, they are heavily dependent on the accuracy of the designer inputs and assumptions. Results can also be difficult to decipher for an inexperienced user. It is best to evaluate computer model projections with results from simplified analysis and/or conventional wisdom to develop a holistic impression of the performance of a building assembly.

REFERENCES AND RESOURCES

Alexander, C., Ishikawa, S., Silverstein, M., with Jacobsen, M., Fiksdahl-King, I., and Angel, S. 1977. *A Pattern Language: Towns, Buildings, Construction*, Oxford, UK: Oxford University Press.

Canada Mortgage and Housing Corporation. 2005. "Wood-frame Envelopes in the Coastal Climate of British Columbia," www.tboake.com/guides/BC_wood.pdf (accessed January 11, 2017).

Fraunhofer Institute for Building Physics. 2016. "What is WUFI?" https://wufi.de/en/software/what-is-wufi/ (accessed January 11, 2017).

Fraunhofer Institute for Building Physics. WUFI®Passive software: https://wufi.de/en/software/wufi-passive/ (accessed January 11, 2017).

Lstiburek, J. 2010. "BSI-001: The Perfect Wall." Building Science Corporation, http://buildingscience.com/documents/insights/bsi-001-the-perfect-wall (accessed January 11, 2017).

Shick, W.L., and Jones, R.A. 1976. "Illinois and Lo-Cal House, C2.3," *Small Homes Council-Building Research Council*, University of Illinois at Urbana-Champaign, Vol. 1, Number 4, Spring 1976.

TenWolde, A., and Bomberg, M. 2009. "Design Tools," Chapter 10, *Moisture Control in Buildings: The Key Factor in Mold Prevention*, 2nd ed. H. Trechsel and M. Bomberg, eds. West Conshohocken, PA: ASTM International, pp. 128–38; www.fpl.fs.fed.us/documnts/pdf2009/fpl_2009_tenwolde001.pdf (accessed January 11, 2017).

WARM blog. 2012. "10 Most Common PHPP Mistakes," www.peterwarm.co.uk/10-most-common-phpp-mistakes/ October 25, 2012 (accessed January 11, 2017).

CHAPTER 2

Foundation Systems and Details

Passive house design standards have brought significant changes to the foundation and ground floor. Not long ago, designers and builders showed little concern for the amount of heat lost from a building owing to the flow downward, against convection. Ventilated and unheated crawl spaces under buildings were a common strategy to control moisture rising from the ground. Insulation between the suspended floor joists may not even have been included in moderate climates. There was limited attention given to punctures through the floor plane that connected the air mass of the house with unheated air in the crawl space or basement below.

As energy performance goals began to rise, the potential for heat loss through the base of the building came into focus. Concrete basement walls, stem walls, and slab edges could no longer be left exposed to the winter air or to frozen soil near the surface. Infiltration of cold air up through the floor was also identified as a problem. The first-order response was to insulate the building perimeter downward to a sufficient depth that the temperature differential between the soil and the foundation was no longer considered a problem. Alternatively, insulation could be extended outward, horizontally, just below grade, to protect the soil mass directly under the building from heat loss to the surface. Combinations of these techniques remain applicable today in the appropriate climate zones.

To meet passive house standards, particularly in a harsh climate, it may be necessary to completely isolate the structure from thermal contact with the soil even as temperatures moderate with depth. Airflow and moisture movement from the ground to the building must be explicitly controlled with appropriate barriers, no longer just a wind-blown crawl space. Perimeter drainage systems have always been required to reduce fluid pressure against the foundation. Good drainage preserves the integrity of the barriers and the embedded materials and it surrounds the building with soil that has a lower thermal conductivity because it is not saturated with water.

The core design challenge in the foundation is to reconcile the inherent conflict between structural continuity and thermal isolation. If a thermal break is established between the building and the ground, this implies a low-conductivity separator some-where in the foundation assembly. At the same time, vertical loads from above must be carried down to bearing through this thermal barrier. In addition, the interface between building and ground must be able to transfer horizontal forces from the wind and resist uplift as well as overturning. All of these various load paths must be established without creating thermal bridges between the interior and the exterior.

Intuition suggests that low-conductivity insulating materials are also low in density and very likely low in compressive strength. How can significant structural loads be transmitted through such materials? Fortunately, there are exceptions that provide a workable balance between the transfer of loads and the transfer of heat. Of particular relevance to foundations are rigid foam insulation products, such as Type IX EPS, that can be embedded below grade. These have bearing capacities that match the underlying soil strength up to moderate levels, such as that of sandy clay.

Designing any building for moderate-to-low soil-bearing capacity means being careful about the distribution of loads. If bearing walls are stretched out along the foundations, this reduces the demands placed on them or the materials directly underneath. By contrast, long span beams supported on columns create concentrated loads that must be dispersed before they can be applied to the ground. Extreme concentrated loads require clustered points of resistance, such as piers or piles, sunk to a stronger, deeper stratum. Such systems are largely beyond the scope of this book. A single exception is the Madrona Passive House case study, in which concrete piers are used to create a stable platform on a steep slope (see Figure 8.8.4 in Chapter 8). The detail examples chosen for this chapter address modest loads that are well distributed over soil with moderate bearing capacity. Collectively, they illustrate a number of distinct approaches to the design of thermally efficient foundations.

The Pumpkin Ridge Passive House illustrates the most direct and obvious strategy, that of surrounding the entire building with insulating material, including all of the foundation (see Figure 2.1.3 below). This means pouring

footings of the appropriate bearing area on top of a layer of foam, as well as surrounding the stem wall with foam, inside and out, from the footing up to grade. Such an approach allows the mass of the foundation, and the backfill piled against it, to hold the building down. It also allows the entire foundation system to participate in resisting lateral forces. Because both the foundation and the structure above are inside the insulation jacket, the steel anchor bolts and tie-down straps connecting the two do not constitute a thermal bridge. This approach is very effective, but it will likely expand the volume of insulating material required, with a potential increase in cost. A similar approach can be seen in the Karuna House case study, with the added challenge of concentrated loads being carried down the steel columns needed to realize the bold design (see Figure 8.6.4 in Chapter 8).

Buildings constructed with flat slabs on grade or slabs that are thickened and turned down at the edges also lend themselves to the fully isolated approach. Structural slabs distribute the superimposed loads and thus avoid concentrations that might tax the substrates. Applied with discipline to the right ground, shallow slab systems can greatly reduce the depth and volume of foundation that must be brought inside the thermal envelope. The VOLKsHouse 1.0 project illustrates this approach (see Figure 2.2.3 below). At VOLKsHouse, rigid foam at the perimeter is placed first to contain the slab edge. The reduction in formwork, labor, and materials helps to offset the cost of the insulation. Case studies of Hayfield House and the Viridescent Building provide additional examples (see Figures 8.5.4 and 8.14.4 in Chapter 8).

At the opposite end of the spectrum, it is possible to draw the thermal envelope tightly around only the occupied portions of the building and exclude the foundation entirely. A specific zone in the foundation can be set up as a thermal break between the superstructure and the concrete footing. Techniques for insulating the floor itself belong to the next chapter. A typical wood light frame construction rests on a relatively small, pressure-treated sill, with limited bearing capacity perpendicular to the grain. A thermal break introduced at the top of the foundation wall may only require a comparable compressive strength, although shear and tension forces are also a factor. Anchor bolts and tie-down rods must reach through this break material and do, therefore, create a thermal bridge. Nevertheless, such a strategy can be effective in climate zones where a deep frost wall is required and yet there is no basement. A distinct thermal break at the top of the concrete relieves the obligation to insulate the entire surface that is in soil contact. The Freeman House provides one example, and the Louisiana Passive House case study provides another (see Figure 2.3.3 below and Figure 8.7.7 in Chapter 8).

There are numerous hybrid strategies through which the concrete foundation is left on the cold side of the insulation jacket or somewhere in between the warm and the cold. In the simplest hybrid, rigid insulation can be extended down both the inside and outside faces of a traditional concrete stem wall. Although this does not eliminate conduction through the bottom of the footing, it reduces the losses nearer the cold surface and preserves a milder temperature regime directly under the floor. The Stellar Apartments demonstrate this principle (Figure 2.4.3 below). At the Full Plane Residence, presented in Chapter 4, insulation runs down both sides of a very tall concrete foundation wall, far enough to make the path to cold longer and less injurious (see Figure 4.3.3).

Hybrid strategies are common in occupied basements, daylight basements, or spaces partially below grade set against the side of a hill. It may be less expensive to construct the thermal layer inside the concrete wall, using studs and an insulating fill; however, this also reduces the available interior space. Where the concrete is acting as a retaining wall, there may be structural reasons to leave it in direct contact with the soil or gravel backfill. The Fineline Residence provides an example (see Figure 2.5.3 below). Typical of this hybrid, the insulation layer that is coming down within or outside the upper wall must cross through the floor junction to pass inside the basement. At this transition, structural connection and thermal isolation must be reconciled, with a design impact on the wall, floor, and foundation systems.

The Jung Haus project improves the thermal performance of the basement wall by using insulating concrete forms (ICFs; see Figure 2.6.3). The structural wall is comple-

mented by overlapping exterior and interior insulation, resulting in continuously high R-values where they are most needed. The Specht Residence building system offers another means of improvement to the basement wall (see Figure 2.7.3 below). Coffered concrete wall elements are precast around blocks of rigid insulation to provide ample structural capacity with a lower thermal conductivity.

Beyond thermal performance, an important role of the foundation in light frame construction is to lift wood-based materials a required distance above grade. Rigid insulation used outside the stem wall is exposed to potential damage in the gap between the earth fill and the wall construction. A simple protection layer can be added over the insulation, provided it is compatible with earth contact.

Developed landscape systems immediately outside the building put further demands on the foundation design, particularly those in close alignment with the interior floor level. These may include decks, paved terraces, raised planters, and rainwater catchment systems. Case studies of the Cowhorn Vineyard Residence, Ankeny Row Net Zero Community, and Uptown Lofts at Fifth illustrate a variety of approaches to this design constraint (see Figures 8.2.4, 8.1.4, and 8.13.4 in Chapter 8). If durable, but heavy, masonry materials are used as an exterior wainscot or veneer cladding, they offer protection of the insulation but require a definite means of support. The Earthship Farmstead case study shows two foundations: a warm one to support the building and a cold one for the masonry (see Figure 8.3.4 in Chapter 8). The Orchards at Orenco uses a thermally mitigated shelf angle to carry the loads of the brick through the insulation to the single warm foundation within (see Figure 8.9.4 in Chapter 8).

In summary, there can be many different foundation types hidden below, although the simple point of contact between the building and the ground is of the greatest visual concern. Direct approaches line up the load-bearing elements, frame walls to footings, as in the Hayfield House and Jung Haus projects. A graceful, effective transition results from applying a thickness of rigid insulation to the outside face of the stem wall that tucks into the shadow of walls and floor plates overhanging above.

2.1.1 The south façade stretches along the crown of the hill with a daylight basement tucked underneath. JEFF AMRAM PHOTOGRAPHY

2.1.2 Installation of rigid foam under the footings. HAMMER & HAND

PUMPKIN RIDGE PASSIVE HOUSE

The Pumpkin Ridge Passive House, nestled in the foothills west of Portland, Oregon, embraces the simplicity of passive house design concepts to deliver superb comfort and efficiency at minimal added cost. It is one of six homes in the Pacific Northwest to be featured by Northwest ENERGY STAR® as a demonstration energy-efficient home. The building engages the hillside spatially but is fully isolated from the ground thermally. The floor slab is cast over Type II EPS insulation, with footings poured on top of Type XIV high-density geofoam EPS. To shorten preparation time and create a level, smooth surface for laying the sheets of geofoam, a flowable fill was used.

PROJECT INFORMATION

Project title: Pumpkin Ridge Passive House

Location: North Plains, Oregon

Size: 3,050 ft.^{2} (283 m^2)

Completion: 2013

Recognition: Certification (PHIUS), 2014 Department of Energy—Zero Energy Ready Home, 2014 Earth Advantage Homes—Platinum Certification, 2014 ENERGY STAR, Super-Efficient Demo

Type: Single-family house

Architect: Scott | Edwards Architecture

Builder: Hammer & Hand Inc.

CPHC: Skylar Swinford, Hammer & Hand

HDD: 4,750 base 65°F (2,639 base 18.3°C)

CDD: 280 base 65°F (156 base 18.3°C)

Annual precipitation: 38 in. (965 mm)

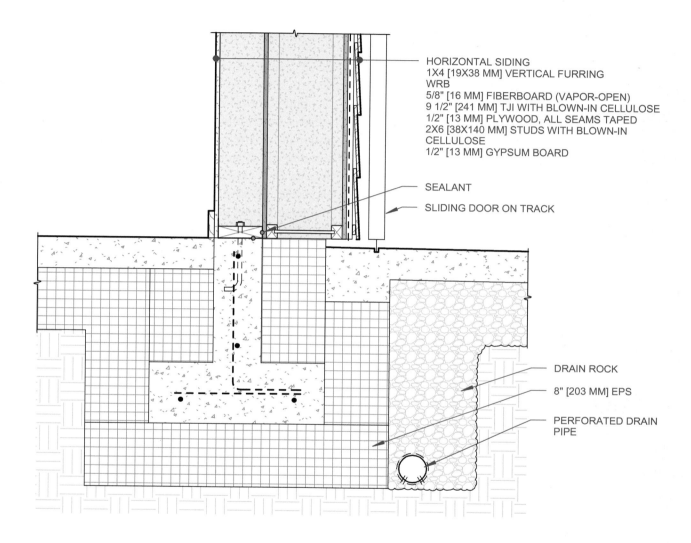

HORIZONTAL SIDING
1X4 [19X38 MM] VERTICAL FURRING
WRB
5/8" [16 MM] FIBERBOARD (VAPOR-OPEN)
9 1/2" [241 MM] TJI WITH BLOWN-IN CELLULOSE
1/2" [13 MM] PLYWOOD, ALL SEAMS TAPED
2X6 [38X140 MM] STUDS WITH BLOWN-IN
CELLULOSE
1/2" [13 MM] GYPSUM BOARD

SEALANT

SLIDING DOOR ON TRACK

DRAIN ROCK

8" [203 MM] EPS

PERFORATED DRAIN
PIPE

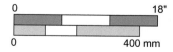

0   18"

0   400 mm

2.1.3 Perimeter footing and stem wall completely isolated within rigid foam insulation.

2.2.1 Thick insulated walls with deeply recessed windows constructed over a slab on grade. AMADEUS LEITNER PHOTOGRPAHY

2.2.2 Preparation for casting of the slab. WAMO STUDIO, LLC

VOLKSHOUSE 1.0

VOLKsHouse 1.0 sits on a site in Santa Fe, New Mexico, with views to the Sangre de Christo Mountains. It is an eco-house for people seeking a viable response to America's overuse of energy resources and the typically higher cost of green construction. Over time, VOLKsHouse LLC will work to advance energy conservation, eco-living, and, in particular, the passive house standard. The construction of the foundation uses a frost skirt perimeter of EPS foam insulation. It is thick enough that no other formwork is needed before the slab is poured. The foundation is wrapped on the exterior with a factory-painted metal sheeting that protects the foam from moisture and bugs. The foam is placed on a bed of sand to allow for drainage and ease of leveling. The project has an EPA-recommended radon system consisting of tubes running under a bed of clean gravel. The gravel layer acts as a capillary break for the additional rigid insulation that will be placed under the slab.

PROJECT INFORMATION

Project title: VOLKsHouse 1.0

Location: Santa Fe, New Mexico

Size: 1,717 ft.^{2} (159.5 m^2)

Completion: 2012

Recognition: Certification (PHI), National Home Buyers Alliance—BuildGreen New Mexico Emerald

Type: Single-family home

Architect: Vahid Mojarrab, WAMO Studio, LLC

Builder: Justin Young, August Construction

CPHC: Graham Irwin, Essential Habitat

HDD: 6,115 base 65°F (3,397 base 18.3°C)

CDD: 339 base 65°F (188 base 18.3°C)

Annual precipitation: 14 in. (355.6 mm)

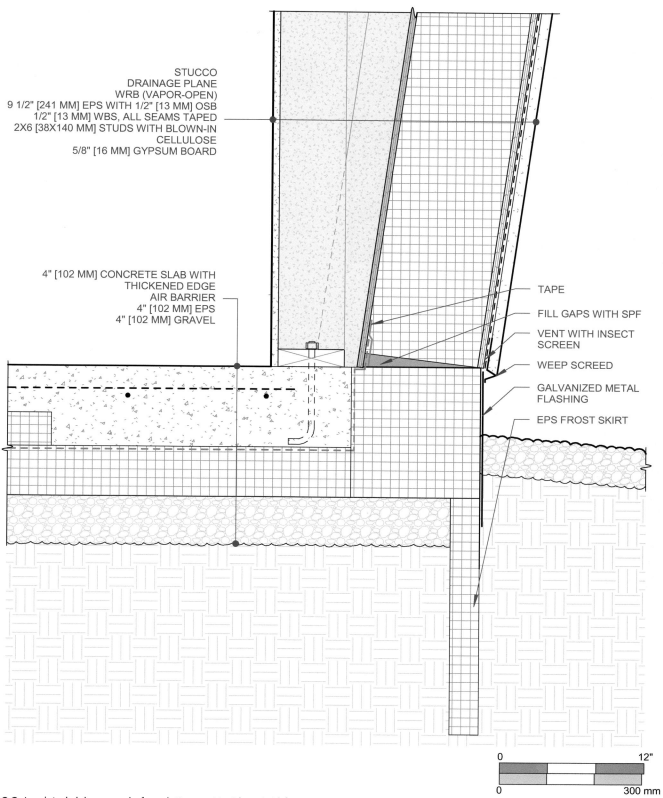

STUCCO
DRAINAGE PLANE
WRB (VAPOR-OPEN)
9 1/2" [241 MM] EPS WITH 1/2" [13 MM] OSB
1/2" [13 MM] WBS, ALL SEAMS TAPED
2X6 [38X140 MM] STUDS WITH BLOWN-IN
CELLULOSE
5/8" [16 MM] GYPSUM BOARD

4" [102 MM] CONCRETE SLAB WITH
THICKENED EDGE
AIR BARRIER
4" [102 MM] EPS
4" [102 MM] GRAVEL

TAPE

FILL GAPS WITH SPF

VENT WITH INSECT
SCREEN

WEEP SCREED

GALVANIZED METAL
FLASHING

EPS FROST SKIRT

0   12"

0   300 mm

2.2.3 Insulated slab on grade foundation cast inside a rigid foam perimeter.

2.3.1 High-performance addition to a traditional house in Maine.
DEREK PORTER, DEREK PORTER STUDIO

2.3.2 Wall framing begins on the concrete perimeter foundation.
BRIGGS KNOWLES ARCHITECTURE+DESIGN

FREEMAN HOUSE

The project is an addition to an 1830 farmhouse, built with the regional practice of aggregated volumes to protect against the cold of central Maine. A fire took the barn in the late twentieth century, leaving only the house. Separated by 200 years and 6 ft., the Freeman addition is an exercise in opposites. The addition follows the vernacular tradition but sets up a dialog between past and present, thick and thin, transparent and opaque, passive and active. The addition is the twin of the original—asymmetrically conjoined, with recognizable features, but different personalities. The original construction is post and beam, hewn and pegged from large timber. The addition is balloon-framed, with truss joists for economy, stiffness, and thermal-bridge-free construction. The 9-in. (229-mm) depth for the wall studs provides a deep cavity for cellulose insulation. The walls of the original are 5-in. (140-mm) thick for an R-14 value. The walls of the addition are 15-in. (381-mm) thick for an R-50 value.

PROJECT INFORMATION

Project title: Freeman House

Location: Freeman, Maine

Size: 1,700 ft.^{2} (157 m^2)

Completion: 2012

Recognition: Passive House planned

Type: Single-family home

Architect: BriggsKnowles Architecture+Design

Builder: Sebastian Tooker Construction

CPHC: Jonathan Knowles, BKAD

HDD: 8784 base 65°F (4880 base 18.3°C)

CDD: 197 base 65°F (109 base 18.3°C)

Annual precipitation: 38 in. (965 mm)

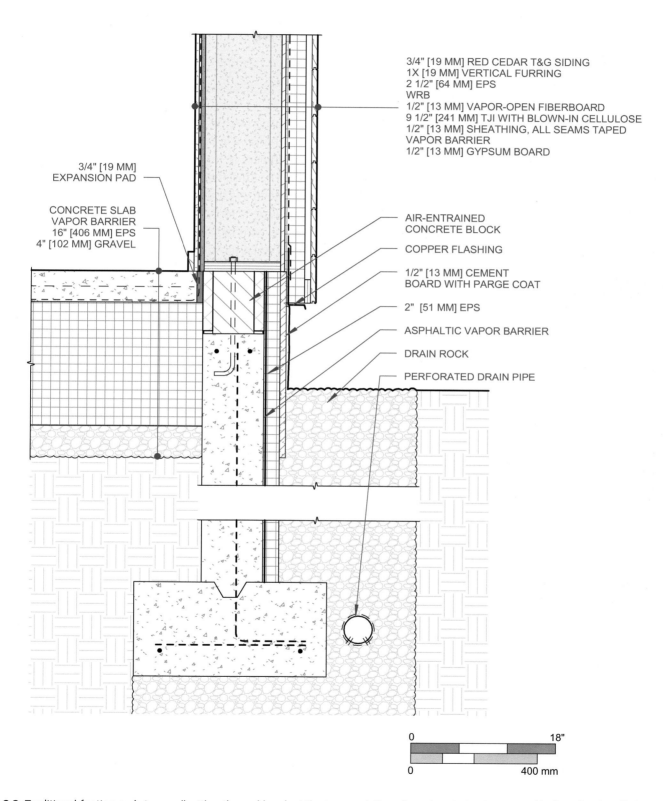

3/4" [19 MM] RED CEDAR T&G SIDING
1X [19 MM] VERTICAL FURRING
2 1/2" [64 MM] EPS
WRB
1/2" [13 MM] VAPOR-OPEN FIBERBOARD
9 1/2" [241 MM] TJI WITH BLOWN-IN CELLULOSE
1/2" [13 MM] SHEATHING, ALL SEAMS TAPED
VAPOR BARRIER
1/2" [13 MM] GYPSUM BOARD

3/4" [19 MM]
EXPANSION PAD

CONCRETE SLAB
VAPOR BARRIER
16" [406 MM] EPS
4" [102 MM] GRAVEL

AIR-ENTRAINED
CONCRETE BLOCK

COPPER FLASHING

1/2" [13 MM] CEMENT
BOARD WITH PARGE COAT

2" [51 MM] EPS

ASPHALTIC VAPOR BARRIER

DRAIN ROCK

PERFORATED DRAIN PIPE

0   18"

0   400 mm

2.3.3 Traditional footing and stem wall with a thermal break at the top consisting of an air-entrained concrete block under the sill plate.

2.4.1 Metal flashing protects the exterior insulation at the stem wall. BERGSUND DELANEY ARCHITECTURE AND PLANNING

2.4.2 Side by side comparator buildings. This one using passive house standards. BERGSUND DELANEY ARCHITECTURE AND PLANNING

STELLAR APARTMENTS

Stellar Apartments is fifty-four-units of affordable family housing in Eugene, Oregon, verified as the first certified passive house, multifamily, affordable housing in the US. This project includes a mixture of one- to three-bedroom townhomes and flats. The complex includes units for National Guard families, and homeless veterans with families, through VetLIFT. All units meet or exceed Earth Advantage Certification, including Energy Star-rated appliances and lighting; U = 0.29 windows; and fresh-air ventilation system for healthy indoor air. One building, of six units, reaches passive house standards as a pilot project to examine its performance compared to a nearly identical neighboring building designed to Earth Advantage. Poor soil drainage mandated a crawlspace. The economical foundation system accommodates raised entry pads for required wheelchair access without thermal bridging.

PROJECT INFORMATION

Project title: Stellar Apartments Passive House

Location: Eugene, Oregon

Size: 6,480 ft.² (602 m²) passive house building; 63,572 ft.² (5,906 m²) entire project

Completion: 2013

Recognition: Certification (PHIUS), Earth Advantage Gold Certification

Type: Multifamily Affordable Housing

Architect: Bergsund DeLaney Architecture and Planning

Builder: Meili Construction Co.

CPHC: Win Swafford, Jan Fillinger

HDD: 4,821 base 65°F (2,678 base 18.3°C)

CDD: 210 base 65°F (117 base 18.3°C)

Annual precipitation: 46 in. (1,168 mm)

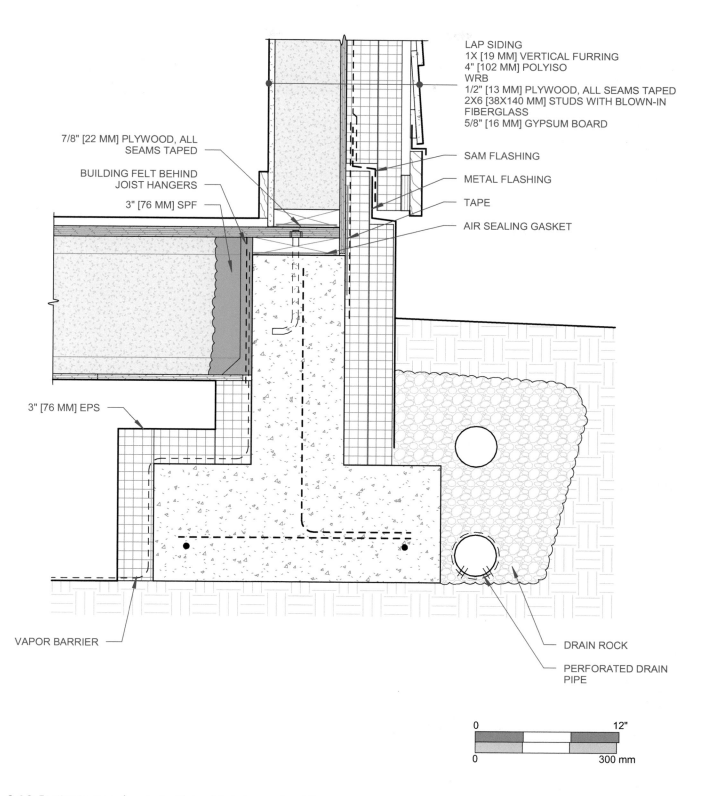

LAP SIDING
1X [19 MM] VERTICAL FURRING
4" [102 MM] POLYISO
WRB
1/2" [13 MM] PLYWOOD, ALL SEAMS TAPED
2X6 [38X140 MM] STUDS WITH BLOWN-IN
FIBERGLASS
5/8" [16 MM] GYPSUM BOARD

SAM FLASHING

METAL FLASHING

TAPE

AIR SEALING GASKET

7/8" [22 MM] PLYWOOD, ALL
SEAMS TAPED

BUILDING FELT BEHIND
JOIST HANGERS

3" [76 MM] SPF

3" [76 MM] EPS

VAPOR BARRIER

DRAIN ROCK

PERFORATED DRAIN
PIPE

0   12"

0   300 mm

2.4.3 Footing in ground contact with insulated stem wall and floor.

2.5.1 House features an elongated plan with occupied basement under the central portion. JON JENSEN PHOTOGRAPHY

2.5.2 Additional retaining walls at the rear to control the hillside. JON JENSEN PHOTOGRAPHY

FINELINE HOUSE

The Fineline House, located in Ashland, Oregon, is a LEED-H Platinum-certified home with exceptional green design and construction features. It is four to five times more efficient than a typical residence of comparable size and configuration. It features state-of-the-art lighting and heating systems and a built-in energy-monitoring system, claiming considerable energy savings and exceptional indoor air quality.

An elongated profile that hugs the site contours, and large expanses of glass facing the view of valley and mountains to the north made the pursuit of passive house certification a challenge. However, the passive house design-build principles were deemed highly relevant nevertheless. PHPP modeling and the key PH building envelope strategies were applied to the final design. Structural insulated panels, thick underslab insulation triple-glazed Unilux windows, and a Zehnder heat recovery ventilator round out a high-performance building.

PROJECT INFORMATION

Project title: Fineline House

Location: Ashland, Oregon

Size: 4,390 ft.² (407m²)

Completion: 2014

Recognition: Passive House planned, LEED-H Platinum, FSC-Chain-of-Custody certificate

Type: Single-family house

Architect: Jan Fillinger

Builder: Green Hammer

CPHC: Alex Boetzel

HDD: 4,323 base 65°F (2,402 base 18.3°C)

CDD: 790 base 65°F (439 base 18.3°C)

Annual precipitation: 20 in. (510 mm)

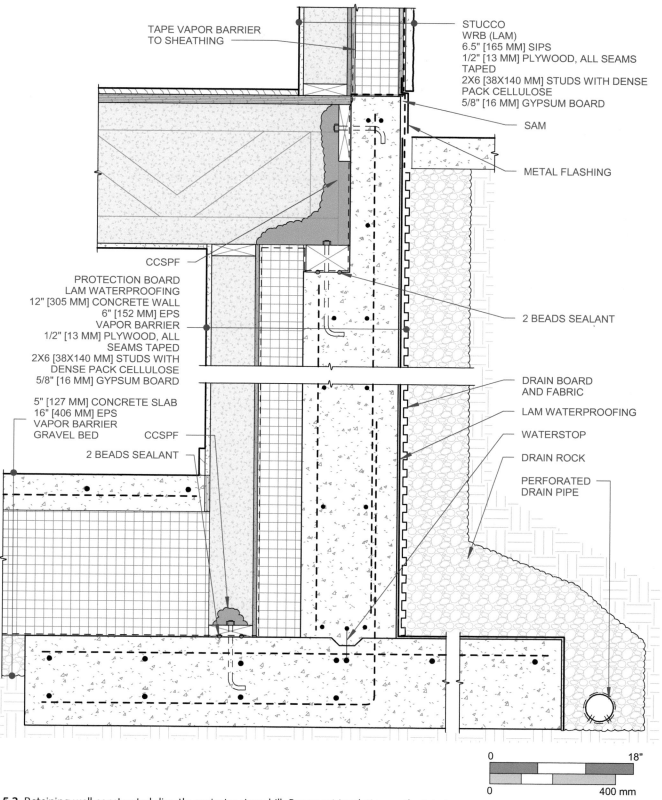

TAPE VAPOR BARRIER
TO SHEATHING

STUCCO
WRB (LAM)
6.5" [165 MM] SIPS
1/2" [13 MM] PLYWOOD, ALL SEAMS
TAPED
2X6 [38X140 MM] STUDS WITH DENSE
PACK CELLULOSE
5/8" [16 MM] GYPSUM BOARD

SAM

METAL FLASHING

CCSPF

PROTECTION BOARD
LAM WATERPROOFING
12" [305 MM] CONCRETE WALL
6" [152 MM] EPS
VAPOR BARRIER
1/2" [13 MM] PLYWOOD, ALL
SEAMS TAPED
2X6 [38X140 MM] STUDS WITH
DENSE PACK CELLULOSE
5/8" [16 MM] GYPSUM BOARD

5" [127 MM] CONCRETE SLAB
16" [406 MM] EPS
VAPOR BARRIER
GRAVEL BED   CCSPF

2 BEADS SEALANT

2 BEADS SEALANT

DRAIN BOARD
AND FABRIC

LAM WATERPROOFING

WATERSTOP

DRAIN ROCK

PERFORATED
DRAIN PIPE

0   18"

0   400 mm

2.5.3 Retaining wall constructed directly against a steep hill. Basement insulation on the interior.

2.6.1 Jung Haus viewed from the south west. KURT JUNG

2.6.2 ICF Basement walls with exterior insulation. KURT AND MAURA JUNG

JUNG HAUS

The Jung Haus is a modern farmhouse situated in the moraine uplands of northwest Oakland County, Michigan, on a site where a nineteenth-century farm house burned down in the 1950s. The foundations of the old stone barn and silo later became garden walls. Insulated concrete forms were used for the basement walls. They were wrapped with an additional layer of insulation inside and out. The heavily insulated walls of the house were constructed using standard 2 x 6 (38 x 140 mm) stud walls, sheathed with a water-resistive air barrier and over-framed with 12-in.-(305-mm-) deep I-joists. The total insulation value of the wall was R-60. The inside chord of the I-joists stands on the shoulder of the ICF wall.

PROJECT INFORMATION

Project title: Jung Haus

Location: Holly, Michigan

Size: 2,300 ft.² (214 m²)

Completion: 2013

Recognition: Certified (PHI), Fine Homebuilding's 2014 Best Energy-Smart Home

Type: Single-family home

Architect: GO Logic

Builder: Energy Wise Homes

CPHC: Think Little

HDD: 6,634 base 65°F (3,686 base 18.3°C)

CDD: 627 base 65°F (348 base 18.3°C)

Annual precipitation: 34 in. (864 mm)

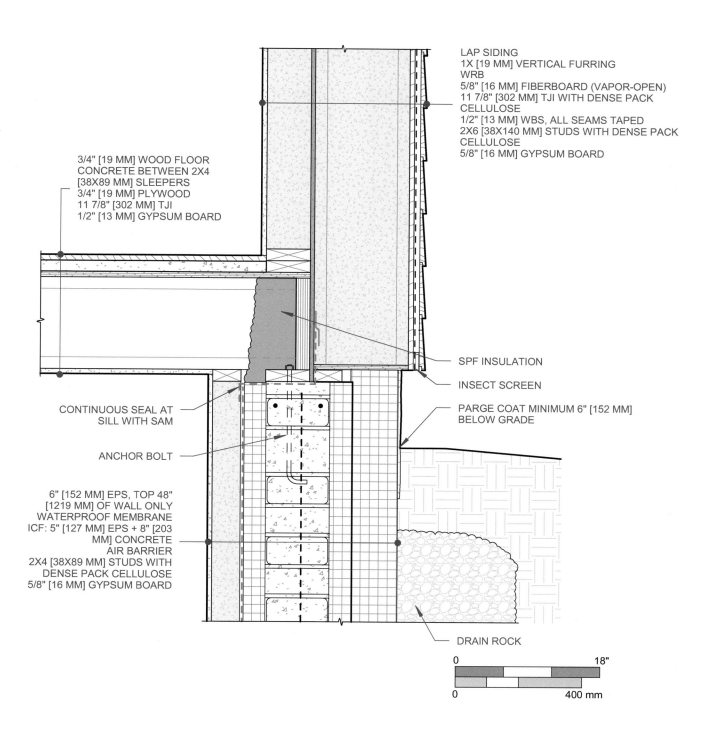

LAP SIDING
1X [19 MM] VERTICAL FURRING
WRB
5/8" [16 MM] FIBERBOARD (VAPOR-OPEN)
11 7/8" [302 MM] TJI WITH DENSE PACK CELLULOSE
1/2" [13 MM] WBS, ALL SEAMS TAPED
2X6 [38X140 MM] STUDS WITH DENSE PACK CELLULOSE
5/8" [16 MM] GYPSUM BOARD

3/4" [19 MM] WOOD FLOOR
CONCRETE BETWEEN 2X4 [38X89 MM] SLEEPERS
3/4" [19 MM] PLYWOOD
11 7/8" [302 MM] TJI
1/2" [13 MM] GYPSUM BOARD

SPF INSULATION

INSECT SCREEN

CONTINUOUS SEAL AT SILL WITH SAM

ANCHOR BOLT

PARGE COAT MINIMUM 6" [152 MM] BELOW GRADE

6" [152 MM] EPS, TOP 48" [1219 MM] OF WALL ONLY
WATERPROOF MEMBRANE
ICF: 5" [127 MM] EPS + 8" [203 MM] CONCRETE
AIR BARRIER
2X4 [38X89 MM] STUDS WITH DENSE PACK CELLULOSE
5/8" [16 MM] GYPSUM BOARD

DRAIN ROCK

0   18"

0   400 mm

2.6.3 Basement walls constructed with insulating concrete forms (ICFs). Additional insulation added inside and out.

2.7.1 Precast basement wall panels placed with a crane.
BUILDSMART/PROSOCO

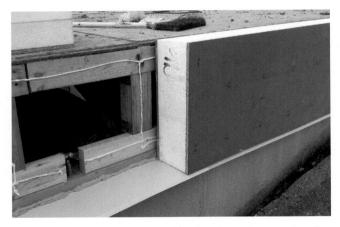

2.7.2 Panelized floor truss assembly placed over basement walls.
BUILDSMART/PROSOCO

SPECHT RESIDENCE

The Specht Residence in Thaxton, Virginia, combines an open floor plan with traditional architectural features for a gracious, modern home experience. Energy savings are realized at virtually no additional construction expense. Ongoing utility bill savings offset any added mortgage payment for financing the modest increase in upfront construction costs. This residence uses an advanced building envelope of prefabricated components and works as an entire system, bringing together structure and insulation as a series of panel systems for the foundation, walls, roof, doors, and windows. This envelope, coupled with ground source heat loop and a solar thermal system, assists this home in achieving 72 percent energy savings compared with a code-built home.

PROJECT INFORMATION

Project title: Specht Residence

Location: Thaxton, Virginia

Size: 1,808 ft.^{2} (175 m^2)

Completion: 2012

Recognition: Certified (PHIUS), Fine Homebuilding's 2014 Best Energy-Smart Home

Type: Single-family home

Architect: Adam Cohen

Builder: Structures Design/Build

CPHC: Adam Cohen

HDD: 4,191 base 65°F (2,328 base 18.3°C)

CDD: 1,124 base 65°F (624 base 18.3°C)

Annual precipitation: 41.25 in. (1,048 mm)

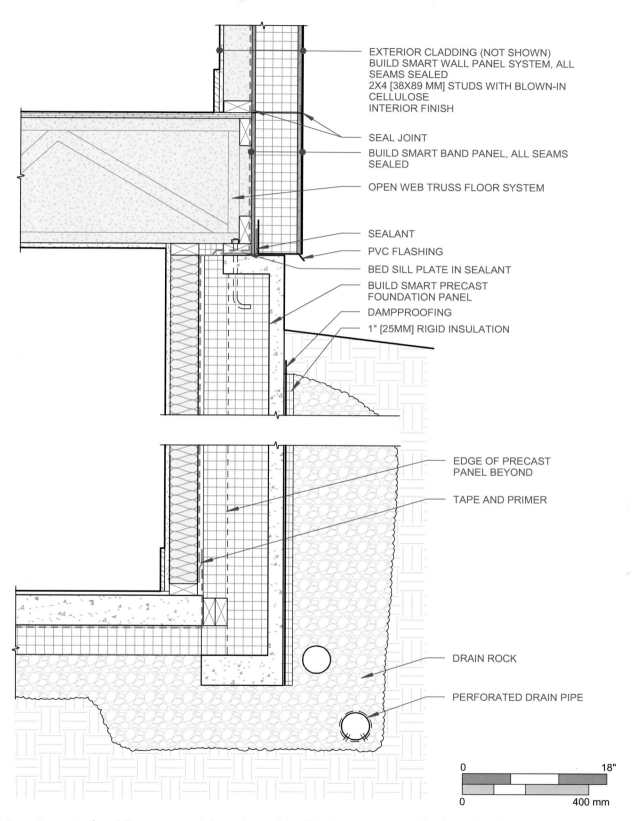

EXTERIOR CLADDING (NOT SHOWN)
BUILD SMART WALL PANEL SYSTEM, ALL
SEAMS SEALED
2X4 [38X89 MM] STUDS WITH BLOWN-IN
CELLULOSE
INTERIOR FINISH

SEAL JOINT

BUILD SMART BAND PANEL, ALL SEAMS
SEALED

OPEN WEB TRUSS FLOOR SYSTEM

SEALANT

PVC FLASHING

BED SILL PLATE IN SEALANT

BUILD SMART PRECAST
FOUNDATION PANEL

DAMPPROOFING

1" [25MM] RIGID INSULATION

EDGE OF PRECAST
PANEL BEYOND

TAPE AND PRIMER

DRAIN ROCK

PERFORATED DRAIN PIPE

0   18"

0   400 mm

2.7.3 Precast concrete foundation using panels formed over slabs of insulation to improve the thermal performance.

CHAPTER 3

Floor Systems

Contemporary wood light frame construction in North America is dominated by the platform frame approach. The first floor is constructed immediately after the basement or foundation, and the succeeding walls are laid out and raised using the floor as a working surface. The chapters in this book reflect this "bottom–up" sequence. During the design process, decisions about the floor construction clearly evolve hand in hand with decisions about the walls above and the foundation below. Although the actual construction is a sequence, design is an iterative process.

Given these complexities, it is useful to begin with the simplest case, that of the intermediate floor with conditioned space above and below. Such floors will interrupt the thermal envelope of the building only at the outer perimeter, if the common platform frame approach is adopted. The insulating wall may pass continuously outside the floor plate, if a balloon frame or internal heavy timber frame is selected.

Platform frame construction can be further broken down according to the location of the load-bearing elements within the overall thickness of the insulated wall—whether closer to the inside face or closer to the outside. If there are two layers of stud framing in the wall, for example, does the intermediate floor rest on the inner or the outer layer? With the line of vertical support closer to the inside of a thick wall, the edge of the floor assembly can be held back from the perimeter, so that it is overlaid by an exterior layer of insulation passing directly from the wall above to the wall below. There is an inevitable density of material at the rim of the floor plate needed to transmit vertical loads and tie the building together in order to resist lateral forces. If all this material gets too close to the exterior surface of the building, it becomes a potential thermal bridge. The Balance Project in this chapter illustrates the thermally efficient approach, in which a plane of load-bearing studs supports the floor from the inside edge of the wall assembly (see Figure 3.1.3 below). This basic strategy is found in most of the case studies in Chapter 8.

As will be seen in the next chapter, climate conditions and construction economy some-times suggest that the floor plates extend to find support near the outside face of the wall. The ends of the perpendicular floor joists then become thermal short circuits, punching through the insulated heart of the wall. This problem can be mitigated by filling the spaces between the joists with insulation. That fill has to be carried a number of feet toward the center of the building, so that the warmth of the interior has further to travel down the axis of the joist, from the point of first contact to the cold, outside end.

In balloon framing, the floor joists are supported by a ledger that is attached to the inside surface of the wall. This largely takes the floor out of contact with the thermal envelope. Skidmore House demonstrates the simplicity and economy that can be achieved with this approach (see Figure 3.2.3 below). Similarly, in a timber frame building wrapped with foam panels, the frame supports the floor entirely on the warm side of the insulation. The common rooms of the Hayfield House case study illustrate this approach (see Figure 8.5.16 in Chapter 8).

At the ground floor of a building, the construction options become both more numerous and more complex. Isolating the floor from heat loss at the perimeter remains the central concern. Many of the relevant options have already been presented in the foundations chapter. As previously described, if the wall, the floor plate, and the foundation are all overlaid with a continuous outer leaf of insulation, then the vertical loads can be transferred from one to the other in a conventional fashion, without concern for thermal bridges.

Insulated concrete slabs on grade can take the place of framed floors. Structural slab foundations are addressed in the previous chapter. Slabs can also be cast inside a perimeter footing, bearing only the floor loads and no superimposed walls or columns. They can easily be placed over a layer of insulating material, bringing them inside the thermal envelope. This is a common strategy in basements. Applied at the first floor, where the concrete can be exposed to direct thermal gains through the windows, the mass of the floor can be used to stabilize interior temperatures and reduce heating demands. The Madrona Passive House case study illustrates this approach at the basement level and at the first floor (see Figures 8.8.4 and 8.8.7 in Chapter 8).

Framed floors at the first level become the thermal envelope of the building when they are suspended above uncontrolled or partially controlled crawl spaces. Relatively deep spanning members can be used to increase the thickness available for insulation. This approach imposes very little penalty beyond a slight increase in the building height. It may pay dividends through the simplification of the floor framing, using longer spans between supports. Manufactured joists are often preferred in the floors to reduce problems of shrinkage, and they are available with substantial depths. In a composite section, the slender web will reduce the thermal bridge effects that ultimately limit the effectiveness of solid sawn framing. This can be seen in the Windy View Passive House (see Figure 3.3.5 below). Engineered trusses offer the same advantage.

Where the floor framing is sized for no more than the depth required by the structural loads, the thermal performance can be augmented by additional layers of insulation being suspended underneath. In the crawl space, free from any compressive loads, a great range of insulating materials will serve. Placement of the extra layer requires additional labor, but it is very effective against thermal losses through the joists. The Midorihaus illustrates this approach in a retrofit project that conserved the solid sawn joists and floor finishes already in place (see Figure 3.4.3 below).

Particular care must be taken when floor systems are directly exposed to the exterior over a significant area. Such conditions arise when recessed porches are cut out of the basic building volume at one level, thermally exposing the underside of the floor above. They also arise when bays or wings of the building cantilever beyond the limits of the level below. Particularly at the cantilever, structural requirements may increase the density of framing lumber at the exposure, increasing the risk of thermal breaks.

Floors of these types may experience changes in temperature from top to bottom that are significantly greater than those found in floors above a crawl space. This gives particular advantage to a second layer of insulated construction below the plane of the structural members. Whether this is achieved with rigid panel products or independently framed and filled, the second layer reduces thermal losses that will occur through the structural layer, regardless of its depth. The Karuna House, both in this chapter and in the case studies, demonstrates these conditions in the extended wings of the upper floor (see Figure 3.5.3 below). The built-up exterior layers of insulation in the walls wrap around the structural elements and continue under the suspended floor.

Exposed floor assemblies require careful consideration of the barriers, in position and detail. The air barrier must be located where the number of penetrations will be manageable. Vapor control must be developed at a point that provides adequate drying potential in both directions. This may be up or down, inward or outward, depending on the climate, season, and direction of exposure. For complex assemblies, a hygrothermal analysis may be advised, with care being taken to avoid two layers of relatively impermeable material that can trap moisture between them.

Floor systems may be exposed upward where the enclosure of a second level steps back to create an outdoor terrace on top of the first. What was an insulated floor transitions into an insulated and walkable roof. This adds water control and drainage to the demands of air, thermal, and vapor control. The greatest challenge comes at the doorsill leading from the warm interior to the terrace. There are many more components to the assembly stacked up outside the threshold, and yet there must be a reasonable continuity in the walking surfaces on the top and the ceiling plane underneath. The Orchard Street House illustrates this condition, as do details in the case studies of the Madrona Passive House and Empowerhouse (see Figure 3.6.3 below and Figures 8.8.13 and 8.4.19 in Chapter 8).

Elevated exterior space can be realized more efficiently with an exterior deck than a roof terrace. If the barriers follow the plane of the wall, the demands on the "floor" assembly are greatly reduced, both inside and out. The case studies of both Karuna House and Saugerties Residence feature use of cantilevered side walls at the extended outdoor space to support deck joists that are parallel to the interior floor joists, allowing a complete separation between the two systems (see Figures 8.6.16 and 8.12.19 in Chapter 8). The Orchards at Orenco uses exterior walls to support decks on three corners, with an exterior post on the fourth (see Figure 8.9.16 in Chapter 8.

3.1.1 Larsen trusses wrap the stud frame structure. NEEDBASED INC.

3.1.2 The garden courtyard at balance project. AMADEUS LEITNER PHOTOGRAPHY

BALANCE PROJECT

The first certified passive house project in New Mexico, the Balance Project, was developed as a unique, mixed-use, infill condominium containing residential and professional office space, including the NEEDBASED design offices. It is named "Balance" to represent the combination of achieving a balance between establishing a professional office, home life, and the highest environmental standards. The project sits within the City of Santa Fe's historic Railyard District and connects to bike trails, city parks, and local shopping and dining. The project features walls with dense-pack cellulose at R-58; slab R-26; roof with cellulose R-98; and high performance Optiwin windows U-0.137 (SHGC 0.63). The second floor bears on the interior stud wall, with blocks of EPS between the floor framing to reduce thermal bridging. Larsen trusses are used on the exterior to provide substantial space for insulation and provide support for cladding.

PROJECT INFORMATION

Project title: Balance Project

Location: Santa Fe, New Mexico

Size: 3,452 ft.² (321 m²) heated; 2,508 ft.² (233 m²) treated floor area

Completion: 2012

Recognition: Certification (PHI), NAHB—Build green/Emerald

Type: NAHB—Build green/Emerald

Architect: Jonah Stanford, NEEDBASED Inc.

Builder: Buck Construction

CPHC: Jonah Stanford, NEEDBASED Inc.

HDD: 6,115 base 65°F (3,397 base 18.3°C)

CDD: 339 base 65°F (188 base 18.3°C)

Annual precipitation: 14 in. (355.6 mm)

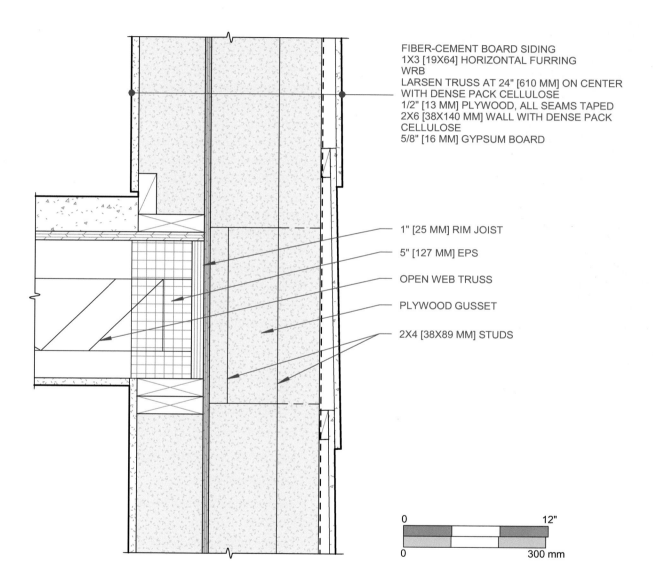

FIBER-CEMENT BOARD SIDING
1X3 [19X64] HORIZONTAL FURRING
WRB
LARSEN TRUSS AT 24" [610 MM] ON CENTER
WITH DENSE PACK CELLULOSE
1/2" [13 MM] PLYWOOD, ALL SEAMS TAPED
2X6 [38X140 MM] WALL WITH DENSE PACK
CELLULOSE
5/8" [16 MM] GYPSUM BOARD

1" [25 MM] RIM JOIST

5" [127 MM] EPS

OPEN WEB TRUSS

PLYWOOD GUSSET

2X4 [38X89 MM] STUDS

0   12"

0   300 mm

3.1.3 Platform framed second floor with an exterior insulation layer contained by a Larsen truss.

3.2.1 South elevation of Skidmore House. JEREMY BITTERMANN PHOTOGRAPHY

3.2.2 Double height living space with balloon framed walls. IN SITU ARCHITECTURE

SKIDMORE HOUSE

Located in a neighborhood of postwar homes in Portland, Oregon, the Skidmore House merges contemporary design with the highest level of energy efficiency. Providing a true live–work condition, two separate buildings address the program requirements while creating a unique transitional space between. High levels of insulation, extremely airtight construction (tested at 0.32 ACH50), high-performing triple-glazed European windows, and a heat recovery ventilator (HRV) allow the structure to meet the passive house standard. The on-grade floors are concrete, providing thermal storage to help stabilize temperatures in the cooling season. EPS insulation wraps down, around, and under the slab on grade foundation, keeping the entire system within the thermal envelope. The upper-floor wood framing is hung from the balloon framed walls with a continuous ledger to minimize thermal bridging and provide a full cavity for insulation.

PROJECT INFORMATION

Project title: Skidmore House

Location: Portland, Oregon

Size: 1,680 ft.^{2} (156 m^2) treated floor area

Completion: 2013

Recognition: Certified (PHIUS), Earth Advantage Platinum

Type: Single-family house

Architect: Jeff Stern, In Situ Architecture

Builder: Jeff Stern, In Situ Architecture

CPHC: Jeff Stern, In Situ Architecture

HDD: 4,222 base 65°F (2,346 base 18.3°C)

CDD: 423 base 65°F (235 base 18.3°C)

Annual precipitation: 46.5 in. (1,181 mm)

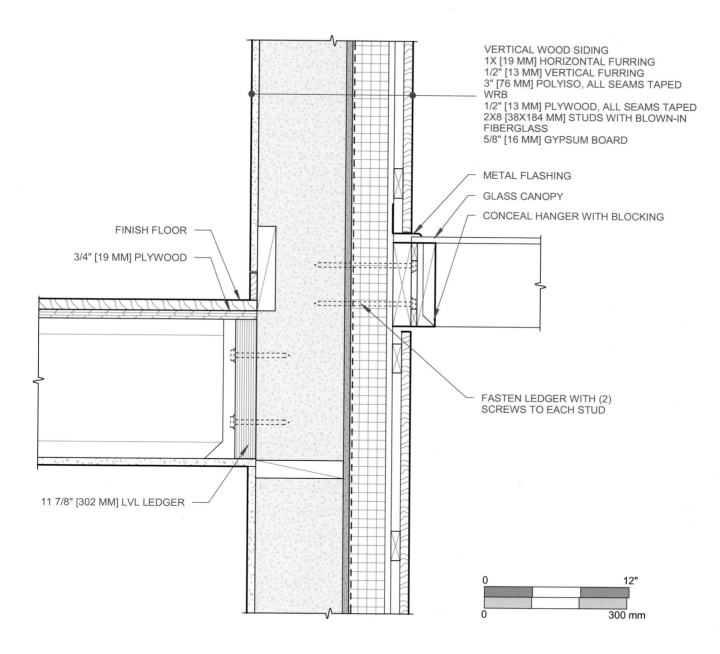

VERTICAL WOOD SIDING
1X [19 MM] HORIZONTAL FURRING
1/2" [13 MM] VERTICAL FURRING
3" [76 MM] POLYISO, ALL SEAMS TAPED
WRB
1/2" [13 MM] PLYWOOD, ALL SEAMS TAPED
2X8 [38X184 MM] STUDS WITH BLOWN-IN
FIBERGLASS
5/8" [16 MM] GYPSUM BOARD

METAL FLASHING

GLASS CANOPY

CONCEAL HANGER WITH BLOCKING

FINISH FLOOR

3/4" [19 MM] PLYWOOD

FASTEN LEDGER WITH (2)
SCREWS TO EACH STUD

11 7/8" [302 MM] LVL LEDGER

0   12"

0   300 mm

3.2.3 Balloon framed second floor with an exterior overlay of rigid insulation.

3.3.1 Windy View from an Oregon hill top. BILYEU HOMES INC.

3.3.2 Sheathed and sealed floor framing. BILYEU HOMES INC.

WINDY VIEW PASSIVE HOUSE

This residence in Philomath, Oregon, commands majestic views of the coastal range and Mary's Peak and combines modern aesthetics with a high-performance building envelope. The house features thickly insulated assemblies, heat recovery ventilation, and an airtight exterior shell that achieved 0.31 ACH50 during the blower door test. A unique and steeply sloping lot proved challenging for several reasons. The customer's need for ADA accessibility at the front door, as well as preserving space for a required emergency vehicle easement, necessitated positioning the house very near the steep slope. Geotechnical engineering requirements made an insulated slab very difficult, if not impossible, and, as a result, a modified crawl space was employed. Northwest Oregon's unique climate zone is one of a few areas in the US where a passively ventilated crawl space performs very well, and it was the right fit for this project.

PROJECT INFORMATION

Project title: Windy View Passive House

Location: Philomath, Oregon

Size: 1,660 ft.^{2} (154 m^2)

Completion: 2015

Recognition: Pre-certified (PHIUS), Net Zero Ready

Type: Single-family home

Architect: Concept by Nathan Good Architects; plans by Bilyeu Homes, Inc.

Builder: Bilyeu Homes, Inc.

CPHC: Blake Bilyeu

HDD: 4,204 base 65°F (2,336 base 18.3°C)

CDD: 412 base 65°F (229 base 18.3°C)

Annual precipitation: 67 in. (1,702 mm)

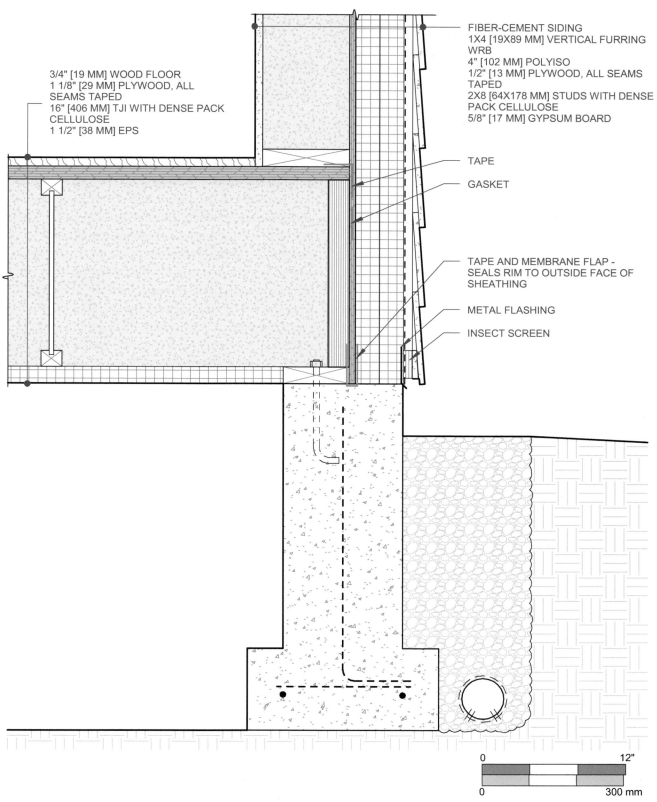

3/4" [19 MM] WOOD FLOOR
1 1/8" [29 MM] PLYWOOD, ALL
SEAMS TAPED
16" [406 MM] TJI WITH DENSE PACK
CELLULOSE
1 1/2" [38 MM] EPS

FIBER-CEMENT SIDING
1X4 [19X89 MM] VERTICAL FURRING
WRB
4" [102 MM] POLYISO
1/2" [13 MM] PLYWOOD, ALL SEAMS
TAPED
2X8 [64X178 MM] STUDS WITH DENSE
PACK CELLULOSE
5/8" [17 MM] GYPSUM BOARD

TAPE

GASKET

TAPE AND MEMBRANE FLAP -
SEALS RIM TO OUTSIDE FACE OF
SHEATHING

METAL FLASHING

INSECT SCREEN

0   12"

0   300 mm

3.3.3 Deep insulated floor assembly spans over an unconditioned crawl space.

3.4.1 Street façade of Midorihaus after renovation. KURT HURLEY

3.4.2 Insulation upgrade in existing crawl space. CHIE KAWAHARA

MIDORIHAUS

This 1922 Craftsman-style bungalow needed extensive repairs when it was purchased, renovated, and upgraded to passive house standards. The subfloor is tongue-and-groove fir, originally covered by linoleum and oak flooring. As part of the rehabilitation, the linoleum was removed, and the exposed fir and existing oak were refinished. To achieve passive house airtightness, and to increase the R-value of the floor assembly without disturbing the finishes, a layer of EPS foam was applied beneath the floor joists and sealed with tape and foam to the mudsill and the interstitial posts. To provide clearance for air-sealing and underfloor insulation, the water supply plumbing was relocated to the middle of the floor cavity, deep within the floor insulation, from below the joists. This also reduced heat loss. This building leakage tested at 22 ACH50 initially, but was reduced to 0.6 ACH50.

PROJECT INFORMATION

Project title: Midorihaus (www.midorihaus.com)

Location: Santa Cruz, California

Size: 1,413 ft.² (131 m²)

Completion: 2012

Recognition: Certification (PHI), 2013 City of Santa Cruz Green Building Award, 2014 Thousand Home Challenge, 2014 Millionth Square Meter of Passive House, 2015 California Senate Certificate of Recognition

Type: Single-family house

Architect: Essential Habitat Architecture

Builder: Santa Cruz Green Builders

CPHC: Graham Irwin, Essential Habitat Architecture

HDD: 3,035 base 65°F (1,700 base 18.3°C)

CDD: 1,385 base 65°F (776 base 18.3°C)

Annual precipitation: 30.66 in. (779 mm)

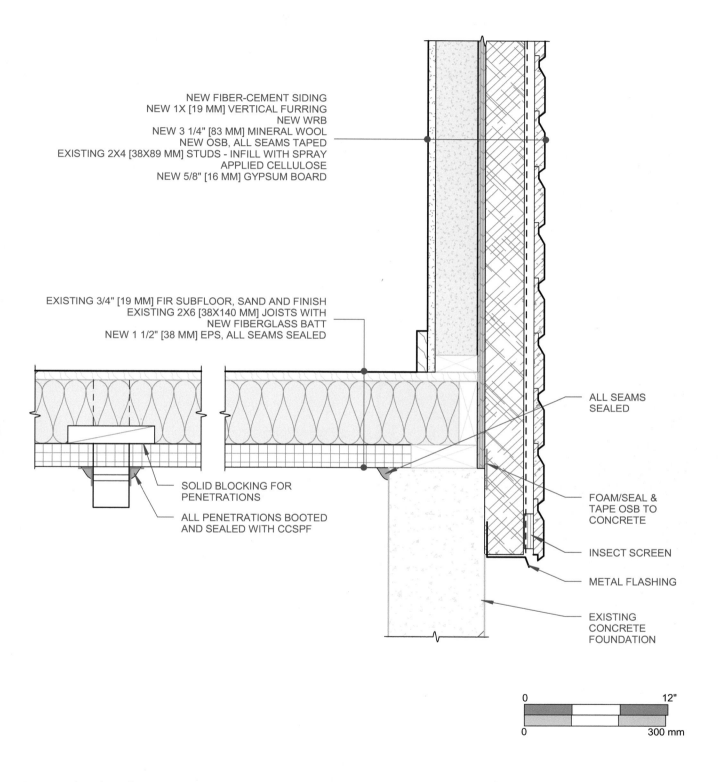

NEW FIBER-CEMENT SIDING
NEW 1X [19 MM] VERTICAL FURRING
NEW WRB
NEW 3 1/4" [83 MM] MINERAL WOOL
NEW OSB, ALL SEAMS TAPED
EXISTING 2X4 [38X89 MM] STUDS - INFILL WITH SPRAY
APPLIED CELLULOSE
NEW 5/8" [16 MM] GYPSUM BOARD

EXISTING 3/4" [19 MM] FIR SUBFLOOR, SAND AND FINISH
EXISTING 2X6 [38X140 MM] JOISTS WITH
NEW FIBERGLASS BATT
NEW 1 1/2" [38 MM] EPS, ALL SEAMS SEALED

SOLID BLOCKING FOR
PENETRATIONS

ALL PENETRATIONS BOOTED
AND SEALED WITH CCSPF

ALL SEAMS
SEALED

FOAM/SEAL &
TAPE OSB TO
CONCRETE

INSECT SCREEN

METAL FLASHING

EXISTING
CONCRETE
FOUNDATION

0   12"

0   300 mm

3.4.3 Rigid insulation layer added under existing, insulated floor joists to reduce thermal bridge effects.

3.5.1 The second floor hovers over a sunken terrace. JEREMY BITTERMAN PHOTOGRAPHY

3.5.2 Steel framing on the east side of the second floor. HAMMER & HAND

KARUNA HOUSE

The Karuna House combines a beautiful site with a sculptural design and exceptionally high energy performance. A unique floor and wall assembly is one of the main reasons for its efficiency, which is exemplified by the detail at a large cantilevered wing. Insulation wraps from underneath the floor, around a beam, and up the wall, providing a continuous thermal envelope. In order to support the cladding through the thick insulation, a layer of custom "J"-shaped over-framing is spaced throughout the insulation. Consisting of a strip of plywood with a small strip of wood nailed to each end, it cuts the amount of thermal bridging to a minimum, while providing ample support for the wood cladding. More details for this house can be found in the case studies of Chapter 8.

PROJECT INFORMATION

Project title: Karuna House

Location: Newberg, Oregon

Size: 3,261 ft.^{2} (303 m^2)

Completion: 2013

Recognition: Certified (PHIUS), LEED for Homes Platinum, Minergie-P-ECO, DOE Zero Energy Ready Home, Earth Advantage Platinum, 2015 First Place—Single Family PHIUS Passive Projects Competition, Beyond Green Award—National Institute of Building Sciences, 2014 Green Home of the Year—*Green Builder Magazine*, 2013 AIA Portland Design Award—2030 Challenge

Type: Single-family house

Architect: Holst Architecture

Builder: Hammer & Hand

CPHC: Dylan Lamar, Green Hammer

HDD: 4,559 base 65°F (2,533 base 18.3°C)

CDD: 300 base 65°F (167 base 18.3°C)

Annual precipitation: 43 in. (1,092 mm)

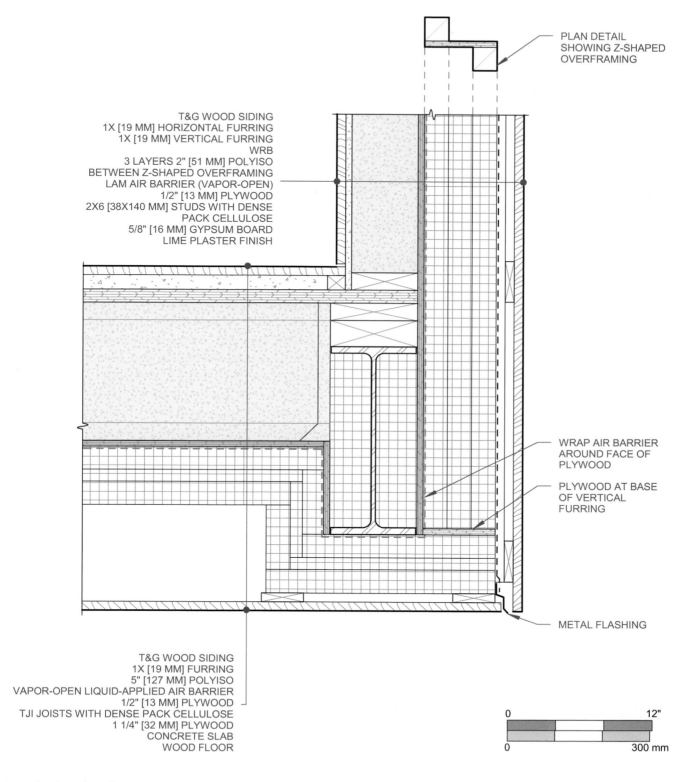

PLAN DETAIL
SHOWING Z-SHAPED
OVERFRAMING

T&G WOOD SIDING
1X [19 MM] HORIZONTAL FURRING
1X [19 MM] VERTICAL FURRING
WRB
3 LAYERS 2" [51 MM] POLYISO
BETWEEN Z-SHAPED OVERFRAMING
LAM AIR BARRIER (VAPOR-OPEN)
1/2" [13 MM] PLYWOOD
2X6 [38X140 MM] STUDS WITH DENSE
PACK CELLULOSE
5/8" [16 MM] GYPSUM BOARD
LIME PLASTER FINISH

WRAP AIR BARRIER
AROUND FACE OF
PLYWOOD

PLYWOOD AT BASE
OF VERTICAL
FURRING

METAL FLASHING

T&G WOOD SIDING
1X [19 MM] FURRING
5" [127 MM] POLYISO
VAPOR-OPEN LIQUID-APPLIED AIR BARRIER
1/2" [13 MM] PLYWOOD
TJI JOISTS WITH DENSE PACK CELLULOSE
1 1/4" [32 MM] PLYWOOD
CONCRETE SLAB
WOOD FLOOR

0   12"

0   300 mm

3.5.3 Steel cantilever beam supports conditioned second story space over an exterior terrace.

3.6.1 Finished view of the recessed bedroom balcony.
JAN FILLINGER, STUDIO-E

3.6.2 Overview of the house from the southeast. JAN FILLINGER, STUDIO-E

ORCHARD STREET HOUSE

The Orchard Street House is a modestly sized home that captures the full potential of existing features of the site. Its geometry and orientation on the long and narrow city lot maximize solar exposure for both the home and the intensively planted garden that provides the owners with a bounty of home-grown food.

A one-car garage topped by a studio apartment sits off the side alley. Both buildings incorporate an elegant, modernized version of the Craftsman style. A 6.3-kW photovoltaic system makes the home net-positive, producing more than twice its annual power needs! The residence has minimal interior air volume, and excess solar gains are managed by a double layer of gypsum board and clay plaster finish throughout the house, as well as a deciduous grapevine shade trellis. However, for the three or four weeks of summer when these measures can't adequately provide full comfort, the owners use a sleeping porch off the second-floor master bedroom, for alfresco slumbering in the balmy night air.

PROJECT INFORMATION

Project title: Orchard Street House

Location: Eugene, Oregon

Size: 1,129 ft.^{2} (105 m^2)

Completion: 2011

Recognition: Certified (PHIUS)

Type: Single-family house

Architect: STUDIO-E Architecture

Builder: EcoBuilding Collaborative of Oregon

CPHCs: Jan Fillinger and Win Swafford

HDD: 4,821 base 65°F (2,678 base 18.3°C)

CDD: 210 base 65°F (117 base 18.3°C)

Annual precipitation: 46 in. (1,168 mm)

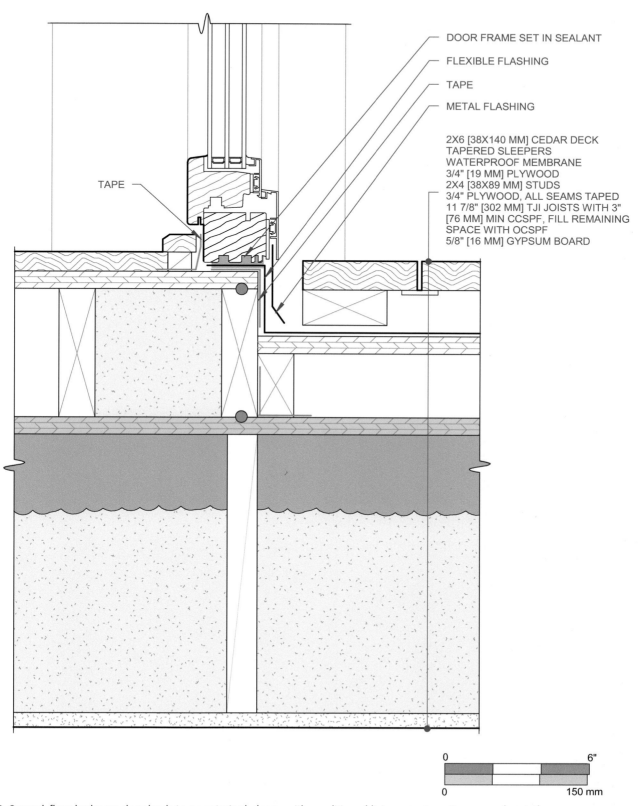

DOOR FRAME SET IN SEALANT

FLEXIBLE FLASHING

TAPE

METAL FLASHING

2X6 [38X140 MM] CEDAR DECK
TAPERED SLEEPERS
WATERPROOF MEMBRANE
3/4" [19 MM] PLYWOOD
2X4 [38X89 MM] STUDS
3/4" PLYWOOD, ALL SEAMS TAPED
11 7/8" [302 MM] TJI JOISTS WITH 3"
[76 MM] MIN CCSPF, FILL REMAINING
SPACE WITH OCSPF
5/8" [16 MM] GYPSUM BOARD

TAPE

0   6"

0   150 mm

3.6.3 Second-floor bedroom door leads to an exterior balcony with conditioned living space continuous underneath.

CHAPTER 4

Wall Systems

The economy and versatility of wood light frame construction is fully demonstrated in the making of walls. Stud walls have evolved as an "open system" in which there are simple rules that govern the relationship between the parts: the structure, the enclosure, and the services of the building. Within this "system," the parts themselves are interchangeable, providing the opportunity to choose from a vast array of alternative elements that have been allowed to evolve to higher levels of cost-effectiveness and performance. The stud wall is a relatively inexpensive container that provides shelter for components that are far less expensive than they would be if they were exposed to wear or damage. The cost savings on electrical wiring, plumbing, small-dimension ductwork, and voluminous insulation materials usually pay for the stud frame that protects them.

So that walls could be made more energy-efficient, they were first given extra thickness, with 2 x 4s (38x 80 mm) being exchanged for 2 x 6s (38 x 140 mm) and 2 x 8s (38 x 184 mm). The larger basic wood sections allowed the total number of studs and plates to be reduced through the discipline of "advanced framing." The size and configuration of elements in a wood frame wall depend to the greatest extent on the characteristics of the insulation materials chosen to fill them. Slender walls require materials with a very high R-value per inch of thickness. Substantially thicker walls consume extra framing material and reduce the indoor space, but they admit use of a much wider range of insulation products that need not perform at such a high level per unit of thickness. Many of these materials offer lower costs and often significantly lower environmental risk.

Owing to the surprisingly powerful influence of thermal bridge effects, the drive to increase wall thickness reaches a point of diminishing returns if there are solid wood studs generating conductive paths all the way through the insulation. For higher levels of performance to be reached, a layered, or multiple-leaf, assembly is needed. The basic strategy consists of a moderately deeper stud cavity coupled with an external overlay of rigid insulation to cut down on the thermal bridges. If the external claddings can be simply fastened through the outer insulation, the structural performance and construction efficiency of the wall remain as they have always been. The Skidmore House illustrates the simplicity of this approach, given the relatively gentle climate of Portland, Oregon (see Figure 4.1.3 below).

The double stud wall also creates a thermal break between the inner and outer surfaces, while using the same, highly familiar construction system throughout. Only one of the walls needs to be organized for load-bearing, and the other generates extra thickness for insulation. It only remains to decide which is which. If the outer leaf is load-bearing, it allows the framing crew to build the house as they always have and then add an additional row of studs inside the completed shell. The one great disadvantage to this approach has been addressed in the previous chapter. Floor framing must pass through the entire thickness of the wall to reach the line of vertical load transfer near the outer surface. The Arlington House, in this chapter, illustrates the use of double studs (see Figure 4.2.3 below). The outer frame is sheathed with plywood, which completes the structural connections in a conventional manner. The Bayside Anchor project—found in Chapter 6, on windows— also uses an exterior load-bearing leaf of studs, even in the harsh winter climate of Maine (see Figure 6.5.3). Despite the potential for heat loss at the floors, the outer leaf could be panelized for the rapid and economical assembly of a large enclosure that could then be finished from within.

If the inner leaf of studs is assigned the load-bearing function, then the outer leaf is free to pass by upper-story floor joists and ceiling joists, providing a continuous outer wrapper of insulation. As the outer leaf sheds the role of primary structure, it can progress from a self-supporting wall, still standing on the foundation or first-floor framing, to a type of curtain wall that is suspended outside the structural frame, with as few points of attachment as possible. Reduction in the points of attachment means reduction in the thermal bridges. The Full Plane Residence includes an outer leaf of studs supported from the bottom by a wood ledger (see Figure 4.3.3 below). The Lone Fir Residence—in Chapter 6, on windows—uses a similar approach, supplemented by long screw fasteners through spacer blocks that tie back to the inner frame at critical points over the height of a multistory building (see Figure 6.2.3).

When the inner leaf of studs is structurally sheathed, with the outer leaf attached frequently and directly to it, the assembly is referred to as "over-framing," rather than as a double stud wall. The over-framing may be accomplished with simple studs or a number of creative alternatives. The Portola Valley Passive House uses over-framing because of the distinct advantages in a retrofit (see Figure 4.4.3 below). The inner leaf, in this case, consists of elegant framing and is left open and visible from the interior. The same strategy may be used to preserve quality interior finishes on a closed wall, if the hygrothermal conditions permit it.

In a new, composite wall assembly, if any specific layer of framing has significant thickness, it can be given enhanced performance by reduction of the conductive cross section at the center of the members. This can be done using manufactured I-joists, with slender but continuous webs, or by means of Larsen trusses in which the webs are broken into short segments, further reducing the conductivity. The Freeman House, presented in both the foundations and windows chapters (Chapters 2 and 6), was realized in a code jurisdiction that allowed the manufactured I-joists to be used as the vertical, load-bearing structure (see Figures 2.3.3 and 6.6.3). The Saugerties Residence case study is similar, with the further refinement that it was panelized (see Figure 8.12.7 in Chapter 8). In many circumstances, a conventional wall of solid rectangular members is used to meet the structural requirements, and the thick, insulating overlay uses optimized framing. In this chapter, the CH2 project I-joists and the MARTak Rest/Work Space uses Larsen trusses (see Figures 4.5.3 and 4.6.3).

From the thermal perspective, the insulating outer layer of the wall should contain as little solid wood as possible. To meet this goal, the proportions of the basic strategy in the Skidmore House can be reversed, reducing the role of the stud wall from the thermal perspective and greatly increasing the thickness of the external insulation. This can be done with sufficiently rigid panels of insulation screw-fastened to the structural wall using furring strips that then provide for the attachment of exterior cladding. A prefabricated variation on this approach is illustrated at the Warren Woods Ecological Field Station, using structural insulated panels (SIPs) to generate the outer layer (see Figure 4.7.3 below).

There are many possible combinations of structural and insulating leafs: thick versus thin, high-performance insulation versus low-tech, low-impact materials. The choice among these options can vary greatly by location, according to the costs of materials and the labor requirements for assembly. The outer edge of the structural leaf is the most common position for the sheathing that resists horizontal loads and provides stability against buckling of the vertical members. Here is the clearest, cleanest opportunity to develop the air barrier in a wall assembly. This can be done by the joints in the sheathing itself being taped, or by a membrane being wrapped over the sheathing. Air barrier membranes are most effective when they have solid backing.

Somewhere in the wall section there may also be moisture control and vapor control systems. The relative position of these elements is governed by climate factors, with the configuration in cold, dry climates being very different than that in hot, humid climates. Recommendations for each climate zone should be reviewed in the specialty literature on barriers, such as the technical papers of John Straube and Joseph Lstiburek, published through the Building Science Corporation.

In broad areas of mixed climate, there are dramatic hygrothermal changes from winter to summer. In the winter, water vapor produced by activities in the build-ing will be driven into the enclosing walls, moving from the warm interior toward the cold exterior. If the building is cooled in the summer months, this vapor drive can reverse, penetrating the walls from the hot, humid exterior and moving toward the cooler and drier interior. The recommended solution for such a circumstance is the one described by Joseph Lstiburek as the "perfect wall," which we discussed in Chapter 1. In this assembly, the plane of vapor control and that of air control are developed in the same place, located at a point of stable temperature deep within the wall section. In this way, vapor being driven outward in the winter, or inward in the summer, will not reach the dew point in either season, and there will be no condensation inside the wall.

Selected wall assemblies should be based on proven models, or carefully checked using hygrothermal analysis software, to correlate the passage of heat and moisture through the wall over the course of a year. There must be no net accumulation of moisture in the wall on an annual basis. The permeability of materials must be carefully selected to promote drying. All materials, especially insulation, must be able to withstand the presence of moisture at whatever level and duration predicted for that location in the wall.

In summary, the logic that prevails for heating climates is to construct an inner structural leaf with sufficient framing density to support and connect the floors and roof, combined with an outer insulating leaf with as little framing density as possible, to reduce thermal bridge effects. The amount of framing material in the outer, insulating leaf of the wall depends on two things: the weight of the exterior finish materials and the way in which the window and door penetrations are developed. Lightweight exterior wall claddings may be attached to furring strips that hang from screws driven through layers of rigid insulation. Heavier claddings, or operable exterior shading systems, may require more a substantial connection to the load-bearing wall within.

4.1.1 Preparation for cladding. Furring strips fastened through rigid insulation to stud wall. IN SITU ARCHITECTURE

4.1.2 Stud framing, sheathed and taped for the air barrier. IN SITU ARCHITECTURE

SKIDMORE HOUSE

As presented in Chapter 3, the Skidmore House in Portland, Oregon meets passive house standards with the slight added costs offset by a series of architectural and material choices. Architect and owner Jeff Stern created two separate volumes, a single-story one for the two studios and a two-story, one-bedroom main house. The space between the volumes, although inside the thermal envelope, acts as an extension of the outdoors, connecting the front porch through to the rear deck. The approach to the construction was simple and direct. The crisp, abstract forms are kept free of eaves or other architectural devices. Balloon framed stud walls on a standard module are filled with blown-in insulation and wrapped in plywood sheathing doubling as the airtight layer. A layer of rigid insulation wraps the plywood and is clad in stained rough-sawn cedar. A high ratio of south-facing glazing maximizes solar gains when needed, and motorized exterior aluminum shades block the excess, producing extremely comfortable temperatures year round.

PROJECT INFORMATION

Project title: Skidmore House

Location: Portland, Oregon

Size: 1,680 ft.^{2} (156 m^2) treated floor area

Completion: 2013

Recognition: Certified (PHIUS), Earth Advantage Platinum

Type: Single-family house

Architect: Jeff Stern, In Situ Architecture

Builder: Jeff Stern, In Situ Architecture

CPHC: Jeff Stern, In Situ Architecture

HDD: 4,222 base 65°F (2,346 base 18.3°C)

CDD: 423 base 65°F (235 base 18.3°C)

Annual precipitation: 46.5 in. (1,181 mm)

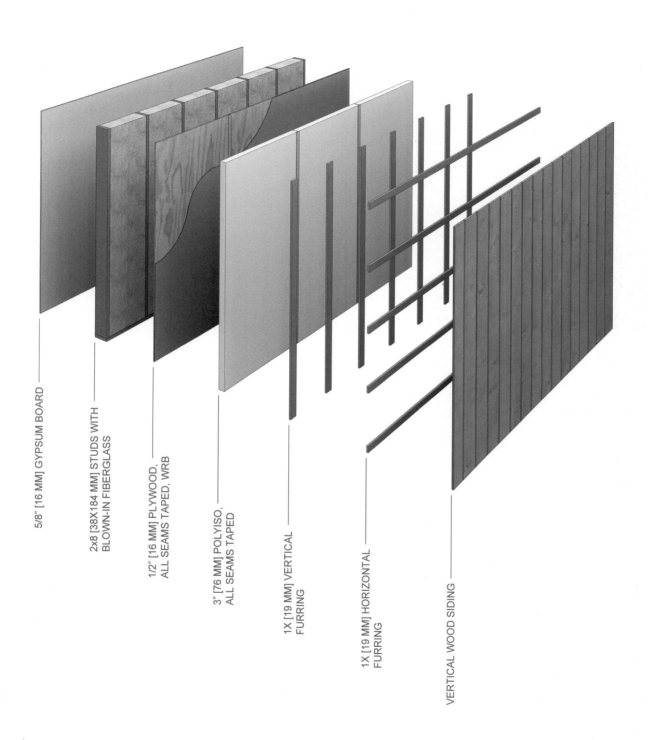

5/8" [16 MM] GYPSUM BOARD

2x8 [38X184 MM] STUDS WITH
BLOWN-IN FIBERGLASS

1/2" [16 MM] PLYWOOD,
ALL SEAMS TAPED, WRB

3" [76 MM] POLYISO,
ALL SEAMS TAPED

1X [19 MM] VERTICAL
FURRING

1X [19 MM] HORIZONTAL
FURRING

VERTICAL WOOD SIDING

4.1.3 Wall framing of deep studs on 24-in. centers. An exterior overlay of rigid insulation is broken only by fasteners that secure the furring strips for the exterior cladding.

4.2.1 Arlington House front entry on northwest elevation.
ERIC VON ECKARTSBERG

4.2.2 Double stud walls with spacing between for high volume insulation. ERIC VON ECKARTSBERG

ARLINGTON HOUSE

The Arlington House is located on a half-acre lot in a verdant neighborhood of Arlington, Virginia, near the Potomac River. The house features elements of the Craftsman style, with a modern interior and a super-energy-efficient envelope. This house design uses traditional, simple forms, with thoughtfully placed windows and overhangs to take advantage of the views and to create a livable, open, and modest plan. The home is constructed with double stud walls, triple-glazed windows, and a well-insulated slab, including innovative detailing throughout. The increased level of performance created by this building system allowed the occupants to significantly downsize their mechanical system and reduce their dependence on fossil fuels.

PROJECT INFORMATION

Project title: Arlington House

Location: Arlington, Virginia

Size: 4,074 ft.^{2} (379 m^2)

Completion: 2015

Recognition: Certified (PHIUS+)

Type: Single-family house

Architect: Kaplan Thompson Architects

Builder: Metro Green, LLC

CPHC: Jesse Thompson, Kaplan Thompson Architects

HDD: 4,613 base 65°F (2,563 base 18.3°C)

CDD: 1,844 base 65°F (base 18.3°C)

Annual precipitation: 44 in. (1,247 mm)

Video series on the project here (nine-part series): www.youtube.com/watch?v=eB8geiBTinQ (accessed January 13, 2017)

https://environment.arlingtonva.us/energy/green-home-choice/how-to-build-a-better-home/ (accessed January 13, 2017)

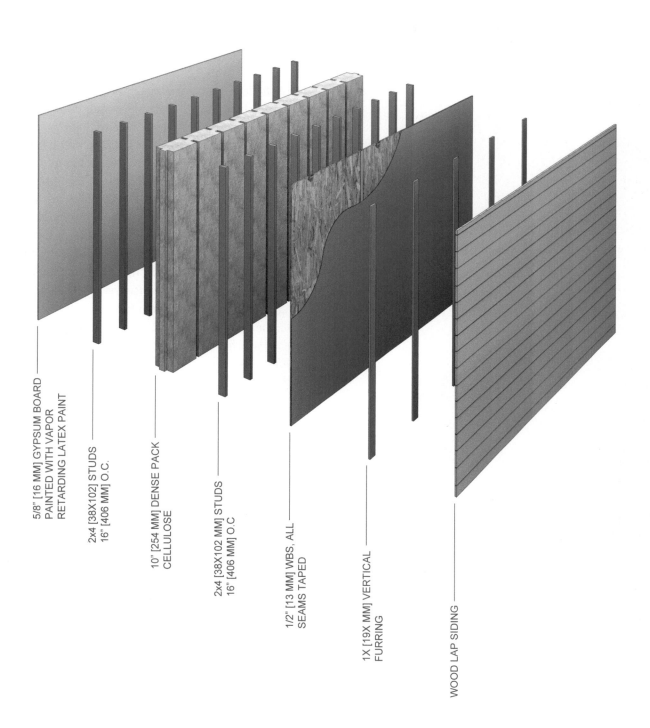

5/8" [16 MM] GYPSUM BOARD PAINTED WITH VAPOR RETARDING LATEX PAINT

2x4 [38X102] STUDS 16" [406 MM] O.C.

10" [254 MM] DENSE PACK CELLULOSE

2x4 [38X102 MM] STUDS 16" [406 MM] O.C

1/2" [13 MM] WBS, ALL SEAMS TAPED

1X [19X MM] VERTICAL FURRING

WOOD LAP SIDING

4.2.3 Double stud walls. Exterior leaf load-bearing, interior leaf added for increased insulation.

4.3.1 West elevation with outer wall leaf extending down to cover the foundation. MITCHELL SNYDER PHOTOGRAPHY

4.3.2 Adding the exterior, non-bearing curtain wall to increase insulation thickness. JRA GREEN BUILDING INC.

FULL PLANE RESIDENCE

The Full Plane Residence meets the Living Building Challenge by uniting a high-performing façade with a comprehensive water collection system and environmentally friendly materials. The house sits on a sloping site in Portland, Oregon, and integrates rainwater cisterns into the foundation. The roof form collects rain for grey water and irrigation. Grey water and storm water are processed within the landscape. The building achieves net zero energy usage by reducing demand. A double layer of studs provides ample insulation, as well as a reduction in thermal bridging. Glazing is reserved for the most important living spaces, improving the overall performance of the envelope. The bulk of the glazing is on the south façade, which is shaded, and also brings the added benefit of passive solar heating on the coldest days of winter. Finally, low-toxicity materials and FSC-certified lumber ensure a minimal environmental impact from the production and use of the materials themselves.

PROJECT INFORMATION

Project title: Full Plane Residence

Location: Portland, Oregon

Size: 1,950 ft.^{2} (181 m^2); 1,729 ft.^{2} (161 m^2) treated floor area

Completion: 2012

Recognition: Passive House planned, LEED Platinum, Living Building Challenge-registered

Type: Single-family house

Architect: Michelle Jeresek while partner at Departure Architecture, now at Ivon Street Studio

Builder: JRA Green Building, Inc.

CPHC: Eric Storm, James Ray Arnold

HDD: 4,222 base 65°F (2,346 base 18.3°C)

CDD: 423 base 65°F (235 base 18.3°C)

Annual precipitation: 46.5 in. (1,181 mm)

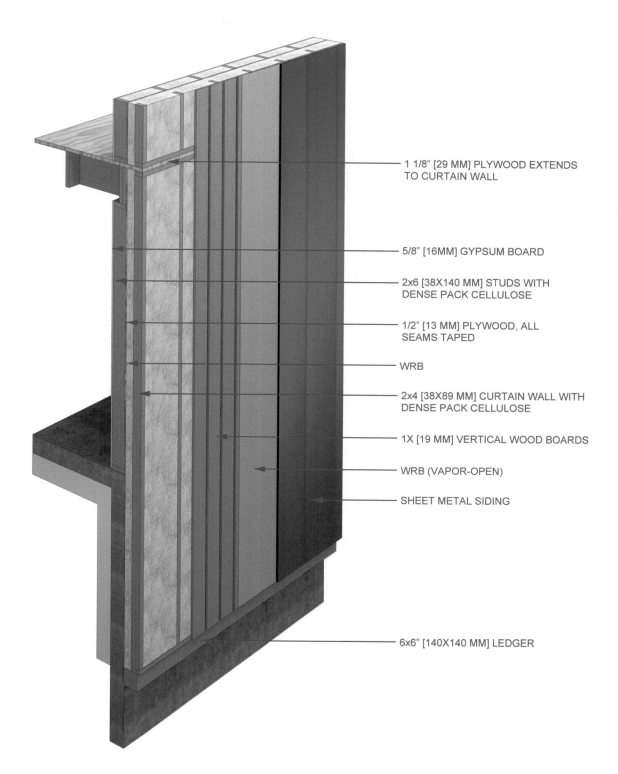

1 1/8" [29 MM] PLYWOOD EXTENDS TO CURTAIN WALL

5/8" [16MM] GYPSUM BOARD

2x6 [38X140 MM] STUDS WITH DENSE PACK CELLULOSE

1/2" [13 MM] PLYWOOD, ALL SEAMS TAPED

WRB

2x4 [38X89 MM] CURTAIN WALL WITH DENSE PACK CELLULOSE

1X [19 MM] VERTICAL WOOD BOARDS

WRB (VAPOR-OPEN)

SHEET METAL SIDING

6x6" [140X140 MM] LEDGER

4.3.3 Load-bearing stud wall stands on concrete foundation. Non-load-bearing curtain wall is supported on a ledger and restrained by the floor sheathing.

PORTOLA VALLEY PASSIVE HOUSE

This all-redwood cabin on the banks of Corte Madera Creek in Portola Valley, California, was originally constructed as a summer cottage during the early twentieth century. Bucking the trend of demolishing small, older homes in the area, the owners decided to keep the old-growth redwood interiors intact and utilize passive house building techniques. These include a super-insulated and airtight exterior envelope, as well as an HRV system that will enable the house to use only modest amounts of generated heat to stay warm in winter. Super-insulated glazing, all-operable windows, and energy-efficient appliances keep energy use at a bare minimum. A future phase to add a photovoltaic array will allow the home to produce enough on-site electricity to make it a net zero energy property. The house achieved 0.6 ACH50 for the airtightness criterion. The owners also did much of the extra testing, from solar analysis to thermal bridge analysis, during construction, with infrared cameras.

4.4.1 Original cabin interior with exposed redwood framing, now serving as the living and dining room. KEVIN KILLEN, EHDD

4.4.2 New exterior stud wall encloses cabin for structural integrity, insulation and services. KEVIN KILLEN, EHDD

PROJECT INFORMATION

Project title: Portola Valley Passive House

Location: Portola Valley, California

Size: 1,765 ft.^{2} (164 m^2)

Completion: 2012

Recognition: Certified (PHI)

Architect: EHDD Architecture

Builder: DeSmidt Builders

CPHC: Graham Irwin, Essential Habitat Architecture

HDD: 2,285 base 65°F (1,269 base 18.3°C)

CDD: 204 base 65°F (113 base 18°C)

Annual precipitation: 41.77 in. (1,061 mm)

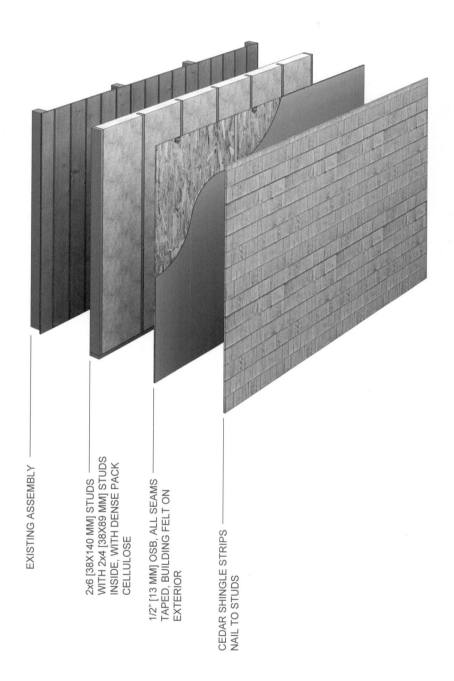

EXISTING ASSEMBLY

2x6 [38X140 MM] STUDS
WITH 2x4 [38X89 MM] STUDS
INSIDE, WITH DENSE PACK
CELLULOSE

1/2" [13 MM] OSB, ALL SEAMS
TAPED, BUILDING FELT ON
EXTERIOR

CEDAR SHINGLE STRIPS
NAIL TO STUDS

4.4.3 Over-framing of the existing structure with stud walls and dense pack insulation.

4.5.1 CH2 Passive House, east elevation, facing the street.
GARRETT DOWNEN

CH2

The CH2 project was a follow-up to PDX Living, LLC's first speculative net zero energy passive house project, the O2Haus. The team decided to use a different, foam-free wall assembly, with non-structural I-joists on the outside of a conventionally framed wood stud wall. The team also came up with a novel method for utilizing the "free" cool air produced by the heat pump water heater in the garage to cool the house on hot days. A thermostat located in the house controls duct dampers that can redirect the cool exhaust air from the heat pump water heater to the HRV intake, distributing cool air throughout the house when it is needed.

4.5.2 Over-framing of the conditioned space, viewed from the northwest. PDX LIVING, LLC

PROJECT INFORMATION

Project title: CH2

Location: Portland, Oregon

Size: 1,670 ft.² (155 m²)

Completion: 2014

Recognition: Built to passive house standards, site net zero energy

Type: Single-family home

Architect: Robert Hawthorne, PDX Living, LLC

Builder: PDX Living, LLC

CPHC: PDX Living, LLC

HDD: 4,222 base 65°F (2,346 base 18.3°C)

CDD: 423 base 65°F (235 base 18.3°C)

Annual precipitation: 46.5 in. (1,181 mm)

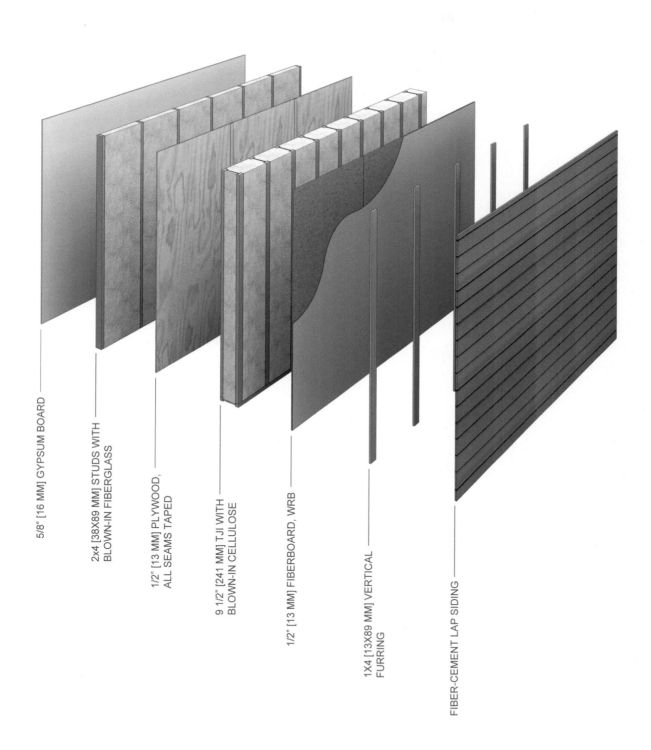

5/8" [16 MM] GYPSUM BOARD

2x4 [38X89 MM] STUDS WITH
BLOWN-IN FIBERGLASS

1/2" [13 MM] PLYWOOD,
ALL SEAMS TAPED

9 1/2" [241 MM] TJI WITH
BLOWN-IN CELLULOSE

1/2" [13 MM] FIBERBOARD, WRB

1X4 [13X89 MM] VERTICAL
FURRING

FIBER-CEMENT LAP SIDING

4.5.3 Standard stud walls and sheathing, over-framed with deep I-joists to create an insulation layer outside the air barrier.

4.6.1 Stud walls overlaid with deep Larsen trusses on the east-facing entry façade. ANDREW MICHLER, BAOSOL

4.6.2 Larsen trusses on the west façade with an outer layer of rockwool insulation. ANDREW MICHLER, BAOSOL

MARTAK REST/WORK SPACE

The MARTak Rest/Work Space is designed to weather the hard winters in a ponderosa pine mountain forest of Colorado and be self-supporting, without purchased electricity. The approach also uses the cradle-to-cradle model by carefully selecting materials that are either fully recyclable or completely organic. The project reused material from an existing shop, including a tire wall foundation. The unique wedge shape is informed and inspired by the local hogback mountains in the area. The angled face of the building increases solar gain, improving performance and reducing materials and cost, while allowing existing trees to provide shade in summer. The Intus triple-glazed windows provide excellent solar gain but reduce thermal losses by over-insulating the frames. An active phase change thermal mass material is used to reduce occurrences of overheating, and exterior thermal shading will be incorporated to reduce swing season solar gains. The house uses no foam and incorporated a broad strategy of fire-wise measures for resiliency.

PROJECT INFORMATION

Project title: MARTak Rest/Work Space

Location: Masonville, Colorado

Size: 1,270 ft.² (118 m²) TFA

Completion: 2015

Recognition: Certified (PHI)

Type: Single-family home

Architect: Andrew Michler, Baosol

Builder: John Parr, Parr Custom Builders Inc.

CPHC: Andrew Michler, Baosol

HDD: 6,228 base 65°F (3,460 base 18.3°C)

CDD: 480 base 65°F (267 base 18.3°C)

Annual precipitation: 15.6 in. (396 mm)

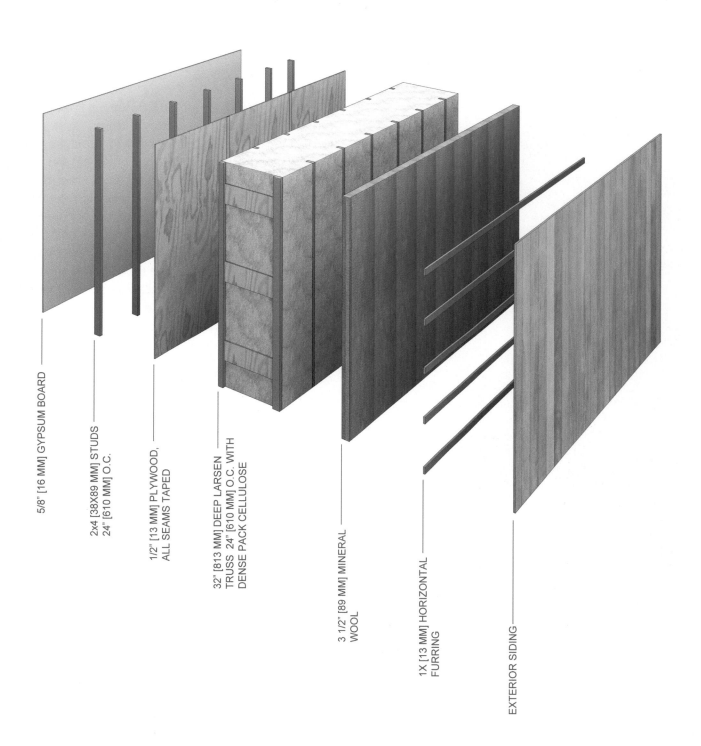

5/8" [16 MM] GYPSUM BOARD

2x4 [38X89 MM] STUDS
24" [610 MM] O.C.

1/2" [13 MM] PLYWOOD,
ALL SEAMS TAPED

32" [813 MM] DEEP LARSEN
TRUSS 24" [610 MM] O.C. WITH
DENSE PACK CELLULOSE

3 1/2" [89 MM] MINERAL
WOOL

1X [13 MM] HORIZONTAL
FURRING

EXTERIOR SIDING

4.6.3 End walls, parallel to the roof span, contain a service space created by open studs and sheathing, then over-framed with extremely deep Larsen trusses.

4.7.1 Installation of SIPs as sheathing of the stud walls.
MICHAEL KLINGER, ENERGYWISE/GO LOGIC, LLC

4.7.2 South elevation with large window wall at seminar space.
TRENT BELL PHOTOGRAPHY

WARREN WOODS ECOLOGICAL FIELD STATION

The Warren Woods Ecological Field Station is the first certified passive house laboratory in North America. Nestled between a forest and grassland, it creates a close relationship between the interior workspaces and test plots outside. Laboratories need precise climate control, so the form of the building is tailored toward maintaining comfortable and consistent conditions. Energy-intensive areas are grouped together on north side, protecting them from unwanted solar gain. The second floor is cantilevered over the laboratory space to further shade this high-use space. Multiple air-sealing materials were used in concert to meet passive house infiltration standards despite the complex building form. Concrete floors help balance temperature swings, and high-performance walls, consisting of load bearing studs sheathed with SIPs keep the building warm during winter.

PROJECT INFORMATION

Project title: Warren Woods Ecological Field Station

Location: Berrien County, Michigan

Size: 2,400 ft.² (223 m²)

Completion: 2014

Recognition: First certified passive house laboratory in North America; Honor Award AIA Maine COTE, 2015; PHIUS Passive Project Award, 2015

Type: Laboratory

Architect: GO Logic

Builder: GO Logic and Ebels Construction

CPHC: GO Logic

HDD: 6,296 base 65°F (3,498 base 18.3°C)

CDD: 564 base 65°F (313 base 18.3°C)

Annual precipitation: 42 in. (1,067 mm)

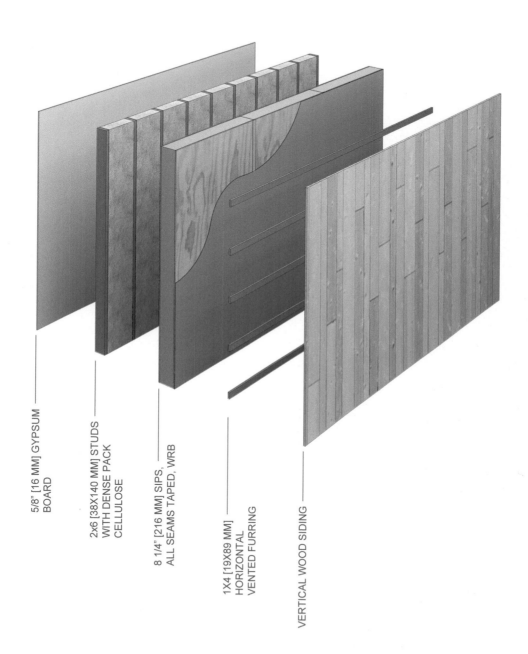

5/8" [16 MM] GYPSUM BOARD

2x6 [38X140 MM] STUDS WITH DENSE PACK CELLULOSE

8 1/4" [216 MM] SIPS, ALL SEAMS TAPED, WRB

1X4 [19X89 MM] HORIZONTAL VENTED FURRING

VERTICAL WOOD SIDING

4.7.3 Insulated wall framing sheathed with sips screwed directly to the studs.

CHAPTER 5

Roof Systems

A simple gable is the classic roof form on small buildings for very good reasons. Rafters cross-tied by ceiling joists in a triangular configuration are structurally effective. Water is shed by the upper surface in a definitive manner, and there is abundant space between and above the joists for insulation. If the attic is ventilated above the insulation, it can accommodate a thick layer of loose blown insulation, such as cellulose. This is a cost-effective means to provide high levels of thermal isolation. With attic ventilation, the airtight layer must be at or near the ceiling. The resulting assembly has long been considered ideal for cold climates.

As performance expectations rise, the limitations of this classic approach become evident. The achievement of a complete air barrier at the ceiling plane is more complex in practice than it might seem in basic concept. In order for the absolute integrity of the airtight layer to be protected, it might be necessary to construct a "utility chase" beneath the air barrier, in the form of a dropped ceiling. With a separation of the airtight layer and the interior ceiling, the penetrations through finish material for light fixtures or junction boxes need not be sealed against air leaks. Where traditional rafters and ceiling joists converge at the exterior bearing walls, it is difficult to reach high levels of insulation because of the limitation on overall thickness. The Midorihaus retrofit vividly illustrates this problem (see Figure 5.1.3 below). The tapered insulation zone at the eave threatens cold spots at the perimeter of the ceiling. It is a condition that met passive house standards in this instance only because of the mild climate.

In more recent construction, the insulation problem has been addressed through the shift from site framing of the roof to prefabricated, trussed rafters, commonly referred to as "trusses." The evolution of the raised "energy heel" truss provides more space for insulation, even at the low edges of the roof. Pressed-plate trusses can be used to create virtually any desired volume for insulation, provided that the building is free to expand toward the sky. They can also be applied to a wide variety of roof shapes: flat planes, low slope sheds, partial attics, and cathedral ceilings, using parallel chord configurations. The Hollis Montessori School combines triangular and parallel chord trusses to create a very large roofscape (see Figure 5.2.3 below). Even though the web members are relatively small in cross section, they are potential thermal bridges. For the same reasons that pertain to the construction of walls, the highest performance levels are reached if a layer of rigid insulation is added over the top of the roof framing.

The desire to occupy space within the volume of the roof tests the limits of the truss-based approach. If the roof is thinner in its construction, more useful space can be captured within a given external volume. Roofs made with I-joists can strike a balance between insulation thickness and usable volume. The Prescott Passive House case study demonstrates this technique, again with an overlay of rigid insulation being used to improve the overall thermal performance (see Figure 8.10.10 in Chapter 8). The New York Street Passive House achieves the same result with traditional, solid sawn rafters (see Figure 5.3.3 below).

As conditions of climate and construction cost vary, the relative contributions of insulation within the structural framing and insulation outside it can be reconsidered and adjusted. The optimal combination will consider insulation types, material costs, and labor requirements. The VOLKsHouse 1.0 project uses a simple flat-roofed box to generate efficiency in the structural framing and sheathing of the building, relying on layers of exterior insulation for most of the thermal performance (see Figure 5.4.3 below).

The Lone Fir Residence applies the concept of over-framing to both the walls and the roof (see Figure 5.5.3 below). There are two framed cavities for insulation, rather than a rigid overlay of more expensive materials. The plywood sheathing on top of the first layer of joists is taped to produce an air barrier that is in a very advantageous position. The framing inside the barrier produces a service cavity for electrical wiring and junction boxes that can be allowed to cut through the finished ceiling. The framing above the air barrier is free to project as a cantilever, without the necessity of a tight seal around each framing member. Other options for articulation of the roof edge will be discussed further on in this chapter.

In mixed climates, the common, central location of all the barriers, which we introduced in Chapter 1 as the "perfect wall," can be applied equally to the making of a "perfect roof." Building on the example of the Lone Fir Residence, both the air barrier and the vapor barrier can be developed at the plane of the structural sheathing in the center of the overall assembly. Insulation to the inside and to the outside will prevent condensation in both the heating and cooling seasons. For drying, the assembly must be vapor open in both directions from the vapor barrier. It is challenging for an assembly to be vapor open to the sky, while providing secure, preferably redundant layers of protection against the rain. Over-framing or additional layers of furring can readily produce a clear ventilation cavity above the insulation and under the potentially impervious layers of the roof. It can be difficult to ventilate complex or low-pitched roofscapes sufficiently, and they must be checked for hygrothermal performance.

If the roof sheathing is unvented, the code usually requires that a layer of "air-impermeable" rigid insulation (typically foam) be applied directly in contact with the bottom or the top of the roof sheathing to prevent interior moisture from condensing there. Another option is the use of a "smart vapor retarder," located close to the interior of the building, that allows for an unvented roof without rigid insulation.

Alternatively, the sheathing can be vented via a narrow, pitched ventilation space between the insulation and the sheathing. In the Hayfield House case study, this is done with a ventilation baffle where the roof geometry begins to restrict the available space (see Figure 8.5.10 in Chapter 8).

The meeting of the wall and the roof is not just a technical challenge but also one of the greatest opportunities to develop the expressive character of a building. For example, the classic Prairie Style of Frank Lloyd Wright features a sheltering roof drawn down over the top of the building, with overhangs and soffits that return horizontally to the head of the windows. These forms are echoed in the common American ranch house. As the roof becomes thicker to provide for more insulation, these traditional relationships are changed. The roof becomes like a hat perched high on the forehead, rather than one with the brim pulled down to better shade the eyes. The visual management of an extremely thick roof assembly can be seen in the elevations of the Orchards at Orenco case study (see Figure 8.9.10 in Chapter 8).

If thick walls, a thick roof, and a continuous air barrier at the sheathing plane are put together, a logical outcome is a building with a pure prismatic form, like the playing pieces in the game of Monopoly. There is no outward expression of the roof thickness, and the window openings are dropped down to a position entirely within the walls, disassociated from the roof. A single layer of sheathing, taped at the joints, provides a secure air barrier of the most direct and efficient form. The New York Street Passive House demonstrates this approach, as does the Prescott Passive House case study (see Figure 5.3.3 below and Figure 8.10.10 in Chapter 8).

In many climate zones, the longevity of the building is dependent upon an overhanging roof that deflects rainfall away from the sidewalls and windows. However, as introduced with the Lone Fir House, projecting rafter tails used to support overhangs must be prevented from bridging the insulation or puncturing the air barrier. This goal could be met if the tight, prismatic gable forms of the New York Street or Prescott houses were surmounted by a light, overhanging canopy that would act as an umbrella. The upper structure could be thermally isolated from the house below by a layer of rigid insulation in between. Alternatively, the insulated, over-framing of the Lone Fir Residence could be applied to a gable form as easily as it was to a low slope shed.

Rather than a full umbrella, brackets can be used to support roof overhangs around the perimeter. If they are attached at the top of the walls, outside the sheathed and sealed volume of the house, only the fasteners need to penetrate the plane of the barriers. The Orchard Street House illustrates this approach, as does the case study of the Louisiana Passive House (see Figure 5.6.3 below and Figure 8.7.9 in Chapter 8). These roof appendages must be designed to resist uplift in high-wind zones.

The protection of the windows from rain and summer sun may be done with accessory elements closer to the openings than the eaves of the primary roof, especially if it is high above. The Cowhorn Vineyard House uses a steel-framed canopy that is attached to a box column developed within the over-framing of the walls. Overhangs and shades applied to the sidewalls can also be seen in the Orchards at Orenco and Ankeny Row Net Zero Community case studies (see Figures 8.9.19 and 8.1.16 in Chapter 8).

A different class of solutions can be explored if the air barrier is folded inward across the top plate of the walls and continued parallel to the ceiling plane, inside the roof construction. This puts all of the roof framing outside the sealed volume of the house, eliminating the concern about rafter tails puncturing the barriers. Pumpkin Ridge Passive House follows this approach, with trusses that integrate a cathedral ceiling, a thick roof, and deep, horizontal soffits in the Frank Lloyd Wright tradition (see Figure 5.7.3 below). There is a shallow service cavity framed in below the air barrier sheathing to accommodate electrical distribution above the gypsum ceiling. Plywood air barriers attached to the bottom chord of roof trusses can also be seen in the Viridescent Building and San Juan Passive House case studies (see Figures 8.14.7 and 8.11.10 in Chapter 8). In the later instance, a starter strip of plywood is attached to the top of the walls before the trusses are placed, in order to develop continuity with the air in the panelized sidewalls.

Living inside the volume of the roof is traditionally enhanced with daylight and views offered by dormers. These are somewhat rare in high-performance roof systems. Dormers are created by cutting and folding the planes of the roof. As the planes grow thicker with insulation, it is difficult to manage the geometry in order to reach a productive combination of the external building volume, the captured interior space, and the clear opening that is created. Extra framing is required where the regular layout of the structure is interrupted, and with that comes the risk of thermal bridges. Air and water barriers can be more difficult to complete. Project Green Home illustrates a simple shed dormer in the mild conditions of Palo Alto, California (see Figure 5.8.3 below). For colder climates, it is perhaps better to adapt and adjust the form of the primary roof, rather than cut though it, or restrict the admission of daylight to strategic spots that can be served with a roof monitor or carefully detailed skylight. The Zero Cottage and Earthship Farmstead use concentrated interventions in the roofscape to introduce light through clerestory windows (see Figure 5.9.3 below and Figure 8.3.16 in Chapter 8). The vertical glass in these examples is easier to control for heat loss and excess solar gain than glass lying in the plane of the roof would be.

5.1.1 Midorihaus Prior to renovation. The expressed rafter tails, roof boards, and brackets are central to the character of the house. ESSENTIAL HABITAT ARCHITECTURE

5.1.2 A deep bed of spray-applied cellulose insulation in the attic. Ventilation at the roof peak. CHIE KAWAHARA

MIDORIHAUS

Presented in Chapter 3, this Craftsman-style house had the original roof, exposed rafter tails, and barge rafters. The ceilings were covered with asbestos-laden material, and so the decision was made to retain the existing roof and to replace the ceilings. The new gypsum board at the ceiling would serve as the airtight layer, with a thick layer of cellulose insulation added above. A significant concern was thermal bridging along the eaves due to narrowed ceiling insulation. The initial intention was to use closed-cell spray foam here, but thermal bridge analysis showed little performance improvement over cellulose. The whole-building analysis ultimately showed little performance impact from this area, and the mild climate rendered interior surface temperatures high enough to prevent condensation, mold, or mildew. In colder climates, it would have been necessary to reframe the roof with a raised heel, or to remove and replace the overhangs after encapsulating the attic with a layer of exterior insulation.

PROJECT INFORMATION

Project title: Midorihaus (www.midorihaus.com)

Location: Santa Cruz, California

Size: 1,413 ft.² (131 m²)

Completion: 2012

Recognition: Certification (PHI), 2013 City of Santa Cruz Green Building Award, 2015 California Senate Certificate of Recognition

Type: Single-family house

Architect: Essential Habitat Architecture

Builder: Santa Cruz Green Builders

CPHC: Graham Irwin, Essential Habitat Architecture

HDD: 3,035 base 65°F (1,700 base 18.3°C)

CDD: 1,385 base 65°F (776 base 18.3°C)

Annual precipitation: 30.66 in. (779 mm)

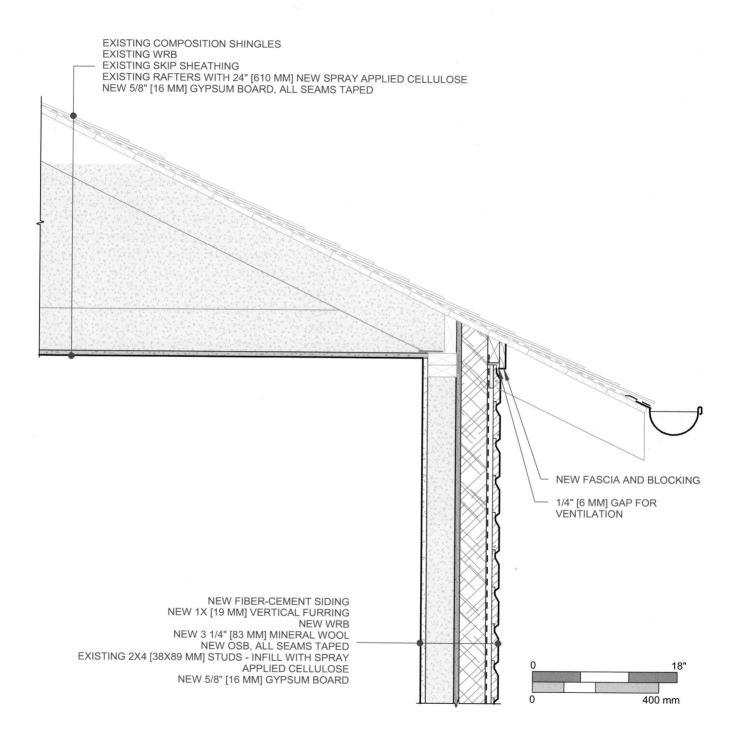

EXISTING COMPOSITION SHINGLES
EXISTING WRB
EXISTING SKIP SHEATHING
EXISTING RAFTERS WITH 24" [610 MM] NEW SPRAY APPLIED CELLULOSE
NEW 5/8" [16 MM] GYPSUM BOARD, ALL SEAMS TAPED

NEW FASCIA AND BLOCKING

1/4" [6 MM] GAP FOR
VENTILATION

NEW FIBER-CEMENT SIDING
NEW 1X [19 MM] VERTICAL FURRING
NEW WRB
NEW 3 1/4" [83 MM] MINERAL WOOL
NEW OSB, ALL SEAMS TAPED
EXISTING 2X4 [38X89 MM] STUDS - INFILL WITH SPRAY
APPLIED CELLULOSE
NEW 5/8" [16 MM] GYPSUM BOARD

0   18"

0   400 mm

5.1.3 Retrofit of a traditional roof and wall assembly. Air barrier developed below and to the inside of the projecting rafter tails.

5.2.1 Large-scale roofscape generated with triangular and parallel chord roof trusses. ERIC ROTH PHOTOGRAPHY

5.2.2 Parallel chord trusses span over an undulating, south-facing wall. WINDY HILL ASSOCIATES

HOLLIS MONTESSORI SCHOOL

The Hollis Montessori School Board and the faculty wanted to set an example for energy efficiency both in the community and nationally. Windy Hill Associates and ZeroEnergy Design collaborated on the first passive house-certified elementary school in the US. The cultural benefits of reaching that standard for a private school outweighed the small cost difference to get from net zero ready to certification. The super-insulated enclosure includes a double stud wall system that provides R-41 dense pack cellulose insulation, an R-111 roof assembly that combines cellulose in the roof trusses and continuous rigid insulation above the roof sheathing, R-54 under the concrete floor slab, and building details to mitigate thermal bridging. High-performance U-0.15 triple-glazed windows/doors offer a SHGC-glass of 0.50 to capture the sun's energy from the southern orientation. The team set performance goals, and all the subcontractors collaborated to make their most energy-efficient building. This was evident during the first blower door test, which achieved an infiltration rate of only 0.26 ACH50, with no changes.

PROJECT INFORMATION

Project title: Hollis Montessori School

Location: Hollis, New Hampshire

Size: 3,030 ft.^{2} (281 m^2)

Completion: 2013

Recognition: Certification (PHI)

Type: School

Architect: Windy Hill Associates

Builder: TMD Construction Services, LLC

CPHC: ZeroEnergy Design

HDD: 6,707 base 65°F (3,726 base 18.3°C)

CDD: 453 base 65°F (252 base 18.3°C)

Annual precipitation: 44 in. (1,118 mm)

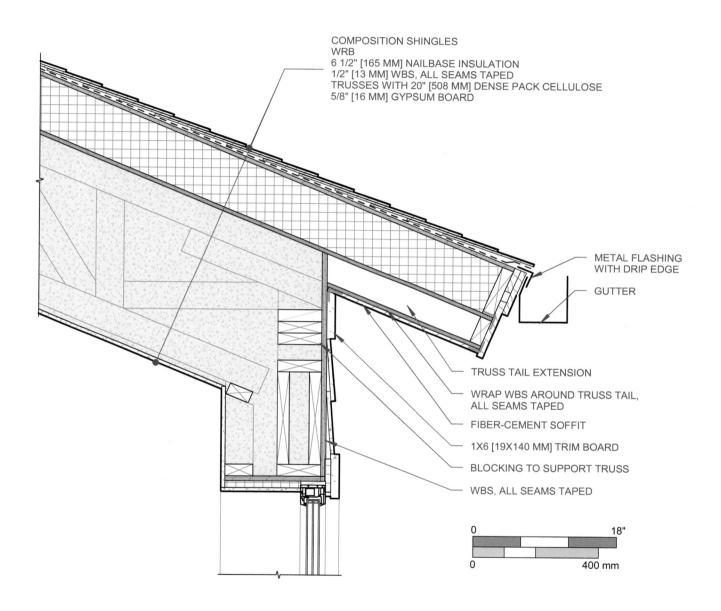

COMPOSITION SHINGLES
WRB
6 1/2" [165 MM] NAILBASE INSULATION
1/2" [13 MM] WBS, ALL SEAMS TAPED
TRUSSES WITH 20" [508 MM] DENSE PACK CELLULOSE
5/8" [16 MM] GYPSUM BOARD

METAL FLASHING
WITH DRIP EDGE

GUTTER

TRUSS TAIL EXTENSION

WRAP WBS AROUND TRUSS TAIL,
ALL SEAMS TAPED

FIBER-CEMENT SOFFIT

1X6 [19X140 MM] TRIM BOARD

BLOCKING TO SUPPORT TRUSS

WBS, ALL SEAMS TAPED

0			18"

0		400 mm

5.2.3 Deep trusses used to create long spans and large insulation volume. Rigid insulation reduces thermal bridge effects due to the truss web members.

5.3.1 Compact gable roof form with inset porches on the south facade. STUDIO 804

5.3.2 Cross ties in tall living space. Stairs to bedroom loft. STUDIO 804

NEW YORK STREET PASSIVE HOUSE

The New York Street Passive House is a design–build achievement by students of Studio 804 at the University of Kansas. It was built on the site of a 1920s-era gas station, and the footings and old fuel tanks left behind were removed under the supervision of personnel from the Kansas Department of Health and Environment. The compact gabled form was constructed with double stud walls and conventional framing of the inhabited roof. An Energy Star Cool Roof-certified standing seam system was installed over rigid foam panels coated with an ice- and water-resistant membrane. This finished the roof assembly, achieving an R-65 insulation value. Upon completion, a 6.1-kW solar panel array was installed via a clip system to the standing seam roof and is expected to offset the energy used in the house.

PROJECT INFORMATION

Project title: New York Street Passive House

Location: Lawrence, Kansas

Size: 1,725 ft.^{2} (160 m^2)

Completion: 2015

Recognition: Certified (PHIUS), LEED Platinum

Type: Single-family house

Architect: Studio 804

Builder: Studio 804

CPHC: Studio 804

HDD: 4,801 base 65°F (2,667 base 18.3°C)

CDD: 1,466 base 65°F (814 base 18.3°C)

Annual precipitation: 36.91 in. (938 mm)

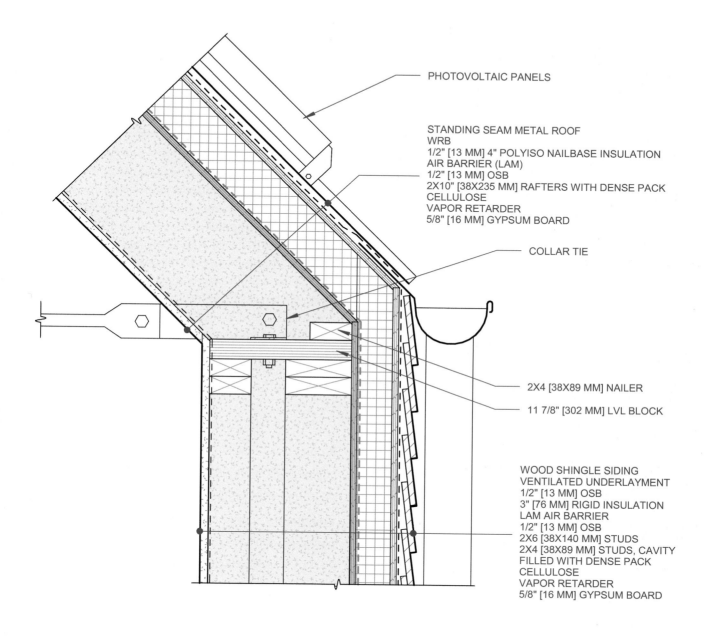

PHOTOVOLTAIC PANELS

STANDING SEAM METAL ROOF
WRB
1/2" [13 MM] 4" POLYISO NAILBASE INSULATION
AIR BARRIER (LAM)
1/2" [13 MM] OSB
2X10" [38X235 MM] RAFTERS WITH DENSE PACK
CELLULOSE
VAPOR RETARDER
5/8" [16 MM] GYPSUM BOARD

COLLAR TIE

2X4 [38X89 MM] NAILER

11 7/8" [302 MM] LVL BLOCK

WOOD SHINGLE SIDING
VENTILATED UNDERLAYMENT
1/2" [13 MM] OSB
3" [76 MM] RIGID INSULATION
LAM AIR BARRIER
1/2" [13 MM] OSB
2X6 [38X140 MM] STUDS
2X4 [38X89 MM] STUDS, CAVITY
FILLED WITH DENSE PACK
CELLULOSE
VAPOR RETARDER
5/8" [16 MM] GYPSUM BOARD

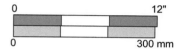

5.3.3 Inhabited roof framed with conventional rafters. Exterior overlay of nailbase insulation.

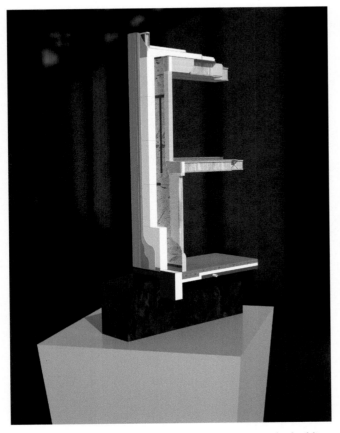

5.4.1 Construction model showing compact, rectangular building form wrapped with insulation. WAMO STUDIO, LLC

5.4.2 Deep roof framing using I-joists, to be filled with cellulose insulation. WAMO STUDIO, LLC

VOLKSHOUSE 1.0

The energy-saving VOLKsHouse 1.0, described in Chapter 2, sets out to provide a model for healthy and comfortable living, combining beauty with economical building techniques and long-term energy savings through passive house construction. In response to making affordable, high-performance housing, the framing for the VOLKsHouse 1.0 is fairly typical, following standard practice for resource efficiency, reducing material costs, and achieving thermal bridge reduction. The house uses traditional strategies such as framing with double-stud corners, headers only on bearing walls, and TJI joists. The flat roof over the volume of the VOLKsHouse 1.0 is constructed with a TJI roofing system filled with cellulose (R-55), over which there is an air barrier/sheathing and thick exterior insulation system.

PROJECT INFORMATION

Project title: VOLKsHouse 1.0

Location: Santa Fe, New Mexico

Size: 1,717 ft.² (159.5 m²)

Completion: 2012

Recognition: Certification (PHI), National Home Buyers Alliance—BuildGreen New Mexico Emerald

Type: Single-family home

Architect: Vahid Mojarrab, WAMO Studio, LLC

Builder: Justin Young, August Construction

CPHC: Graham Irwin, Essential Habitat

HDD: 6,115 base 65°F (3,397 base 18.3°C)

CDD: 339 base 65°F (188 base 18.3°C)

Annual precipitation: 14 in. (355.6 mm)

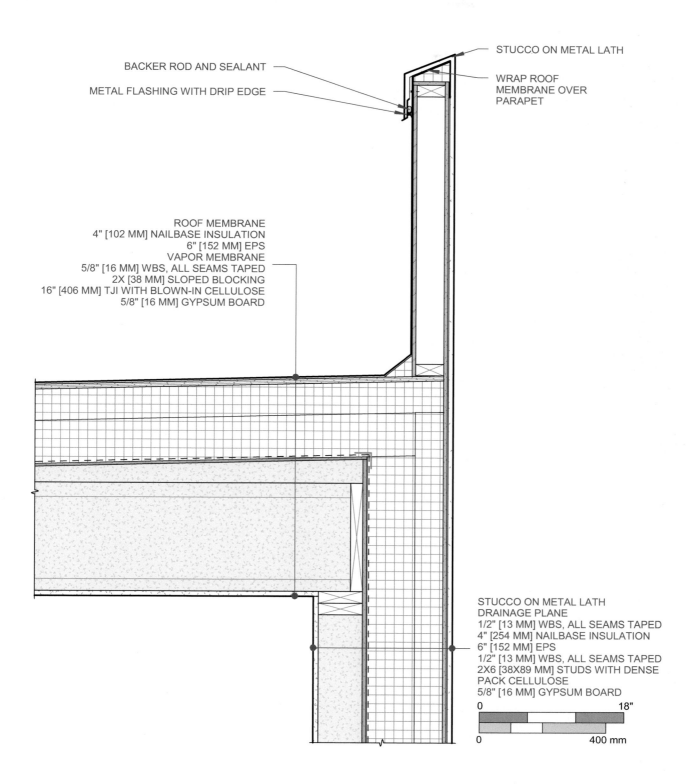

STUCCO ON METAL LATH

BACKER ROD AND SEALANT

WRAP ROOF
MEMBRANE OVER
PARAPET

METAL FLASHING WITH DRIP EDGE

ROOF MEMBRANE
4" [102 MM] NAILBASE INSULATION
6" [152 MM] EPS
VAPOR MEMBRANE
5/8" [16 MM] WBS, ALL SEAMS TAPED
2X [38 MM] SLOPED BLOCKING
16" [406 MM] TJI WITH BLOWN-IN CELLULOSE
5/8" [16 MM] GYPSUM BOARD

STUCCO ON METAL LATH
DRAINAGE PLANE
1/2" [13 MM] WBS, ALL SEAMS TAPED
4" [254 MM] NAILBASE INSULATION
6" [152 MM] EPS
1/2" [13 MM] WBS, ALL SEAMS TAPED
2X6 [38X89 MM] STUDS WITH DENSE
PACK CELLULOSE
5/8" [16 MM] GYPSUM BOARD

0   18"

0   400 mm

5.4.3 Low slope roof with air barrier sheathing. Exterior overlaid with two layers of rigid insulation.

5.5.1 South-side roof overhang with shading at window heads. BEN GATES AND MARGO RETTIG

5.5.2 Construction of the overhanging roof frame. BEN GATES AND MARGO RETTIG

LONE FIR RESIDENCE

When Ben Gates and Margo Rettig set out to design and build their own house, they wanted to build something small, efficient, and cost-effective, but they knew that radiant heating was complex and expensive. At the time, Katrin Klingenberg of PHIUS was demonstrating how building designers could eliminate costly mechanical systems by focusing on insulation, airtightness, and heat recovery ventilation. Ben and Margo proceeded to design to the passive house standard and were the first to permit a passive house design in the City of Portland, Oregon. They looked abroad for solutions, while innovating a unique double-wall assembly to eliminate thermal bridging and utilize local wood. The unvented attic assembly of the roof required a building code appeal so that a similar double framing and insulation strategy could be utilized in lieu of code-required foam insulation.

PROJECT INFORMATION

Project title: Lone Fir Residence

Location: Portland, Oregon

Size: 1,820 ft.^{2} (170 m^2)

Permitted: 2010

Recognition: Pre-certified

Type: Single-family home and attached accessory dwelling unit

Architect: Owner

Builder: Owner and Green Hammer (core and shell)

CPHC: Owner

HDD: 4,222 base 65°F (2,346 base 18.3°C)

CDD: 423 base 65°F (235 base 18.3°C)

Annual precipitation: 46.5 in. (1,181 mm)

Blower door result: 0.45 ACH50

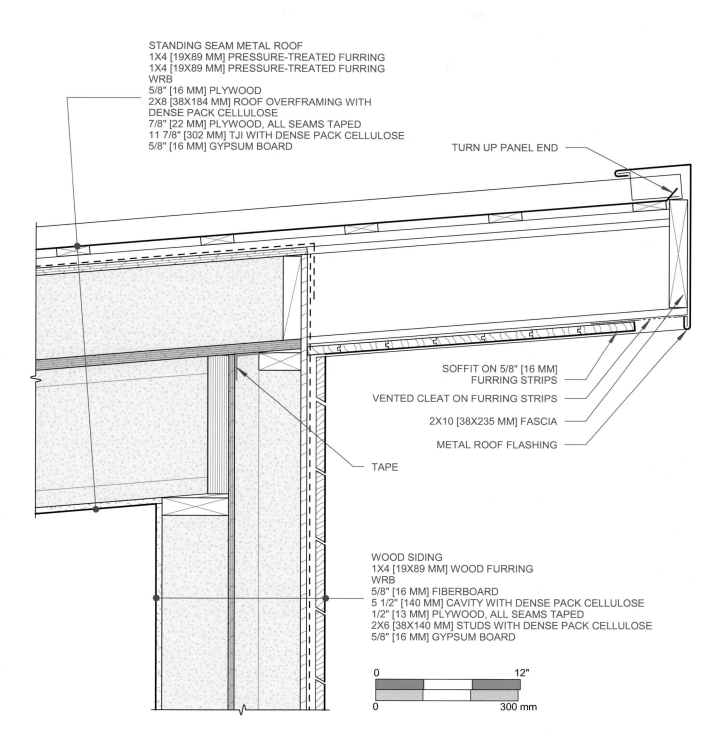

STANDING SEAM METAL ROOF
1X4 [19X89 MM] PRESSURE-TREATED FURRING
1X4 [19X89 MM] PRESSURE-TREATED FURRING
WRB
5/8" [16 MM] PLYWOOD
2X8 [38X184 MM] ROOF OVERFRAMING WITH
DENSE PACK CELLULOSE
7/8" [22 MM] PLYWOOD, ALL SEAMS TAPED
11 7/8" [302 MM] TJI WITH DENSE PACK CELLULOSE
5/8" [16 MM] GYPSUM BOARD

TURN UP PANEL END

SOFFIT ON 5/8" [16 MM]
FURRING STRIPS

VENTED CLEAT ON FURRING STRIPS

2X10 [38X235 MM] FASCIA

METAL ROOF FLASHING

TAPE

WOOD SIDING
1X4 [19X89 MM] WOOD FURRING
WRB
5/8" [16 MM] FIBERBOARD
5 1/2" [140 MM] CAVITY WITH DENSE PACK CELLULOSE
1/2" [13 MM] PLYWOOD, ALL SEAMS TAPED
2X6 [38X140 MM] STUDS WITH DENSE PACK CELLULOSE
5/8" [16 MM] GYPSUM BOARD

0   12"

0   300 mm

5.5.3 Shed roof constructed with I-joists and air barrier sheathing. overhangs generated with a second layer of framing.

5.6.1 Steel connector screwed through insulation to framing.
JAN FILLINGER, STUDIO-E

5.6.2 Roof bracket at ridge. Application of finish cladding.
JAN FILLINGER, STUDIO-E

ORCHARD STREET HOUSE

As described in Chapter 3, the Orchard Street House is a moderately sized residence in a quiet residential neighborhood in Eugene, Oregon. Graceful wood joinery adorns the eaves, colonnaded arcade, trellises, and gates. Muscular basalt bases support tapering wood columns, and beautifully textured finishes define interior and exterior wall surfaces. A robust stone masonry wall base and landscape constructions root the house to its site. The cozy and welcoming feel of its interior is enhanced by an earthy palette of eco-friendly materials and textures used throughout the house. Clay plaster walls and ceilings, cork and white oak flooring, and sustainably sourced and repurposed wood trims complete the alliance of exceptional sustainability and stylish craftsmanship. Attention to detailing is also expressed in exterior structural elements, including roof edges. The gable ends are supported by gently curved timber braces fastened to the structure with custom-shaped steel brackets designed to minimize thermal bridging, while providing both essential structure and visual delight.

PROJECT INFORMATION

Project title: Orchard Street House

Location: Eugene, Oregon

Size: 1,129 ft.^{2} (105 m^2)

Completion: 2011

Recognition: Certified (PHIUS)

Type: Single-family house

Architect: STUDIO-E Architecture

Builder: EcoBuilding Collaborative of Oregon

CPHCs: Jan Fillinger and Win Swafford

HDD: 4,821 base 65°F (2,678 base 18.3°C)

CDD: 210 base 65°F (117 base 18.3°C)

Annual precipitation: 46 in. (1,168 mm)

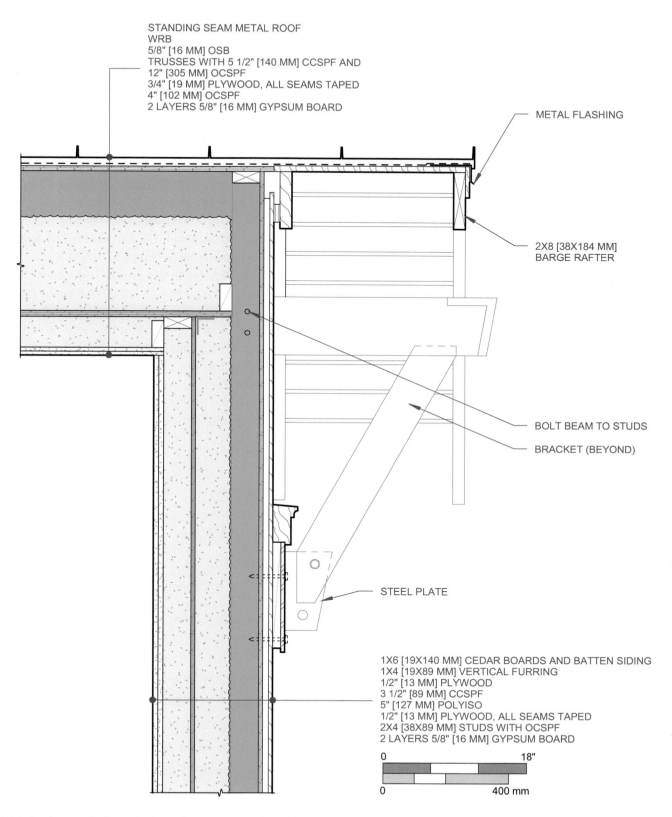

STANDING SEAM METAL ROOF
WRB
5/8" [16 MM] OSB
TRUSSES WITH 5 1/2" [140 MM] CCSPF AND
12" [305 MM] OCSPF
3/4" [19 MM] PLYWOOD, ALL SEAMS TAPED
4" [102 MM] OCSPF
2 LAYERS 5/8" [16 MM] GYPSUM BOARD

METAL FLASHING

2X8 [38X184 MM]
BARGE RAFTER

BOLT BEAM TO STUDS

BRACKET (BEYOND)

STEEL PLATE

1X6 [19X140 MM] CEDAR BOARDS AND BATTEN SIDING
1X4 [19X89 MM] VERTICAL FURRING
1/2" [13 MM] PLYWOOD
3 1/2" [89 MM] CCSPF
5" [127 MM] POLYISO
1/2" [13 MM] PLYWOOD, ALL SEAMS TAPED
2X4 [38X89 MM] STUDS WITH OCSPF
2 LAYERS 5/8" [16 MM] GYPSUM BOARD

0   18"

0   400 mm

5.6.3 Brackets applied outside the air barrier support the gable end roof extension.

5.7.1 Large overhanging roof volume generated with trusses.
HAMMER & HAND

5.7.2 Truss configuration creates cathedral ceiling in main rooms.
HAMMER & HAND

PUMPKIN RIDGE PASSIVE HOUSE

First introduced in Chapter 2, the Pumpkin Ridge Passive House in North Plains, Oregon, uses a vaulted scissor roof truss design. The interior air barrier is taped sheathing at the lower chord of the trusses. The insulation above is loose-fill cellulose. The wall assembly of R-60 insulation value is provided by two thick layers of high-density insulation, 9.5 in. (241 mm) in a Larsen truss system to the exterior, and 5.5 in. (140 mm) contained by the 2 x 6 (38 x 140 mm) stud wall on the inside. The air barrier follows vertically up the outside of the structural wall to the underside of the vaulted truss. It is a standard vented truss assembly, and so the air barrier must pass between the top plate of the wall and the truss. The wall is capped with OSB slightly beyond the interior framing to achieve a good air seal with the interior sheathing at the ceiling.

PROJECT INFORMATION

Project title: Pumpkin Ridge Passive House

Location: North Plains, Oregon

Size: 3,050 ft.² (283 m²)

Completion: 2013

Recognition: Certification (PHIUS), 2014 Department of Energy—Zero Energy Ready Home, 2014 Earth Advantage Homes—Platinum Certification, 2014 ENERGY STAR, Super-Efficient Demo

Type: Single-family house

Architect: Scott | Edwards Architecture

Builder: Hammer & Hand Inc.

CPHC: Skylar Swinford, Hammer & Hand

HDD: 4,750 base 65°F (2,639 base 18.3°C)

CDD: 280 base 65°F (156 base 18.3°C)

Annual precipitation: 38 in. (965 mm)

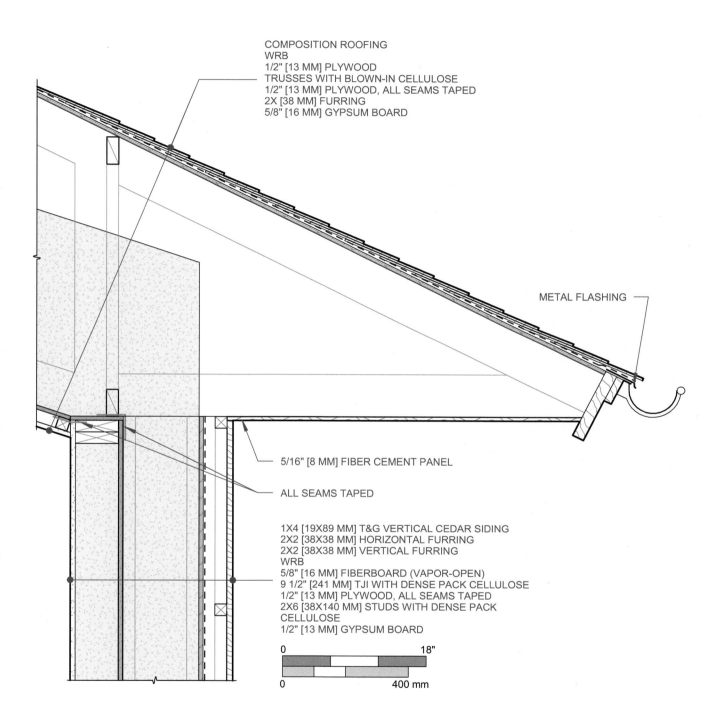

COMPOSITION ROOFING
WRB
1/2" [13 MM] PLYWOOD
TRUSSES WITH BLOWN-IN CELLULOSE
1/2" [13 MM] PLYWOOD, ALL SEAMS TAPED
2X [38 MM] FURRING
5/8" [16 MM] GYPSUM BOARD

METAL FLASHING

5/16" [8 MM] FIBER CEMENT PANEL

ALL SEAMS TAPED

1X4 [19X89 MM] T&G VERTICAL CEDAR SIDING
2X2 [38X38 MM] HORIZONTAL FURRING
2X2 [38X38 MM] VERTICAL FURRING
WRB
5/8" [16 MM] FIBERBOARD (VAPOR-OPEN)
9 1/2" [241 MM] TJI WITH DENSE PACK CELLULOSE
1/2" [13 MM] PLYWOOD, ALL SEAMS TAPED
2X6 [38X140 MM] STUDS WITH DENSE PACK
CELLULOSE
1/2" [13 MM] GYPSUM BOARD

0   18"

0   400 mm

5.7.3 High heel scissors truss with air barrier sheathing attached to the bottom chord. Projecting roof framing outside the control layers.

5.8.1 Shed dormer admits south light to the living space.
ARKIN TILT ARCHITECTS

5.8.2 West façade with shed dormer visible at the right.
EDWARD CALDWELL PHOTOGRAPHY

PROJECT GREEN HOME

Project Green Home is the result of ambitious client goals for a building that is a "Beyond-LEED-Platinum," Net Zero Energy, and Passive House certified. It features four bedrooms plus a "senior suite" that opens to the outdoors. The design is traditional, but also uncompromisingly modern, from its open floor plan to its well-sealed envelope and advanced, high-efficiency heating system. Although the rooms are relatively small, they open up to each other in section for balanced daylight and spatial interest. The simple, two-story, gabled form varies across its length, most prominently in a play loft that opens to the living space below. This provides increased daylight, and passive ventilation by way of mechanically operated skylights that allow heat to escape from much of the house. The tall gable contains attic space plus play lofts above the kids' bedrooms.

PROJECT INFORMATION

Project title: Project Green Home

Location: Palo Alto, California

Size: 2,043 ft.² (190 m²)

Completion: 2011

Type: Single-family home

Recognition: Certified (PHIUS); 2012 EcoHome Design, Sustainable Excellence, Merit Award; 2012 *Environmental Design + Construction*, Excellence in Design Residential Award

Architect: Arkin Tilt Architects

Builder: Josh Moore, Red Company

CPHC: Dan Johnson

HDD: 2,830 base 65°F (1,572 base 18.3°C)

CDD: 305 base 65°F (169 base 18.3°C)

Annual precipitation: 15.3 in. (389 mm)

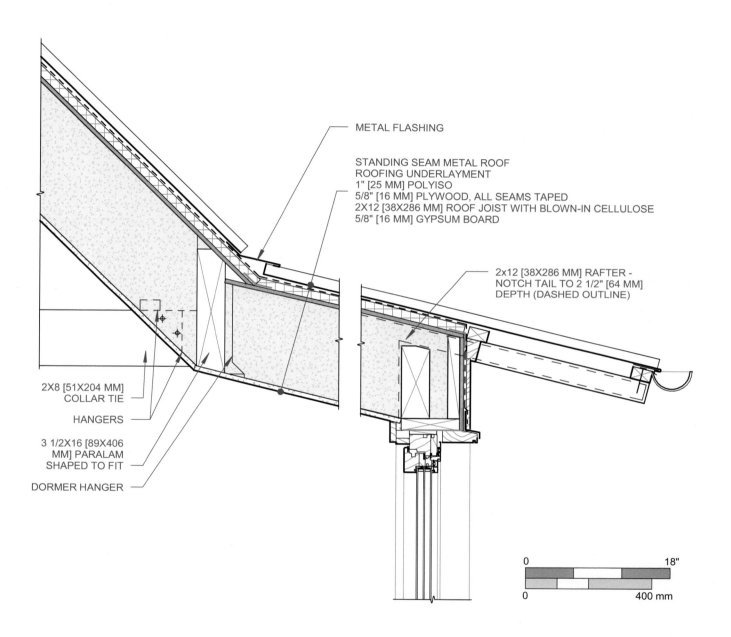

METAL FLASHING

STANDING SEAM METAL ROOF
ROOFING UNDERLAYMENT
1" [25 MM] POLYISO
5/8" [16 MM] PLYWOOD, ALL SEAMS TAPED
2X12 [38X286 MM] ROOF JOIST WITH BLOWN-IN CELLULOSE
5/8" [16 MM] GYPSUM BOARD

2x12 [38X286 MM] RAFTER -
NOTCH TAIL TO 2 1/2" [64 MM]
DEPTH (DASHED OUTLINE)

2X8 [51X204 MM]
COLLAR TIE

HANGERS

3 1/2X16 [89X406
MM] PARALAM
SHAPED TO FIT

DORMER HANGER

0   18"

0   400 mm

5.8.3 Conventional shed dormer framing with exterior layer of rigid insulation to combat thermal bridge effects.

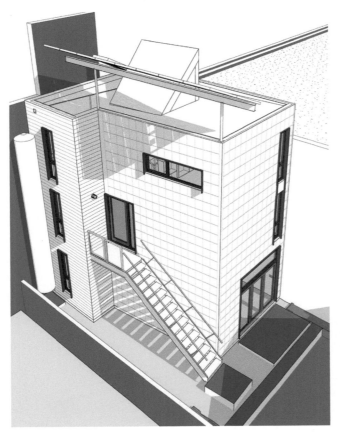

5.9.1 Zero Cottage constructed against neighboring buildings.
DAVID BAKER ARCHITECTS

5.9.2 West Elevation viewed from main house. MATTHEW MILLMAN

ZERO COTTAGE

Zero Cottage in San Francisco is an exploration of compact, sustainable urban development and a contemporary approach to living and working. The cottage is composed of a 712 ft.^{2} (66 m^2) living space set over a 430 ft.^{2} (40 m^2) workshop. It pairs with an existing building to complete a flexible, mixed-use compound that also includes a two-bedroom flat, studio apartment, and storefront space. The building uses salvaged and new metal shingles that slide into custom metal clips and can be quickly moved or replaced. Planter box panels add a playful functionality and are relocated throughout the seasons. The passive house assemblies include charred wood siding made with maple flooring salvaged from a previous project. The vegetated roof features a drought-tolerant garden, composting, urban agriculture, a "bread-box" solar water heater, and a 3-kW photovoltaic system that generates more energy than the cottage uses. The roof also features a clerestory monitor for top lighting which is operable and can be used for ventilation.

PROJECT INFORMATION

Project title: Zero Cottage

Location: San Francisco, California

Size: 1,044 ft.^{2} (97 m^2)

Completion: 2013

Recognition: Certified (PHIUS), LEED for Homes Platinum, Zero Net Energy Building

Type: Mixed use

Architect: David Baker Architects

Builder: Falcon Five Design Build, Jon Landon

CPHC: Prudence Ferreira, Integral Impact

HDD: 2,708 base 65°F (1,504 base 18.3°C)

CDD: 142 base 65°F (79 base 18.3°C)

Annual precipitation: 23.6 in. (600 mm)

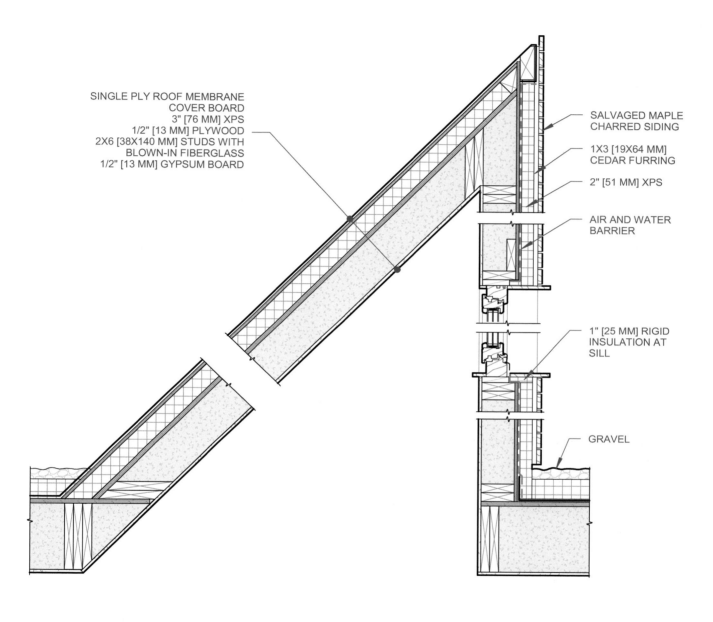

SINGLE PLY ROOF MEMBRANE
COVER BOARD
3" [76 MM] XPS
1/2" [13 MM] PLYWOOD
2X6 [38X140 MM] STUDS WITH
BLOWN-IN FIBERGLASS
1/2" [13 MM] GYPSUM BOARD

SALVAGED MAPLE
CHARRED SIDING

1X3 [19X64 MM]
CEDAR FURRING

2" [51 MM] XPS

AIR AND WATER
BARRIER

1" [25 MM] RIGID
INSULATION AT
SILL

GRAVEL

0   24"

0   600 mm

5.9.3 South facing clerestory windows in projecting roof monitor above central atrium space.

CHAPTER 6

Openings for Windows and Doors

The character of a building is greatly influenced by the position of the window within the thickness of the wall. Traditional windows were set back from the surface, with a deep, sloping sill at the base. This helped to protect the wood sash from exposure to the rain. It also expressed the substance and security of the enclosure. Contemporary, mass-produced windows, with durable materials on the exterior, have been applied closer to the outer surface of the wall. This has allowed them to be attached directly to the structural sheathing with nailing flanges.

The layered construction of a passive house wall presents numerous options regarding the position of the window within a very thick wall. Passive house windows are best located somewhere near the thermal center of the wall. This reduces diagonal shortcuts through the corner of the insulation that could occur if the window were to be mounted fully to the inside or outside of the opening. High-performance windows rarely have nailing flanges, allowing the designer to place the window in the most effective position. Flange material is usually more conductive than either the glazing unit or the wall, so that retaining it is counterproductive.

Even where there is the freedom to choose otherwise, windows often remain closely associated with the structural sheathing plane at the load-bearing portion of the wall. This offers a direct connection for the transfer of wind loads. If the air barrier is developed at the sheathing, this proximity facilitates closure at the interface between window and wall. Finally, the rough opening at the sheathing plane is a stable shape, less likely to distort and accidentally stress the window.

Window details from the Stellar Apartments demonstrate the basic approach (see Figure 6.1.3 below). The glazing unit is secured with clips rather than nailing flanges, but the position in the wall is nearly the same, close to the sheathing. The insulating glass unit is centered thermally, given the overlay of rigid insulation. Of particular note, the air and water barriers are carried under and up at the sill to complete a back dam. Sealant is applied at the inside edge of the window unit. Water working through the joints in the frame is prevented from passing to the interior either by capillary action or air pressure differential. In this example, the rigid insulation around the window opening is concealed with metal flashing. A gasket behind the flashing is used to reduce thermal transfer from the solid structure to the exterior.

At Lone Fir Residence, the outer insulation is placed within a non-bearing curtain wall that is thermally isolated from the bearing structure (see Figure 6.2.3 below). The outer curtain of studs provides secure backing for cladding, applied over vapor-permeable sheathing. The framed opening in the outer leaf of studs is enlarged, leaving room for rigid insulation that reduces thermal bridges across the corners. Hayfield House uses structural insulated panels as the outer leaf of insulation (see Figure 8.5.13 in Chapter 8). Their inherent rigidity provides a secure base for the trim, without solid framing members near the exterior surface. Rigid insulation is brought over the wood window frame to the limit imposed by the exterior metal cladding. This lapping of the thermal barrier at the window is a modest form of "over-insulation," something that can be more pronounced at the head and the jambs. It is difficult to increase at the sill, where metal flashing tucks under or into the base of the frame. Classic window treatments maintain a consistent reveal of the frame on all four sides, but high-performance objectives suggest otherwise. Hayfield House strikes a balance, with a reasonable contrast in the amount of frame revealed at the head and the sill.

At Madrona Passive House, the external layers of insulation and rainscreen cladding are moderately thick, providing space for operable shading devices at the head of the window, behind the exterior finishes (see Figure 6.3.3 below). Jung Haus uses over-framing with I-joists to create a cavity for dense-pack cellulose rather than rigid insulation (see Figure 6.4.3 below). As the thermal center of the wall moves outward, the window moves out with it. This is achieved with a 2 x 10 (38 x 235-mm) window buck and a projecting plywood surround, or throat. The goal is to control the shape of the opening and maintain a firm connection back to the structural leaf of the wall, while minimizing the cross section of material that bridges the thermal insulation. Window reveals both inside and out express the substance of the wall in both directions. Rain driven against the window must be carried back out to the surface, and the exterior window surround must have durable finishes. Moderation of the depth of the recesses allows them to be completed with reasonable dimensions of material.

The Viridescent Building case study again demonstrates the use of a full-depth plywood throat at the window opening, but, in this case, the window is moved all the way to the outside (see Figure 8.14.16 in Chapter 8). A flanged frame is used to create a secure overlap at the water-resistant barrier, giving priority in this instance to water over the optimized thermal consideration. Bayside Anchor uses plywood gussets to tie together a double stud wall (see Figure 6.5.3 below). The exterior leaf of studs is load-bearing, and the plywood throat at the window allows the unit to be secured near the center of the wall, more or less independent of the structural configuration.

Windows pressed into the corner of a room present design opportunities and technical challenges. To capture a diagonal view, or strengthen the connection to the outdoors, the building corner between window units needs to be slender. It is difficult to locate the glass in the thermal center of a thick wall when that wall is folded at 90°. Adding to the complexity, there is usually a load-bearing structure somewhere nearby, competing for space. The corner window in the Madrona Passive House case study embodies a thoughtful response to these issues (see Figure 8.8.19 in Chapter 8). First, the adjacent frames are pushed together, as suggested in Chapter 1. Wood structure is replaced with a slender steel tube to reduce the bulk. Finally, the window units are over-insulated on the exterior to reduce the amount of frame material exposed to the cold.

The living-room corner at Karuna House uses an offset steel structure to bring vertical support at the corner into the warm interior, eliminating it as a thermal bridge (see Figure 8.6.19 in Chapter 8). A similar approach is used with steel elements in the south- and east-facing curtain walls in the Earthship Farmstead case study (see Figure 8.3.7 in Chapter 8). Viridescent Building uses laminated veneer lumber (LVL) mullions to secure a broad expanse of glazing (see Figure 8.14.19 in Chapter 8). These are wrapped with rigid insulation to provide a thermal break, while at least partially over-insulating the window frame from the interior.

In the Freeman House, the corner window is inverted so that the adjacent glazing units form a right angle on the exterior face rather than the interior (see Figure 6.6.3 below). Cutting into the volume of the house dramatically expresses the thickness of the wall while responding creatively to basic principles. The load-bearing structure is removed from the outside corner, with a cantilevered header buried in the thick wall above the opening. The walls run past the window jambs, lining up the thermal centers of solid and glass even as they are perpendicular to one another. The final inside corner again puts the frames directly together, with over-insulation from the interior.

Passive house applications beyond the detached, single-family house bring with them a host of new issues of material and detail. The Tighthouse Brownstone is the transformation of a Brooklyn row house using steel and concrete masonry in the backyard elevation (see Figure 6.7.3 below). Mineral wool insulation over masonry is a staple of European retrofits. The Uptown Lofts on Fifth is multifamily housing that applies the perfect wall concept, with insulation in the cavity outside the combined air, water, and vapor barriers. This occurs with both a rainscreen cladding system and a masonry veneer (see Figures 8.13.13 and 8.13.16 in Chapter 8). At the veneer, a loose lintel and other miscellaneous angles are used to support the masonry units around the window opening with a minimum of thermal compromise.

Contemporary standards of practice for multifamily apartments and condominiums place a much greater emphasis on the control of water entry at the window interface and through the window itself. Some of this is in conflict with passive house objectives. The Orchards at Orenco window details show a continuous sill pan folded over an aluminum back dam (see Figure 8.9.13 in Chapter 8). The air seal is developed at the interior edge of the window frame, with an open passage to the exterior to allow any accumulated water to weep back out. The window unit and the sill are supported on insulated shims to promote drainage. Passive house principles discourage an open channel of cold air penetrating so deeply into the wall section. Subsills in passive houses usually interlock with the exterior face of the window unit, but often without a backup system behind them. The challenge in all cases is to maintain the integrity of the air barrier and

thermal control layers at the interface between the window and the wall. This must be done without compromise to weather-resistance systems that rely on redundant layers, free drainage, and drying to be fully effective.

Door openings present all of the challenges of windows, with a few in addition. The connection of doors to the structural frame is even more important because of the impact loads when they swing shut. A door must be located toward the interior edge of a deep wall section if it is to be in-swinging and free to open beyond 90°. This requires a solution to issues of closing the wall thickness at the head and the jambs. The deep sill at the bottom of a door has to exclude water and it must be strong enough to support foot traffic or a hand truck moving in appliances. The door sill is a particular challenge if it is to provide safe passage over the threshold and barrier-free design. The building foundation, floor system, walls, and exterior walk surface all come together in close proximity. Finish surfaces must align inside and out, while the thermal, water, and air control remain intact. Among these, the control of water is particularly influential. The access door to a roof deck at Madrona Passive House (see Figure 8.8.13 in Chapter 8) illustrates the necessary components: an upstand at the edge of the walkable roof system, a through wall pan at the sill, provision for drainage, a back dam, and a sealant at the inside edge of the frame to complete the air barrier. Variations on these themes can be found in many of the case studies.

Doors are a necessary and inevitable thermal compromise, due to the framing that surrounds them and the potential for leaks at the air seals. They can repay some of this deficit if they contribute daylight and positive solar gain, excepting the sheltering roof expected at principal entrances. Excess solar gain must be avoided with seasonally adaptive shading devices. The Warren Woods Ecological Field Station uses a system of folding shade screens to protect a wall of glass, with dramatic effect (see Figure 6.8.3 below). Rolling screens cover both windows and doors at the Hayfield House, whereas Madrona Passive House uses external louvers to do the same (see Figures 8.5.16 and 8.8.16 in Chapter 8).

6.1.1 Sheet metal window surround projects through the depth of the exterior insulation. BERGSUND DELANEY ARCHITECTURE AND PLANNING

6.1.2 Sheet metal jamb and sill extensions fastened through a neoprene gasket. BERGSUND DELANEY ARCHITECTURE AND PLANNING

STELLAR APARTMENTS

Stellar Apartments, Eugene, Oregon consists of twelve buildings with one, two, and three bedroom townhome-style apartments and flats. All units meet or exceed Earth Advantage Certification and have double-glazed windows. However, one building (six units), built to the passive house standard, appears similar in all ways to its neighboring Earth Advantage building, except for the triple-glazed windows, shading devices, HRVs, increased insulation, and infiltration rate of 0.5 ACH50. Casement windows are installed within the wood frame portion of the wall, with the outer face of the frame 1-in. (25-mm) proud of the exterior plywood sheathing. A metal surround is attached to the wall to encapsulate the 4-in. (100-mm) thick exterior foam insulation, with multiple layers of protection against water.

PROJECT INFORMATION

Project title: Stellar Apartments Passive House

Location: Eugene, Oregon

Size: 6,480 ft.^{2} (602 m^2) passive house building; 63,572 ft.^{2} (5,906 m^2) entire project

Completion: 2013

Recognition: Certification (PHIUS), Earth Advantage Gold Certification

Type: Multifamily affordable housing

Architect: Bergsund Delaney Architecture and Planning

Builder: Meili Construction Co.

CPHC: Win Swafford, Jan Fillinger

HDD: 4,821 base 65°F (2,678 base 18.3°C)

CDD: 210 base 65°F (117 base 18.3°C)

Annual precipitation: 46 in. (1,168 mm)

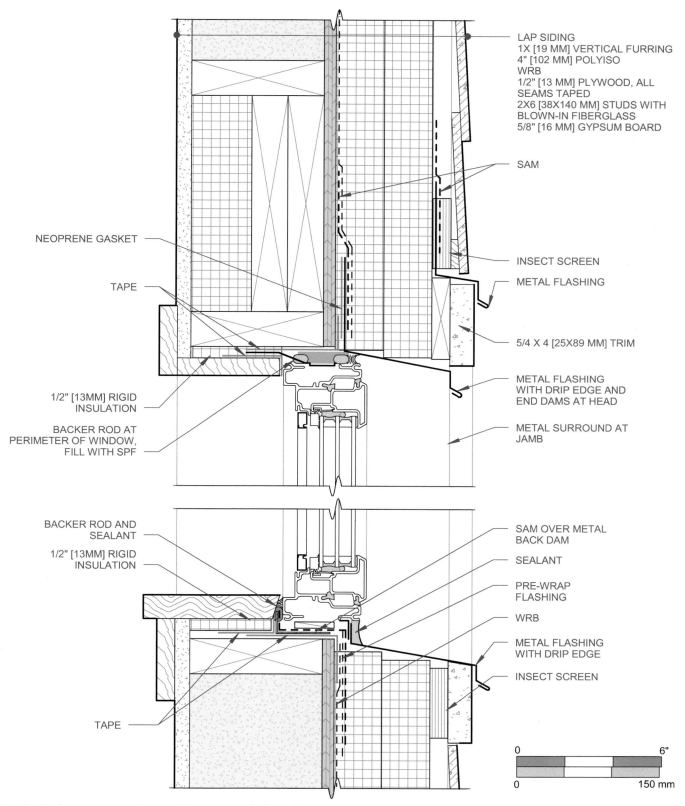

LAP SIDING
1X [19 MM] VERTICAL FURRING
4" [102 MM] POLYISO
WRB
1/2" [13 MM] PLYWOOD, ALL
SEAMS TAPED
2X6 [38X140 MM] STUDS WITH
BLOWN-IN FIBERGLASS
5/8" [16 MM] GYPSUM BOARD

SAM

INSECT SCREEN

METAL FLASHING

5/4 X 4 [25X89 MM] TRIM

METAL FLASHING
WITH DRIP EDGE AND
END DAMS AT HEAD

METAL SURROUND AT
JAMB

NEOPRENE GASKET

TAPE

1/2" [13MM] RIGID
INSULATION

BACKER ROD AT
PERIMETER OF WINDOW,
FILL WITH SPF

BACKER ROD AND
SEALANT

1/2" [13MM] RIGID
INSULATION

SAM OVER METAL
BACK DAM

SEALANT

PRE-WRAP
FLASHING

WRB

METAL FLASHING
WITH DRIP EDGE

INSECT SCREEN

TAPE

0   6"

0   150 mm

6.1.3 Window units secured to rough opening with clips. Sill protected by back dam and sealant. Drainage to exterior.

6.2.1 Window opening framed in non-bearing exterior curtain wall. BEN GATES AND MARGO RETTIG

6.2.2 Window unit with sheet metal surround and rainscreen cladding. BEN GATES AND MARGO RETTIG

LONE FIR RESIDENCE

Lone Fir Residence, presented in Chapter 5, uses advanced framing with 2 x 6 (38 x 140-mm) studs, sheathed with ⅝-in. (16-mm) plywood. An additional curtain wall of 2 x 4 (38 x 80-mm) studs, sheathed with ½-in. (13-mm) fiberboard, was added and tied in at each level to provide a 2-in. (51-mm) air gap between walls. Both wall cavities were filled with cellulose insulation. FSC-certified framing lumber and cedar siding were sourced from Sustainable Northwest Wood. Triple-glazed wood windows from Unilux allow tilt (hopper) and turn (casement) operation. Motorized exterior shades from Hella block unwanted summer heat. An HRV from Zehnder provides 350 CFM of filtered, fresh air. All of these strategies allow the house to be heated through the winter by a few King Electric 500-W (model KCE) radiant heaters, a simple solution the owners were able to install themselves.

PROJECT INFORMATION

Project title: Lone Fir Residence

Location: Portland, Oregon

Size: 1,820 ft.² (170 m²)

Permitted: 2010

Recognition: Pre-certified

Type: Single-family home and attached accessory dwelling unit

Architect: Owner

Builder: Owner and Green Hammer (core and shell)

CPHC: Owner

HDD: 4,222 base 65°F (2,346 base 18.3°C)

CDD: 423 base 65°F (235 base 18.3°C)

Annual precipitation: 46.5 in. (1,181 mm)

Blower door result: 0.45 ACH50

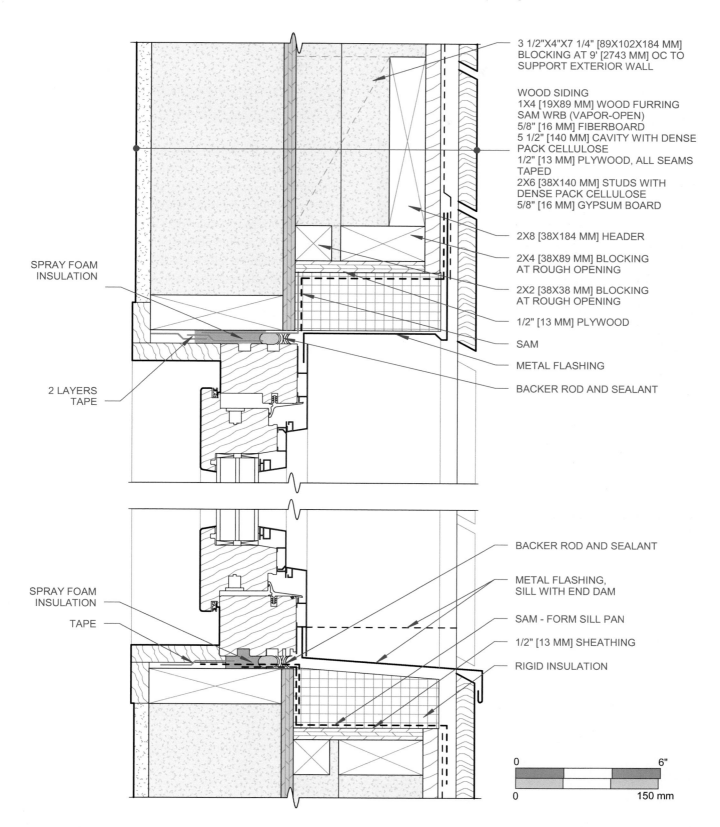

3 1/2"X4"X7 1/4" [89X102X184 MM] BLOCKING AT 9' [2743 MM] OC TO SUPPORT EXTERIOR WALL

WOOD SIDING
1X4 [19X89 MM] WOOD FURRING
SAM WRB (VAPOR-OPEN)
5/8" [16 MM] FIBERBOARD
5 1/2" [140 MM] CAVITY WITH DENSE PACK CELLULOSE
1/2" [13 MM] PLYWOOD, ALL SEAMS TAPED
2X6 [38X140 MM] STUDS WITH DENSE PACK CELLULOSE
5/8" [16 MM] GYPSUM BOARD

2X8 [38X184 MM] HEADER

2X4 [38X89 MM] BLOCKING AT ROUGH OPENING

2X2 [38X38 MM] BLOCKING AT ROUGH OPENING

1/2" [13 MM] PLYWOOD

SAM

METAL FLASHING

BACKER ROD AND SEALANT

SPRAY FOAM INSULATION

2 LAYERS TAPE

SPRAY FOAM INSULATION

TAPE

BACKER ROD AND SEALANT

METAL FLASHING, SILL WITH END DAM

SAM - FORM SILL PAN

1/2" [13 MM] SHEATHING

RIGID INSULATION

0   6"

0   150 mm

6.2.3 Window unit aligns with structural wall. Oversized opening in outer curtain wall provides space for blocks of rigid insulation.

6.3.1 Window head flashing shelters operable shades. Prepared for rainscreen cladding. HAMMER & HAND

6.3.2 Completed exterior window treatment. HAMMER & HAND

MADRONA PASSIVE HOUSE

At the edge of the Madrona neighborhood in Seattle, this contemporary home uses the highest-performance building techniques to create a beautiful, healthy, environmentally responsive, and resource-efficient house. The house is designed as a series of volumes, with large, ZOLA aluminum-clad windows that allow daylight, ventilation, and expansive views, yet conceal an external shade system to prevent overheating from the sun. The project aims to respect the environmentally critical site and achieve the high performance of the passive house energy standard. Well versed in advocacy work for climate change mitigation, the owner stated, "If the house costs 10, 15, or even 20 percent more to build in a climate-friendly way, then it's reasonable for others with some extra money to replicate, especially if the 10th or 20th such house in Seattle costs only a few percent more to build in a climate-friendly way." Additional details for this house are located Chapter 8.

PROJECT INFORMATION

Project title: Madrona Passive House

Location: Seattle, Washington

Size: 3,766 ft.² (152 m²) treated floor area

Completion: 2015

Recognition: Certified (PHIUS), ILFI Net Zero Energy Building Certification

Type: Single-family house

Architect: SHED Architecture & Design

Builder: Hammer & Hand

CPHC: Daniel Whitmore, Hammer & Hand

HDD: 4,280 base 65°F (2,378 base 18.3°C)

CDD: 279 base 65°F (155 base 18.3°C)

Annual precipitation: 38 in. (965 mm)

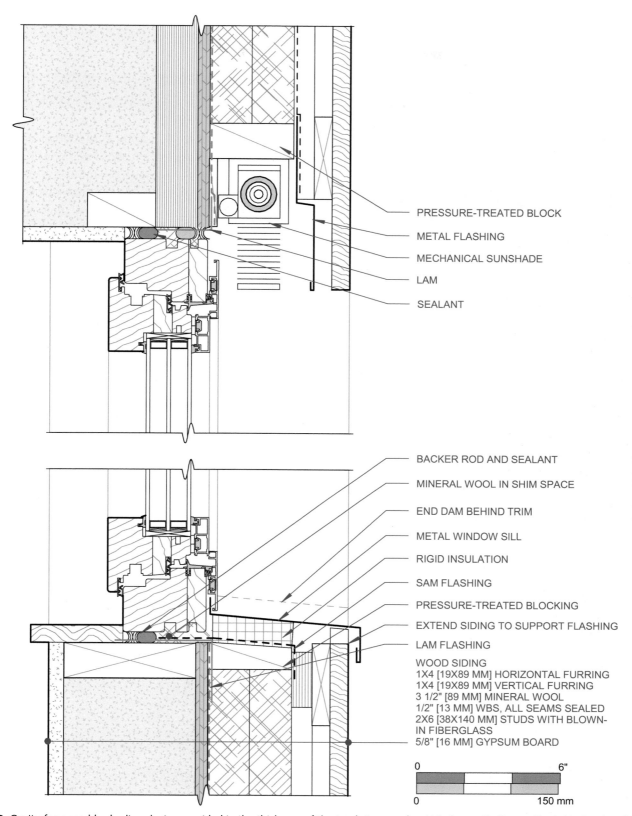

PRESSURE-TREATED BLOCK

METAL FLASHING

MECHANICAL SUNSHADE

LAM

SEALANT

BACKER ROD AND SEALANT

MINERAL WOOL IN SHIM SPACE

END DAM BEHIND TRIM

METAL WINDOW SILL

RIGID INSULATION

SAM FLASHING

PRESSURE-TREATED BLOCKING

EXTEND SIDING TO SUPPORT FLASHING

LAM FLASHING

WOOD SIDING
1X4 [19X89 MM] HORIZONTAL FURRING
1X4 [19X89 MM] VERTICAL FURRING
3 1/2" [89 MM] MINERAL WOOL
1/2" [13 MM] WBS, ALL SEAMS SEALED
2X6 [38X140 MM] STUDS WITH BLOWN-
IN FIBERGLASS
5/8" [16 MM] GYPSUM BOARD

0   6"

0   150 mm

6.3.3 Cavity for operable shading device provided in the thickness of the insulation overlay. Window unit aligns with air barrier sheathing.

6.4.1 Plywood throat and window buck at opening. Installing I-joist over-framing. KURT AND MAURA JUNG

6.4.2 Window installation, prepared for casing and lap siding. KURT AND MAURA JUNG

JUNG HAUS

Previously introduced in Chapter 2, the Jung Haus features walls that were constructed traditionally and sheathed with a water-resistive air barrier. Later, a 12-in.- (305-mm-) thick insulated wall was added to the outside to achieve an overall insulation value of R-60, including the windows. The designers used a number of innovative products that made the design and scope possible in the harsh climate of Michigan. The system consists of a series of panels and tape that effectively manages moisture, air sealing, and structural durability (Huber engineered Wood ZIP System). This made it easier to overlay 12-in.-deep I-joists on the exterior of a standard 2 x 6 (38 x 140-mm) stud wall to complete the insulated walls of the house. A deep "box" was framed through the wall to prepare for installation of the triple-glazed windows (Kneer-Sudfenster). After attachment, the edges of the window frames were taped and over-insulated.

PROJECT INFORMATION

Project title: Jung Haus

Location: Holly, Michigan

Size: 2,300 ft.² (214 m²)

Completion: 2013

Recognition: Certified (PHI), Fine Homebuilding's 2014 Best Energy-Smart Home

Type: Single-family home

Architect: GO Logic

Builder: Energy Wise Homes

CPHC: Think Little

HDD: 6,634 base 65°F (3,686 base 18.3°C)

CDD: 627 base 65°F (348 base 18.3°C)

Annual precipitation: 34 in. (864 mm)

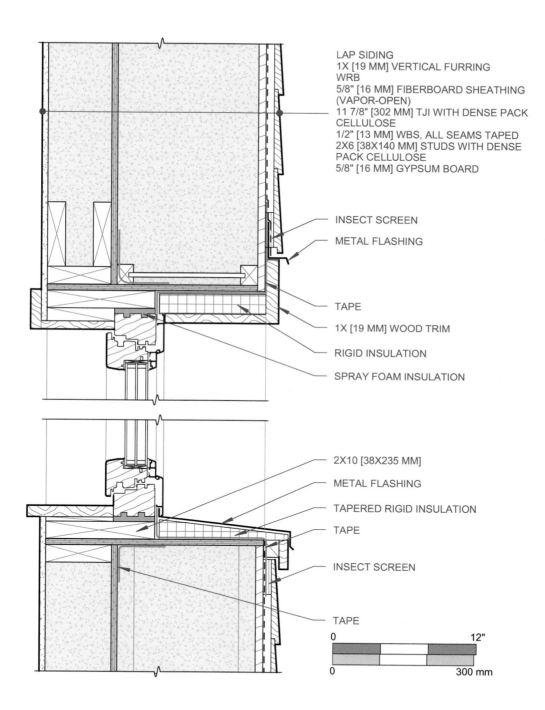

LAP SIDING
1X [19 MM] VERTICAL FURRING
WRB
5/8" [16 MM] FIBERBOARD SHEATHING (VAPOR-OPEN)
11 7/8" [302 MM] TJI WITH DENSE PACK CELLULOSE
1/2" [13 MM] WBS, ALL SEAMS TAPED
2X6 [38X140 MM] STUDS WITH DENSE PACK CELLULOSE
5/8" [16 MM] GYPSUM BOARD

INSECT SCREEN

METAL FLASHING

TAPE

1X [19 MM] WOOD TRIM

RIGID INSULATION

SPRAY FOAM INSULATION

2X10 [38X235 MM]

METAL FLASHING

TAPERED RIGID INSULATION

TAPE

INSECT SCREEN

TAPE

0 ——————— 12"
0 ——————— 300 mm

6.4.3 Deep over-framing with I-joists secured with a plywood throat at the opening. Window unit mounted on a wood buck to reach thermal center of wall.

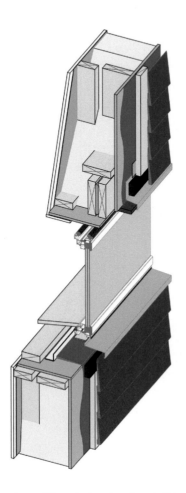

6.5.1 Cutaway view of the window head and sill in a double stud wall. KAPLAN THOMPSON ARCHITECTS

6.5.2 Bayside Anchor affordable housing complex. KAPLAN THOMPSON ARCHITECTS

BAYSIDE ANCHOR

Kaplan Thompson Architects won a competition, sponsored by Deutsche Bank and Enterprise Community Partners Inc., for forty-five units of multifamily affordable housing. Partnering with Avesta Housing, Portland Housing Authority, Wright-Ryan Construction, John Anton Consulting, and the Maine Affordable Housing Coalition, the team set out to prove that first costs of development and long-term costs over the life of a building can both be lowered. Strategies include: PHIUS+ energy savings, off-site prefabrication, shorter time frames, more efficient use of labor, and lowered embodied energy of construction. "State of the shelf" technologies achieve ambitious energy savings at market rate construction costs of $140 per square foot. These include double stud wall construction, with dense-packed cellulose insulation protected by a smart vapor retarder, energy recovery ventilators, vinyl triple-glazed casement windows, and conventional rigid insulation for the roof and slab. The project targets 0.05 CFM50 per square foot of enclosure, or 0.35 ACH50.

PROJECT INFORMATION

Project title: Bayside Anchor

Location: Portland, Maine

Size: 37,800 ft.² (3,511 m²) total project

Completion: 2016

Recognition: Pre-Certified (PHIUS)

Type: Multifamily housing

Architect: Kaplan Thompson Architects

Builder: Wright-Ryan Construction

CPHC: Jesse Thompson

HDD: 7,082 base 65°F (3,934 base 18.3°C)

CDD: 365 base 65°F (203 base 18.3°C)

Annual precipitation: 47.33 in. (1,202 mm)

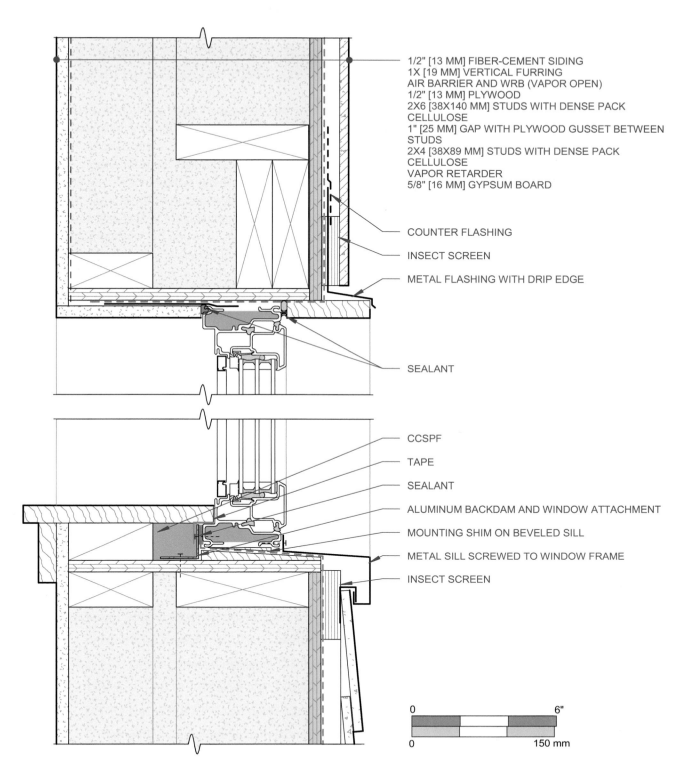

1/2" [13 MM] FIBER-CEMENT SIDING
1X [19 MM] VERTICAL FURRING
AIR BARRIER AND WRB (VAPOR OPEN)
1/2" [13 MM] PLYWOOD
2X6 [38X140 MM] STUDS WITH DENSE PACK
CELLULOSE
1" [25 MM] GAP WITH PLYWOOD GUSSET BETWEEN
STUDS
2X4 [38X89 MM] STUDS WITH DENSE PACK
CELLULOSE
VAPOR RETARDER
5/8" [16 MM] GYPSUM BOARD

COUNTER FLASHING

INSECT SCREEN

METAL FLASHING WITH DRIP EDGE

SEALANT

CCSPF

TAPE

SEALANT

ALUMINUM BACKDAM AND WINDOW ATTACHMENT

MOUNTING SHIM ON BEVELED SILL

METAL SILL SCREWED TO WINDOW FRAME

INSECT SCREEN

0   6"

0   150 mm

6.5.3 Plywood gussets tie double stud walls together with a minimal thermal cross section. Gussets provide mounting surface for window unit.

6.6.1 View of recessed corner window from the southwest.
DEREK PORTER, DEREK PORTER STUDIO

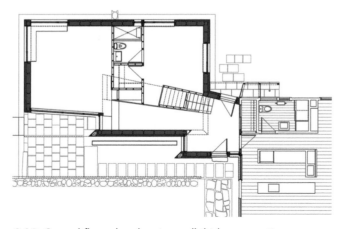

6.6.2 Ground floor plan showing wall thickness meeting corner window. BRIGGS KNOWLES ARCHITECTURE+DESIGN

FREEMAN HOUSE

The Freeman passive house addition to a 200-year-old farmhouse, described in Chapter 2, follows vernacular traditions and uses exterior materials to tie together ideas of the past with new ideas for energy efficiency. The original house has symmetrically arrayed openings for the general illumination of the interior. The apertures in the addition are individually placed to make connections between the existing house, the addition, and the landscape and to provide daylight throughout. The shape of the addition, along with the placement of the windows, provides a panorama of the mountains. The view is offered at several moments—the same view appearing as a continuation. Although the windows from the original loose heat, the new windows provide surplus energy on an annual basis. The striking corner opening surrounds the largest windows with thick, insulating walls.

PROJECT INFORMATION

Project title: Freeman House

Location: Freeman, Maine

Size: 1,700 ft.^{2} (157 m^2)

Completion: 2012

Recognition: Passive House planned

Type: Single-family home

Architect: Briggs Knowles Architecture+Design

Builder: Sebastian Tooker Construction

CPHC: Jonathan Knowles, BKAD

HDD: 8,784 base 65°F (4,880 base 18.3°C)

CDD: 197 base 65°F (109 base 18.3°C)

Annual precipitation: 38 in. (965 mm)

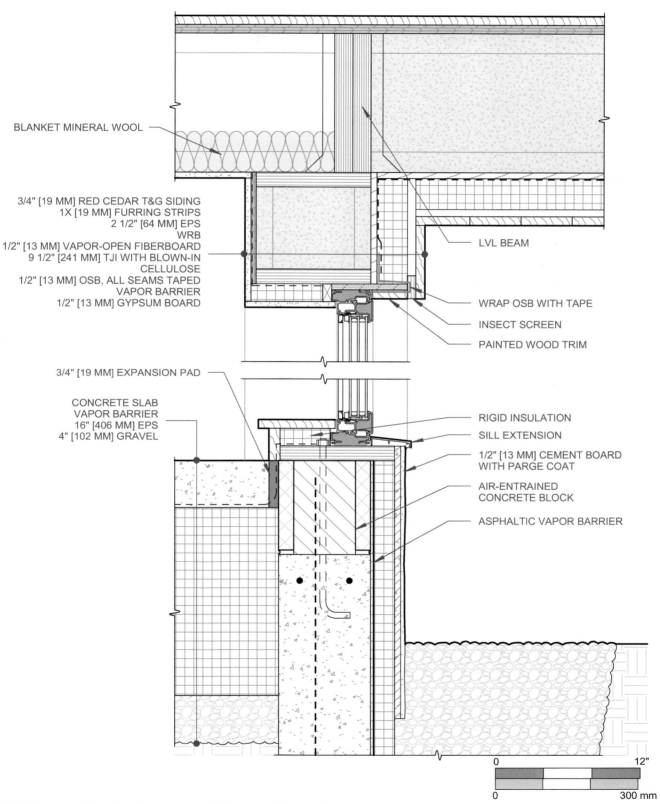

BLANKET MINERAL WOOL

3/4" [19 MM] RED CEDAR T&G SIDING
1X [19 MM] FURRING STRIPS
2 1/2" [64 MM] EPS
WRB
1/2" [13 MM] VAPOR-OPEN FIBERBOARD
9 1/2" [241 MM] TJI WITH BLOWN-IN
CELLULOSE
1/2" [13 MM] OSB, ALL SEAMS TAPED
VAPOR BARRIER
1/2" [13 MM] GYPSUM BOARD

LVL BEAM

WRAP OSB WITH TAPE

INSECT SCREEN

PAINTED WOOD TRIM

3/4" [19 MM] EXPANSION PAD

CONCRETE SLAB
VAPOR BARRIER
16" [406 MM] EPS
4" [102 MM] GRAVEL

RIGID INSULATION

SILL EXTENSION

1/2" [13 MM] CEMENT BOARD
WITH PARGE COAT

AIR-ENTRAINED
CONCRETE BLOCK

ASPHALTIC VAPOR BARRIER

0   12"

0   300 mm

6.6.3 Window wall developed in a recess with the second floor continuous above.

6.7.1 New rear elevation with fiber cement rainscreen.
HAI ZHANG

6.7.2 Metal cover plate conceals zone of mineral wool insulation.
FETE NATURE ARCHITECTURE, PLLC

TIGHTHOUSE BROWNSTONE

This retrofit is the first certified passive house project in New York City. The project adds a new rear façade, third floor, and roof terrace. It features high-performance materials, airtightness, and an HRV ventilation system. The third floor has an angled roof, with the ridge optimized due south for solar thermal and photovoltaic panels. There is no gas service. All lighting is LED or fluorescent. Two triple-glazed skylights bring natural light to the internal stair volume and thus into the middle of the building, through perforated metal stairs and glass partitions. The windows are tilt-and-turn style fabricated by a European manufacturer, Schuco Thermoplus, and certified for passive house use. Five blower door tests were conducted over the course of construction to learn about airtightness levels, and the final blower door test for certification at the end of the project achieved a 0.38 ACH50.

PROJECT INFORMATION

Project title: Tighthouse Brownstone

Location: Brooklyn, New York

Size: 2,203 ft.² (204 m²; treated floor area)

Completion: 2012

Recognition: Certified (PHI), 2015 AIA NY Chapter COTE Honorable Mention Award, 2014 International Passive House Design Award

Type: Single-family home

Architect: FNA/Fete Nature Architecture, PLLC

Builder: WM Dorvillier & Co.

CPHC: ZeroEnergy Design

HDD: 4,828 base 65°F (2,682 base 18.3°C)

CDD: 978 base 65°F (543 base 18.3°C)

Annual precipitation: 46.25 in. (1,174.24 mm)

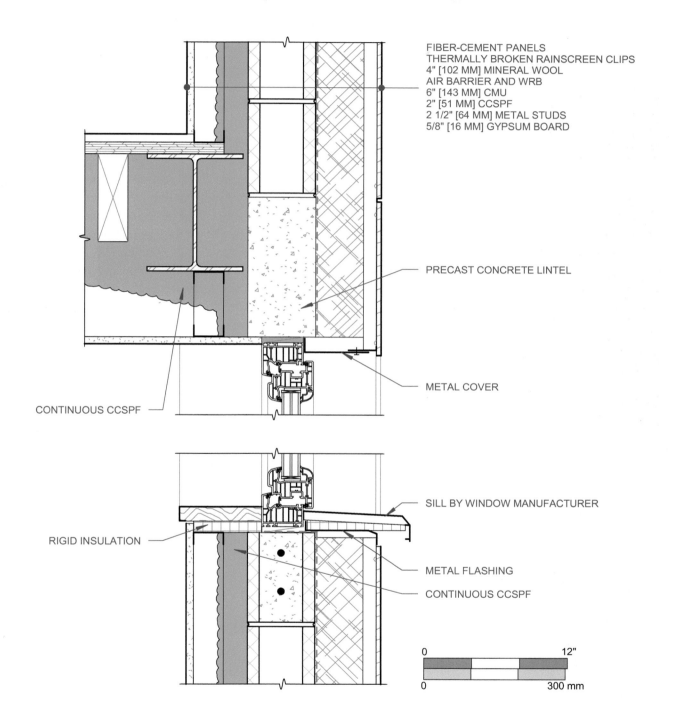

FIBER-CEMENT PANELS
THERMALLY BROKEN RAINSCREEN CLIPS
4" [102 MM] MINERAL WOOL
AIR BARRIER AND WRB
6" [143 MM] CMU
2" [51 MM] CCSPF
2 1/2" [64 MM] METAL STUDS
5/8" [16 MM] GYPSUM BOARD

PRECAST CONCRETE LINTEL

METAL COVER

CONTINUOUS CCSPF

SILL BY WINDOW MANUFACTURER

RIGID INSULATION

METAL FLASHING

CONTINUOUS CCSPF

0   12"

0   300 mm

6.7.3 Window units installed in a masonry wall with an exterior overlay of mineral wool insulation.

6.8.1 Folding metal screen covers south side windows and doors.
TRENT BELL PHOTOGRAPHY

6.8.2 Installation of wood cladding over heads of doors and windows. MICHAEL KLINGER, ENERGYWISE/GO LOGIC, LLC

WARREN WOODS ECOLOGICAL FIELD STATION

The Warren Woods Ecological Field Station was introduced in Chapter 4. The windows are strategically sized and located to provide sufficient views and daylight, while keeping unwanted solar gain in check. One exception is a large expanse of glass along the main conference space on the ground floor, which opens up to views of the forest. Excessive solar gain can be controlled by closing a series of perforated metal screens, serving as a visual counterpoint to the rustic wood siding on the façade. The building envelope performs well enough to allow the heat generated by the lab equipment to warm the entire building, and yet it overheats the space in which it is housed. Rather than increasing the levels of air conditioning within the lab, an in-line fan was installed between the lab and conference space to allow the excess heat to be removed and used to condition the rest of the building.

PROJECT INFORMATION

Project title: Warren Woods Ecological Field Station

Location: Berrien County, Michigan

Size: 2,400 ft.^{2} (223 m^2)

Completion: 2014

Recognition: First certified Passive House laboratory in North America; 2015 AIA Honor Award recipient from AIA Maine COTE, 2015; PHIUS Passive Project Award, 2015

Type: Laboratory

Architect: GO Logic

Builder: GO Logic and Ebels Construction

CPHC: GO Logic

HDD: 6,296 base 65°F (3,498 base 18.3°C)

CDD: 564 base 65°F (313 base 18.3°C)

Annual precipitation: 42 in. (1,067 mm)

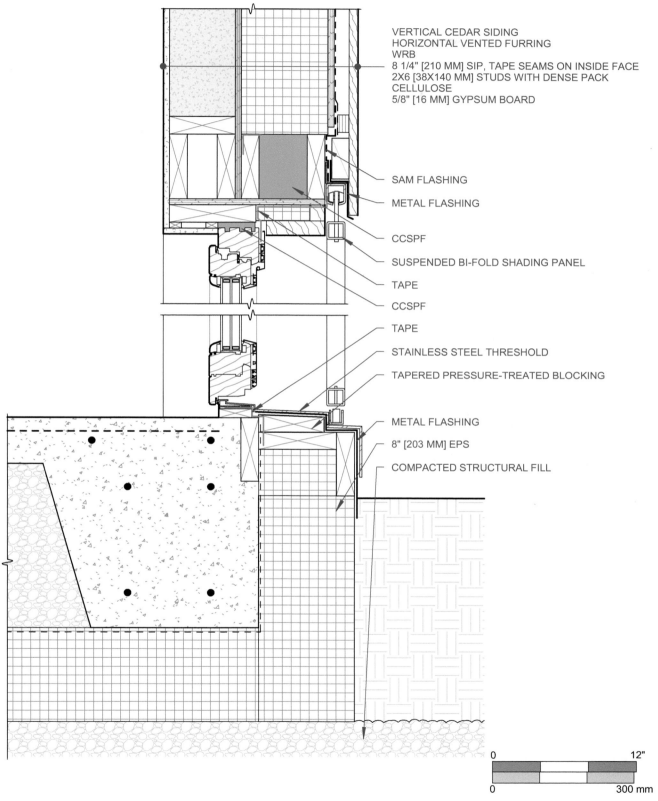

VERTICAL CEDAR SIDING
HORIZONTAL VENTED FURRING
WRB
8 1/4" [210 MM] SIP, TAPE SEAMS ON INSIDE FACE
2X6 [38X140 MM] STUDS WITH DENSE PACK CELLULOSE
5/8" [16 MM] GYPSUM BOARD

SAM FLASHING

METAL FLASHING

CCSPF

SUSPENDED BI-FOLD SHADING PANEL

TAPE

CCSPF

TAPE

STAINLESS STEEL THRESHOLD

TAPERED PRESSURE-TREATED BLOCKING

METAL FLASHING

8" [203 MM] EPS

COMPACTED STRUCTURAL FILL

0   12"

0   300 mm

6.8.3 Door at slab edge with stainless steel sill extension. Bifold sliding screens suspended from a track tucked behind the cladding.

CHAPTER 7

Openings: Mechanical, Plumbing, and Electrical

Passive house performance standards require that the integrity of the air barrier and thermal isolation layer be maintained completely and consistently. As mechanical, electrical, and plumbing systems are integrated into the design, the first goal is to eliminate punctures through the air barrier and cold bridges across the insulation in so far as possible. If the passage of service systems through the envelope cannot be eliminated, such events must be reduced in number and effectively controlled.

In the past, openings in the building envelope for the passage of service systems were considered a minor energy loss. They were often ignored in favor of simple, low-cost approaches to systems installation. Common system components and traditions of practice that evolved in this context can be hard to replace or change, particularly when they are reinforced by requirements of the building codes. As one example, sanitary vents are large-diameter, often loosely fitted pipes that pass through the envelope, introducing a column of cold air into the building. Forced air heating systems may rely on the convenience of unheated crawl spaces to distribute large-dimension ductwork across the plan. Outlet louvers are cut through the floor in each room. The fireplace, enduring symbol of hearth and home, has long been recognized as an energy liability. Without doors and combustion make-up air, the flue draws heat from the house long after the positive thermal contribution has died away.

The first method to eliminate punctures in the envelope is to question the need for a given system to engage the envelope at all. A traditional clothes dryer takes conditioned air from the house and pushes it out through a relatively large hole in the wall. This has been the most convenient way to expel the moisture from wet clothes. By contrast, a condensing dryer attacks both of the former problems. Using various means of condensation, these devices extract only the water and recycle the hot air, either back to the space or back to the machine. The hole in the side of the house is eliminated (see Figure 7.1). Similarly, air admittance valves can be used to prevent siphoning of the water trap in sanitary drains. They replace the connection to a ventilation stack, eliminating that column of cold air and the hole in the roof (see Figure 7.2).

7.1 A condensing dyer does not need to be vented to the exterior. BILYEU HOMES INC.

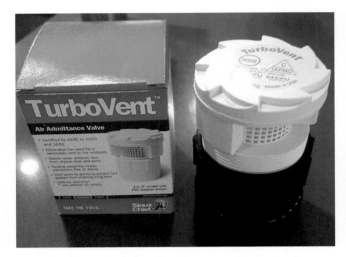

7.2 Air admittance valves replace the connection to a sanitary vent. BILYEU HOMES INC.

Code requirements for bathroom and kitchen ventilation are not so easily resolved. The combustion products associated with cooking can be reduced by use of an induction range. Many passive house designers use ductless range hoods to filter smoke and grease particles, without the direct expulsion of conditioned air to the exterior. A written code appeal may be needed to obtain relief from the explicit requirement for a ducted range hood. Passive house design consultants for the Ankeny Row Net Zero Community were able to demonstrate that the HRV specified would provide more kitchen ventilation than the nominal code requirement and was therefore acceptable as "Alternative Materials and Methods" (Lamar and Everhart, n.d.).

There are systems that must be associated with the building envelope and are not so easily eliminated. The prime example is electrical service. Building codes require electrical outlets at regular intervals, including along the length of exterior walls. Boxes and cables compromise insulation to some extent and regularly puncture the interior finish surface, making it difficult to develop an air or vapor barrier at that location. The preferred strategy involves the development of the critical barriers in a wall or a roof to the outside of any embedded systems. A review of the wall assemblies discussed in Chapter 4 reveals that many of them fulfill this objective. If the air barrier is developed at the sheathing plane on the outside of the initial stud cavity, and an additional leaf of insulation is added to the outside of that, then the electrical distribution system is contained well within the controlled perimeter of the building. Combining the vapor barrier with the air barrier on the face of the sheathing produces a "perfect wall" for mixed climates. The stud cavity is then left vapor open to the interior, and punctures through the interior finish are no longer a great concern. Hygrothermal analysis must confirm the seasonal drying potential at a specific building site.

The MARTak Rest/Work Space dramatically makes this point (see Figure 4.6.3 in Chapter 4). The insulation thickness is developed with deep over-framing using Larsen trusses, plus a continuous layer of mineral wool, all outside the air barrier. The interior stud cavity is not expected

7.3 Service distribution using the wall cavity inside the taped air barrier. The exterior is over-framed and insulated. ANDREW MICHLER, BAOSOL

to contribute to the thermal performance of the wall and can therefore be filled with service systems (see Figure 7.3). In more moderate climates, the exterior leaf may not carry such a high insulation value, but, if it contributes a substantial portion of the total wall performance, there is less concern about displacing insulation with pipes in the inner stud cavity. The Warren Woods Ecological Field Station uses SIPs to protect the inner stud wall, whereas the Full Plane Residence uses a wood framed curtain wall outside the load bearing studs and air barrier sheathing (see Figures 4.7.3 and 4.3.3 in Chapter 4). The San Juan Passive House is a slightly complex variation, because the wall panels were prefabricated off-site (see Figure 8.11.7 in Chapter 8). There are two independent stud cavities in the panels, with the air barrier roughly at the middle. This allows the interior cavity to be open to the addition of service systems, like the other strategies that follow this model.

As previously noted, the logic of the perfect wall applies equally to the perfect roof. The hygrothermal advantages in mixed climates and the service distribution advantages extend to both cases. Light fixtures recessed into the ceiling generally demand a larger void than wall outlets. Fortunately, roof joists are usually deeper than wall studs. If the sheathing on top of the structural joists is the air barrier, all of that space is available for systems. Chapter 5 demonstrates that there are many ways to develop the water, vapor, and thermal control layers stacked on top

of the sheathing, and all outside the service cavity in the ceiling. The VOLKsHouse 1.0 uses superimposed layers of rigid insulation, whereas the Lone Fir Residence uses a second leaf of roof framing (see Figures 5.4.3 and 5.5.3 in Chapter 5). In the single-story volume appended to the Hayfield House, a shed roof acts as a voluminous umbrella over the structural framing and sheathing of the box below (see Figure 8.5.19 in Chapter 8).

The roof assembly suggests a second general approach, when the air barrier turns inward at the top of the wall and travels along the underside of the spanning structure. In this class of solutions, a service cavity of virtually any depth can be created by the ceiling surface being framed at some distance below the control layers. In extreme cases, the ceiling can be literally suspended, at intervals, from the structure above. Pumpkin Ridge Passive House demonstrates a minimal cavity accomplished with furring (see Figure 5.7.3 in Chapter 5). Windy View Passive House, illustrated in this chapter, uses additional framing at the ceiling to accommodate more than just wiring (see Figure 7.4). Viridescent Building demonstrates a much greater available volume (see Figure 8.14.13 in Chapter 8). The San Juan Passive House creates service space within the depth of the roof truss, but only as needed. The air barrier attached to the lower truss chords is folded up into the space between to generate a passage for ducts, crossing the house parallel to the structure (see Figure 7.5).

7.4 Taped sheathing attached to the lower chord of roof trusses. Non-structural ceiling joists create a service cavity. BILYEU HOMES INC.

7.5 Sheathing folds up into the cavity between trusses to create a duct chase inside the air barrier. ARTISANS GROUP

7.6 Mechanical equipment located in a fully conditioned attic space. GO LOGIC LLC

Attic storage is expected in a building with a gable roof, but access to it creates a genuinely large opening in the ceiling plane. This can be addressed by creation of a substantially larger version of the service ceiling. If the air and thermal control layers follow the roof pitch, horizontal ceiling joists create an attic void entirely within the controlled perimeter of the house. At Hayfield House, there are cathedral ceilings in the bedrooms, with an attic above the bathrooms and closets (see Figure 7.6). The space is large enough to contain the HRV unit and a web of distribution ducts (see Figure 7.7). Working in plan, rather than section, the equivalent to this approach is a central service closet or the use of thickened interior partitions for systems distribution well inside the envelope. Space under or adjacent to stairs has the advantage of easy communication using walls that carry up through multiple levels (see Figure 7.8).

Activities, services, or systems that do not need to be in fully conditioned space may be relocated outside the controlled perimeter of the building. This brings two benefits: it reduces the volume and cost of the controlled zone and eliminates the need for those activities to interact with the control barriers of the envelope. Attic storage of durable items can be located above the air and thermal control layers. The double benefit accrues if access to the attic is also from the exterior, eliminating the characteristic passage through the ceiling. Similarly,

7.7 Heat recovery ventilator and associated ductwork installed in the warm attic. STEVEN TOOMEY AND ANNE DECKER

7.8 Service runs following an interior wall at the back of a staircase. STEVEN TOOMEY AND ANNE DECKER

7.9 Laundry machines in a mudroom outside the rear door of the house. GREEN HAMMER

unheated crawl spaces can be reached from outside the conditioned portion of the building. In a permissive climate, laundry rooms and utility spaces that normally ventilate directly to the exterior can be moved outside the primary air and thermal barriers. The access door that serves such a space must be insulated and tightly sealed. If that door also provides a useful exit from the house, then a partially conditioned buffer space on the outside will reduce the losses through an opening that was already planned (see Figure 7.9). The vernacular architecture of many regions features a "summer kitchen" designed to remove the heat of a continuously fired stove from inside the dwelling. This migratory pattern remains an option if cooking with gas or charcoal is considered desirable, whereas the heat and ventilation problems are not. Grilling on the back deck is the simplest present form of this tradition.

Certain systems simply must pass through the envelope, as they tie to the infrastructure of the site. These include sanitary drains, electrical feeds, and water supplies. Large-diameter pipes can be treated individually as they pass up from the ground or out through the roof (see Figures 7.10 and 7.11). Where there is a cluster of large pipes, the minimum spacing between them depends on the material that will be used to create the seal and whether it can flow into tight dimensions (see Figure 7.12). If tape or adhered membrane flashing must be worked between

7.10 Sanitary drain sealed at the vapor barrier under a slab on grade foundation. STEVEN TOOMEY AND ANNE DECKER

the pipes, they have to be spaced so that they are essentially acting separately.

As cables or tubes get smaller, there is a greater incentive to cluster them in order to save labor. First, a large-diameter sleeve is passed through the barriers, with appropriate attention to the air seal (see Figure 7.13). Next, the cluster of small-diameter elements is threaded through the sleeve (see Figure 7.14). Finally, all of the voids within the length of the sleeve are filled, using spray foam to complete the seal (see Figure 7.15).

7.11 Sanitary vent sealed at membrane serving as the vapor barrier and temporary roof. WALSH CONSTRUCTION CO.

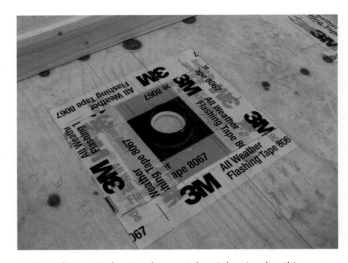

7.13 Sealing a single pipe sleeve at the air barrier sheathing. BILYEU HOMES INC.

7.12 Clustered electrical conduits sealed with mastic that flows between all of the elements. WALSH CONSTRUCTION CO.

Occasionally, a small-diameter element acts alone, such as the electrical supply cable to an exterior light fixture. Here, it is possible to seal a patch of elastic membrane material over the hole in the air barrier sheathing and push the cable through a small slit in the membrane (see Figure 7.16). Not all of the challenges to the air barrier arise from the mechanical and electrical systems. Some of them derive from structural requirements, such as the need to tie walls and floors to the foundation in zones of high wind or seismic activity (see Figure 7.17).

7.14 Collecting a group of supply lines in a single opening. BILYEU HOMES INC.

7.15 Foam-filled sleeves prevent air leakage. BILYEU HOMES INC.

Finally, there are apertures that could be avoided, but are introduced into the design by preference for a lifestyle. Fireplaces and woodstoves are not often needed in a passive house. If they are considered desirable, they must be carefully managed. Make-up air to fuel the fire must not be drawn from the conditioned volume of the house. There are several options: the sealed combustion stove with direct supply and exhaust, an independent but coordinated air inlet near the stove to make up for the exhaust without stirring the entire room, and various types of automated damper to make either of the previous options more effective. The same thinking can be applied to lifestyle options in the kitchen, such as an electrical

7.16 A single electrical cable passes through the air barrier. Preparing to seal a larger sleeve. BILYEU HOMES INC.

7.17 Sealing the floor assembly, including a threaded hold-down that will connect to the walls above. BILYEU HOMES INC.

Some systems have a specific responsibility to connect the interior of the house to the exterior. These must be designed and detailed to prevent any inadvertent leaks that are not explicitly controlled by the system. The HRV is a primary example. Tightly sealed, insulated supply and exhaust ducts bring fresh air in and send stale air out (see Figure 7.18). It is the responsibility of the device to manage energy exchange between them. Clearly, the shorter the link from the HRV to the exterior, the better. Sealing the large-diameter penetrations through the envelope is an extension of previous techniques.

7.18 The intake and exhaust of the hrv must reach the exterior through insulated, airtight ducts. HAMMER & HAND

7.19 An insulated pet door with a double magnetic seal passed the blower door test. BILYEU HOMES INC.

interlock that will not let the fan in the range hood run until a nearby window is cracked open.

Last of all, passive house consultant Blake Bilyeu, of Salem, Oregon, was able to install a pet door with a seal sufficient to pass the blower door test (see Figure 7.19).

REFERENCES AND RESOURCES

Lamar, D., and Everhart, T. (n.d.). "Kitchen Exhaust Ventilation with HRV at Ankeny Row," Northwest Eco-Building Guild, www.ecobuilding.org/code-innovations/case-studies/kitchen-exhaust-by-continuous-ventilation-with-hrv-at-ankeny-row (accessed January 22, 2017).

CHAPTER 8

Case Studies

The case studies in this chapter offer an opportunity to examine projects in greater depth than do the individual entries in the previous chapters. In each study, the featured details are selected from basic building conditions: foundations, floors, walls, roof, windows, and doors. The studies expand on the array of design options laid out in the opening chapters, plus they demonstrate how the specific strategies used for key assemblies must relate well to each other across a single project.

The selection also includes details that respond to the unique requirements of the project design and contribute to its success in terms of performance, constructability, or aesthetic intent. Certain details make the design possible, while they also demonstrate how passive house principles can be worked through even in complex or particular situations.

Where it was possible, the case studies were chosen to cut across building types and site conditions. They are most often, but not exclusively, residential. There are rural and urban sites, freestanding buildings and attached townhouses. Some are multistory, multifamily apartment structures. Multifamily housing is, at present, a tremendous area of growth in passive house design. In response to these different settings, there are a range of construction strategies. These include: site building, pre-cut timber frames, manufactured components, off-site panelizing, utility cores, and full modules.

For the book as a whole, an effort has been made to represent a variety of climate zones, from New Mexico to Michigan. Each of the climate conditions is summarized by including the heating degree days (HDD) and the cooling degree days (CDD) for their respective sites. There are a great number of candidate projects in the Pacific Northwest, the Mid-Atlantic region, and New England. Because of the effort to meet the other criteria, case studies from these regions predominate.

The final inventory derived from a network of architects and certified passive house consultants who have completed a number of projects. They have also made frequent contributions to technical seminars and passive house conferences around the country. In the end, these are projects with interesting stories to tell. Together, they speak of the creative opportunity that can be found in high-performance design to the passive house standard.

8.1.1 Ankeny Row townhouses facing south to the street. There Is a courtyard and a second row of units behind.
JON JENSEN PHOTOGRAPHY

The owners of Ankeny Row are retiring couples with a strong desire to age in-place in the heart of the city, while minimizing their living expenses and environmental footprint. On a quarter-acre, brownfield property in the Buckman neighborhood of Portland, Oregon, they planned a co-housing community consisting of six townhomes, a common room, and a shared courtyard. The project's location, in an existing urban neighborhood, on a designated bicycle route, and in close proximity to public transportation allows the owners to live a car-free lifestyle if they choose. The owners wanted the community to feel welcome and connected to the co-housing project. Therefore, the townhouses are accessed through a pronounced pedestrian entrance, defining the Ankeny streetscape, further enhancing neighborhood walkability, and keeping "eyes on the street." The common courtyard is designed in relation to the townhouses to afford ample private, semi-private, and public outdoor rooms, offering a full gradient of social experience. Balconies, for example, allow residents to take advantage of the sun in privacy or simply engage in people watching. The open floor plans of each unit encourage informal gatherings centered around the dining and kitchen areas. First-story master suites allow the owners to live entirely on one floor if desired or needed. The units are designed with a super-insulated, airtight envelope, daylit through large, triple-glazed windows, have superior indoor air quality through a constant supply of fresh filtered air via HRVs, and have acoustic isolation from urban noise. In this way, livability is improved, while the carbon footprint is nearly eliminated. A small rooftop solar photovoltaic array is expected to allow Ankeny Row to produce as much energy as the buildings will consume on an annual basis, or more. In the first 9 months of operation, the community was on track to produce an excess of energy for its first year.

ANKENY ROW NET ZERO COMMUNITY

PROJECT INFORMATION

Project title: Ankeny Row Net Zero Community

Location: Portland, Oregon

Size: 10,200 ft.^{2} (948 m^2); seven units

Completion: 2015

Recognition: Passive House planned (not certified), FSC-COC certification, Earth Advantage Platinum

Type: Multifamily homes (co-housing)

Architect: Daryl Rantis and Dylan Lamar

Builder: Green Hammer

CPHC: Dylan Lamar

HDD: 4,222 base 65°F (2,346 base 18.3°C)

CDD: 423 base 65°F (235 base 18.3°C)

Annual precipitation: 46.5 in. (1,181 mm)

8.1.2 Entry path to internal courtyard. Storm-water planter to the right. JON JENSEN PHOTOGRAPHY

8.1.3 Casting the slab on grade foundation behind the planter.
GREEN HAMMER

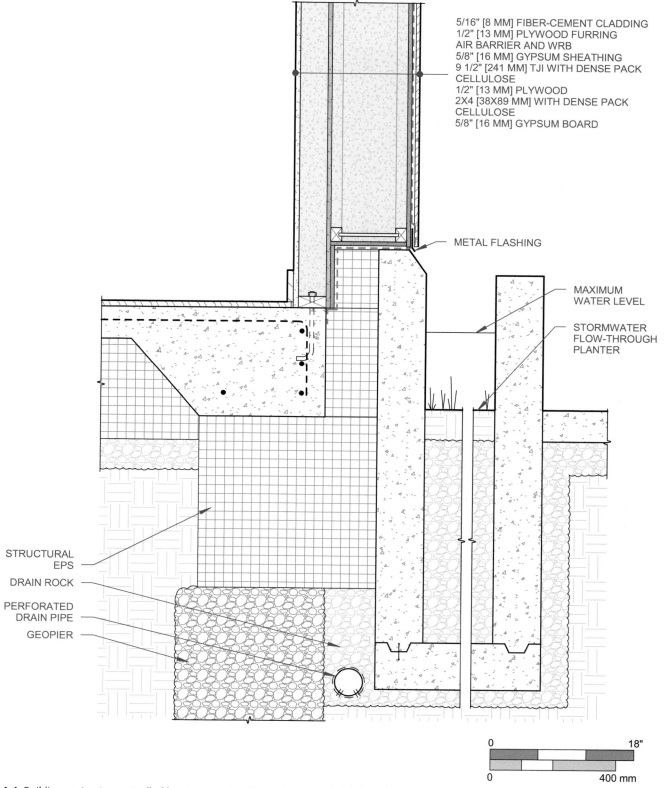

5/16" [8 MM] FIBER-CEMENT CLADDING
1/2" [13 MM] PLYWOOD FURRING
AIR BARRIER AND WRB
5/8" [16 MM] GYPSUM SHEATHING
9 1/2" [241 MM] TJI WITH DENSE PACK CELLULOSE
1/2" [13 MM] PLYWOOD
2X4 [38X89 MM] WITH DENSE PACK CELLULOSE
5/8" [16 MM] GYPSUM BOARD

METAL FLASHING

MAXIMUM WATER LEVEL

STORMWATER FLOW-THROUGH PLANTER

STRUCTURAL EPS

DRAIN ROCK

PERFORATED DRAIN PIPE

GEOPIER

8.1.4 Building perimeter controlled by storm-water planter. Thickened slab foundation isolated inside on rigid insulation.

8.1.5 South-facing roof overhangs at the street. EVAN STRAVERS

8.1.6 Preparation of the south façade for cladding.
GREEN HAMMER

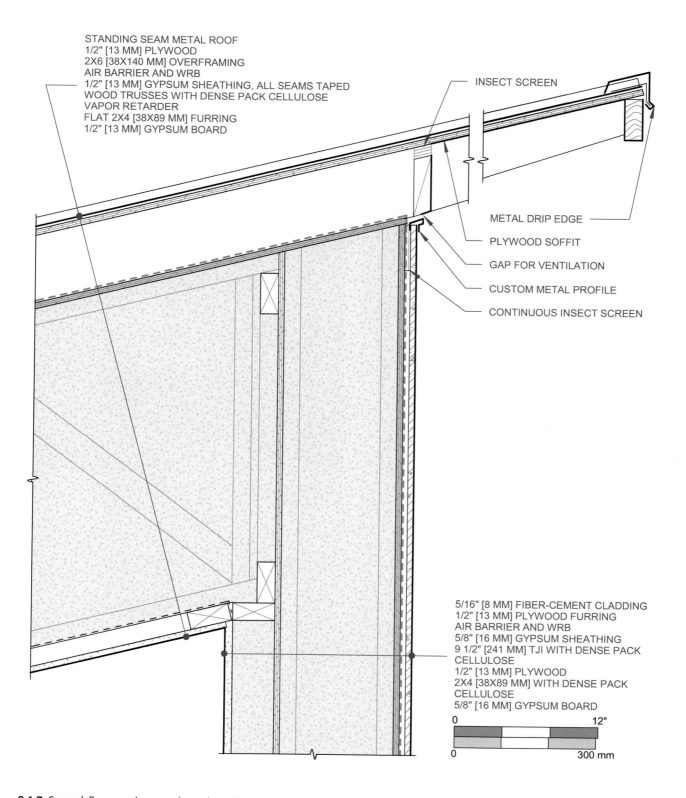

STANDING SEAM METAL ROOF
1/2" [13 MM] PLYWOOD
2X6 [38X140 MM] OVERFRAMING
AIR BARRIER AND WRB
1/2" [13 MM] GYPSUM SHEATHING, ALL SEAMS TAPED
WOOD TRUSSES WITH DENSE PACK CELLULOSE
VAPOR RETARDER
FLAT 2X4 [38X89 MM] FURRING
1/2" [13 MM] GYPSUM BOARD

INSECT SCREEN

METAL DRIP EDGE

PLYWOOD SOFFIT

GAP FOR VENTILATION

CUSTOM METAL PROFILE

CONTINUOUS INSECT SCREEN

5/16" [8 MM] FIBER-CEMENT CLADDING
1/2" [13 MM] PLYWOOD FURRING
AIR BARRIER AND WRB
5/8" [16 MM] GYPSUM SHEATHING
9 1/2" [241 MM] TJI WITH DENSE PACK
CELLULOSE
1/2" [13 MM] PLYWOOD
2X4 [38X89 MM] WITH DENSE PACK
CELLULOSE
5/8" [16 MM] GYPSUM BOARD

0   12"

0   300 mm

8.1.7 Second-floor overhang and supplementary shading protects south-facing windows.

8.1.8 Window unit recessed behind insulated over-framing.
GREEN HAMMER

8.1.9 Mockup of window trim and sidewall cladding.
GREEN HAMMER

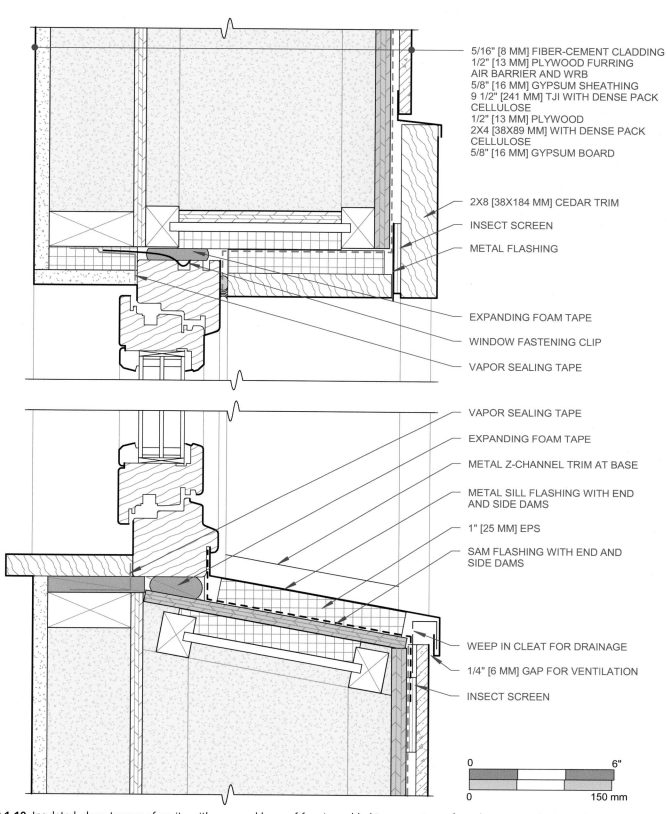

5/16" [8 MM] FIBER-CEMENT CLADDING
1/2" [13 MM] PLYWOOD FURRING
AIR BARRIER AND WRB
5/8" [16 MM] GYPSUM SHEATHING
9 1/2" [241 MM] TJI WITH DENSE PACK
CELLULOSE
1/2" [13 MM] PLYWOOD
2X4 [38X89 MM] WITH DENSE PACK
CELLULOSE
5/8" [16 MM] GYPSUM BOARD

2X8 [38X184 MM] CEDAR TRIM

INSECT SCREEN

METAL FLASHING

EXPANDING FOAM TAPE

WINDOW FASTENING CLIP

VAPOR SEALING TAPE

VAPOR SEALING TAPE

EXPANDING FOAM TAPE

METAL Z-CHANNEL TRIM AT BASE

METAL SILL FLASHING WITH END
AND SIDE DAMS

1" [25 MM] EPS

SAM FLASHING WITH END AND
SIDE DAMS

WEEP IN CLEAT FOR DRAINAGE

1/4" [6 MM] GAP FOR VENTILATION

INSECT SCREEN

0   6"

0   150 mm

8.1.10 Insulated, deep truss roof cavity with a second layer of framing added to generate roof overhangs outside the air barrier.

8.1.11 Internal courtyard with two-story units along the north edge. JON JENSEN PHOTOGRAPHY

8.1.12 Preparation of the second-floor roof deck. GREEN HAMMER

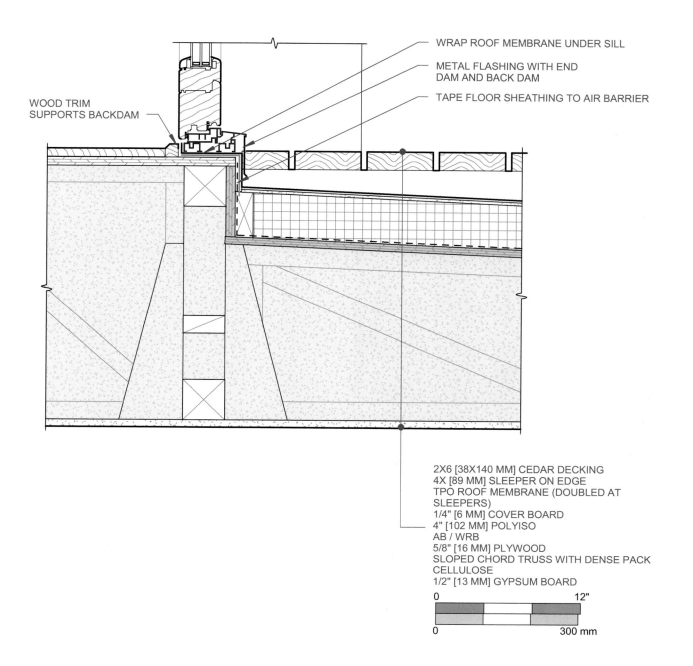

WRAP ROOF MEMBRANE UNDER SILL

METAL FLASHING WITH END
DAM AND BACK DAM

TAPE FLOOR SHEATHING TO AIR BARRIER

WOOD TRIM
SUPPORTS BACKDAM

2X6 [38X140 MM] CEDAR DECKING
4X [89 MM] SLEEPER ON EDGE
TPO ROOF MEMBRANE (DOUBLED AT
SLEEPERS)
1/4" [6 MM] COVER BOARD
4" [102 MM] POLYISO
AB / WRB
5/8" [16 MM] PLYWOOD
SLOPED CHORD TRUSS WITH DENSE PACK
CELLULOSE
1/2" [13 MM] GYPSUM BOARD

0   12"

0   300 mm

8.1.13 Timber bracket supports second-floor balcony. Blocking and fastener systems reduce penetrations of the air barrier.

8.1.14 Second-floor overhang and shading on the south façade.
EVAN STRAVERS

8.1.15 Exposed timber framing above the living room. South
window on the left. JON JENSEN PHOTOGRAPHY

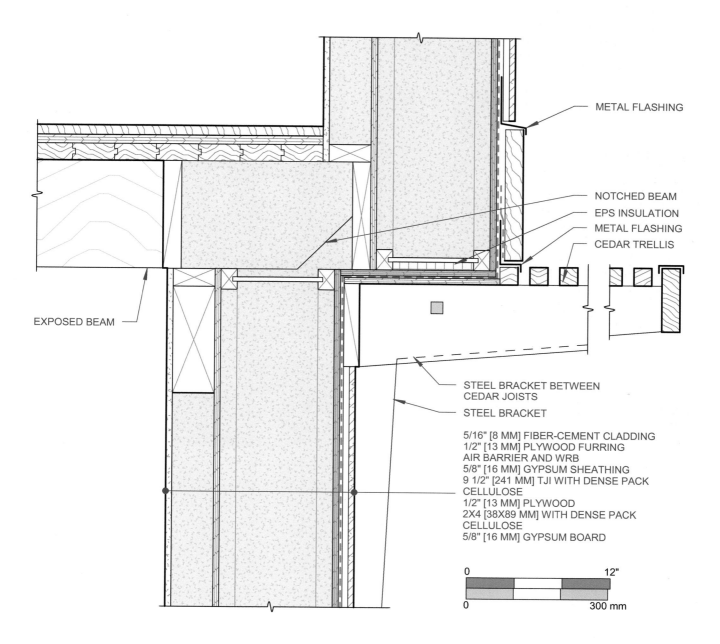

METAL FLASHING

NOTCHED BEAM
EPS INSULATION
METAL FLASHING
CEDAR TRELLIS

EXPOSED BEAM

STEEL BRACKET BETWEEN
CEDAR JOISTS
STEEL BRACKET

5/16" [8 MM] FIBER-CEMENT CLADDING
1/2" [13 MM] PLYWOOD FURRING
AIR BARRIER AND WRB
5/8" [16 MM] GYPSUM SHEATHING
9 1/2" [241 MM] TJI WITH DENSE PACK
CELLULOSE
1/2" [13 MM] PLYWOOD
2X4 [38X89 MM] WITH DENSE PACK
CELLULOSE
5/8" [16 MM] GYPSUM BOARD

0   12"

0   300 mm

8.1.16 Truss girder supports level interior floor and roof deck trusses that are sloped to drain. Exterior walk surface meets door sill.

8.1.17 Second-floor balconies on the street façade. Steel plate guardrails. EVAN STRAVERS

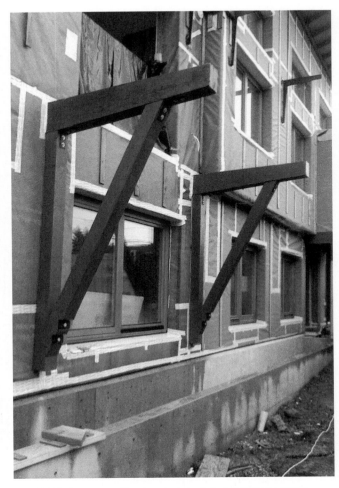

8.1.18 Timber supporting brackets installed. GREEN HAMMER

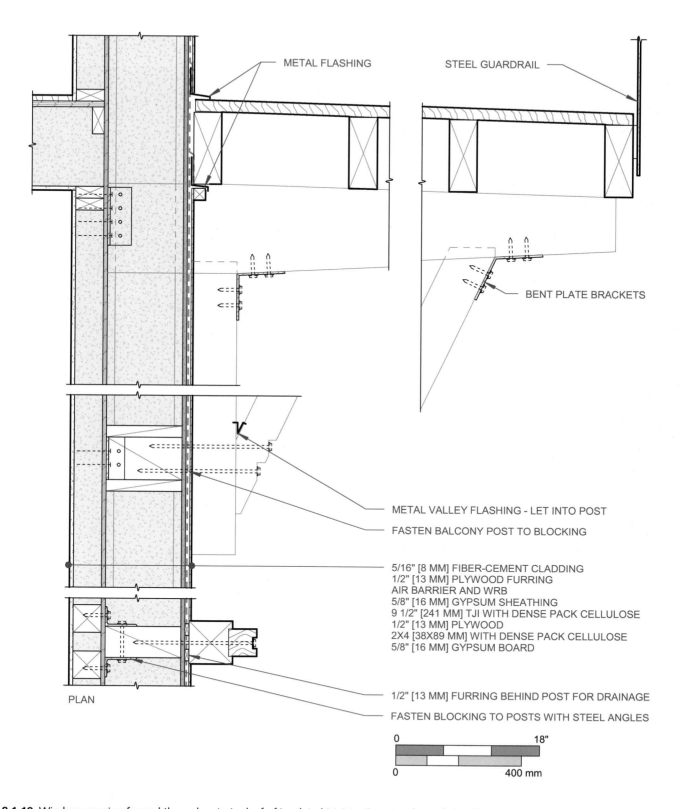

METAL FLASHING

STEEL GUARDRAIL

BENT PLATE BRACKETS

METAL VALLEY FLASHING - LET INTO POST

FASTEN BALCONY POST TO BLOCKING

5/16" [8 MM] FIBER-CEMENT CLADDING
1/2" [13 MM] PLYWOOD FURRING
AIR BARRIER AND WRB
5/8" [16 MM] GYPSUM SHEATHING
9 1/2" [241 MM] TJI WITH DENSE PACK CELLULOSE
1/2" [13 MM] PLYWOOD
2X4 [38X89 MM] WITH DENSE PACK CELLULOSE
5/8" [16 MM] GYPSUM BOARD

1/2" [13 MM] FURRING BEHIND POST FOR DRAINAGE

FASTEN BLOCKING TO POSTS WITH STEEL ANGLES

PLAN

0   18"

0   400 mm

8.1.19 Window opening framed through exterior leaf of insulated I-joists. Over-insulation behind the window surround.

8.2.1 Extruded from the rugged environment of the Cowhorn Estate, the angular volumes of the Main Residence (left) and the Guest Cottage (right) split apart to open a path to the front door. STUDIO-E ARCHITECTURE AND HOPPER ILLUSTRATION

Overlooking the Applegate Valley in Southern Oregon, Cowhorn Vineyard and Garden is a Demeter-certified biodynamic winery that expresses the owners' deep commitment to environmentally responsible practices. "Biodynamic farming" works to enhance and support the dynamic nature of the first 12 in. (305 mm) of the Earth's skin, the soil. Vineyard owners Barbara and Bill Steele broke ground in 2015 for a new tasting room and a residence. Both buildings share an angular style that highlights their connection to the natural elements of the landscape. They were designed to incorporate many of the same ambitious sustainability goals. The tasting room is striving for Petal Certification in the Living Building Challenge, and the residence is a certified passive house.

The home is tucked into the forested hillside, above the vineyard in the valley, 300 ft. (91.4 m) below. Composed of a number of faceted building shapes strung along an internal spine, the various volumes contain the great room, a utilitarian pod (with mudroom, pantry, mechanical room, and den), the master-suite pod, and an exercise pod (with gym and endless pool). Each element is clad with a ventilated rainscreen of dark-stained cedar slats or random-width fiber-cement lap siding. The black standing-seam roofing continues down one wall of each building volume.

Outside, the main residence and the guest cottage pivot apart to reveal the entrance. Inside, a walnut wood-clad central spine cleaves the private wing from the public space. A black marble floor contrasts with pure white walls throughout the house. The kitchen, dining, and living spaces gather in one airy volume, brightly illuminated by generous glazing that frames stunning views to the valley and mountains beyond.

The thermal strategy includes a wall sandwich of 2 x 6 (38 x 140-mm) interior studs with 9.5-in. (241-mm) wood I-joists screwed to each stud. Outboard of the structure, waxed fiberboard sheathing serves as both air

COWHORN VINEYARD HOUSE

PROJECT INFORMATION

Project title: Cowhorn Vineyard House

Location: Jacksonville, Oregon

Size: 2,300 ft.² (214 m²)

Completion: 2016

Recognition: Pre-certified (PHIUS), FSC Certified

Type: Single-family house

Architect: Jan Fillinger

Builder: Green Hammer

CPHC: Dylan Lamar

HDD: 4,264 base 65°F (2,369 base 18.3°C)

CDD: 834 base 65°F (463 base 18.3°C)

Annual precipitation: 19 in. (483 mm)

barrier and water-resistive barrier. Floors and roofs are built with deep wood trusses, and the entire envelope was dense-packed with cellulose insulation. There are extraordinary quadruple-glazed ZOLA windows and doors. A Zehnder HRV, ducted mini-split heat pump, and LED lighting help to bring the house within reach of its net zero energy goal.

8.2.2 Floor trusses inside rigid insulation. Wood blocks tie floor sheathing to concrete perimeter. GREEN HAMMER

8.2.3 Over-framing with I-joists laps the concrete perimeter wall.
GREEN HAMMER

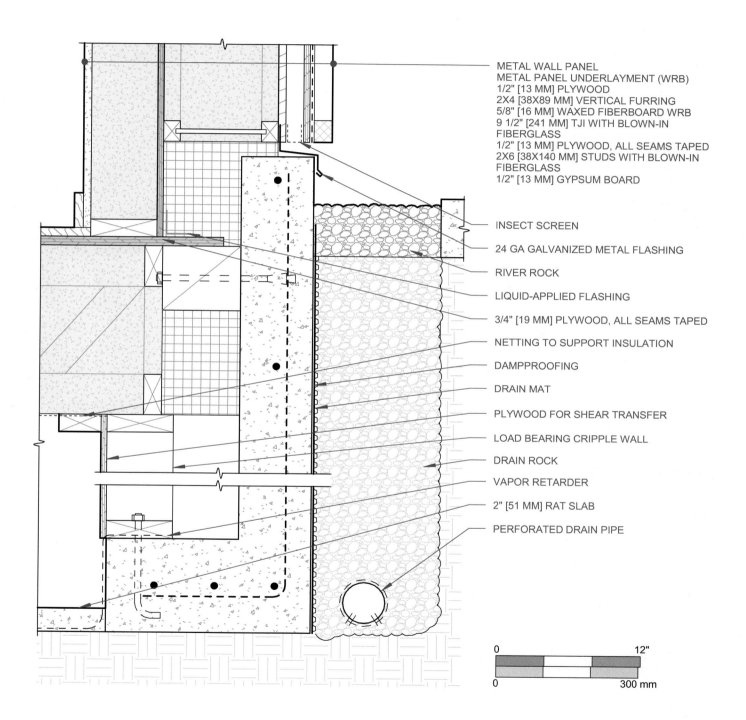

METAL WALL PANEL
METAL PANEL UNDERLAYMENT (WRB)
1/2" [13 MM] PLYWOOD
2X4 [38X89 MM] VERTICAL FURRING
5/8" [16 MM] WAXED FIBERBOARD WRB
9 1/2" [241 MM] TJI WITH BLOWN-IN FIBERGLASS
1/2" [13 MM] PLYWOOD, ALL SEAMS TAPED
2X6 [38X140 MM] STUDS WITH BLOWN-IN FIBERGLASS
1/2" [13 MM] GYPSUM BOARD

INSECT SCREEN

24 GA GALVANIZED METAL FLASHING

RIVER ROCK

LIQUID-APPLIED FLASHING

3/4" [19 MM] PLYWOOD, ALL SEAMS TAPED

NETTING TO SUPPORT INSULATION

DAMPPROOFING

DRAIN MAT

PLYWOOD FOR SHEAR TRANSFER

LOAD BEARING CRIPPLE WALL

DRAIN ROCK

VAPOR RETARDER

2" [51 MM] RAT SLAB

PERFORATED DRAIN PIPE

0   12"

0   300 mm

8.2.4 Deep floor trusses supported by wood stud cripple wall. Concrete perimeter wall retains grade.

8.2.5 Shed roof overhangs generated by top chord of trusses. GREEN HAMMER

8.2.6 Air seal developed at truss chords. Prepared for installation of over-framing. GREEN HAMMER

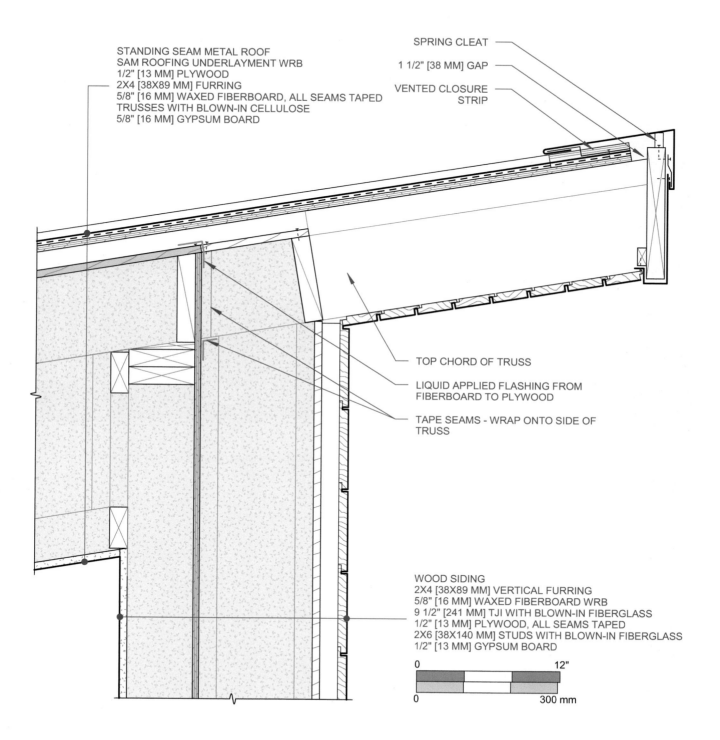

STANDING SEAM METAL ROOF
SAM ROOFING UNDERLAYMENT WRB
1/2" [13 MM] PLYWOOD
2X4 [38X89 MM] FURRING
5/8" [16 MM] WAXED FIBERBOARD, ALL SEAMS TAPED
TRUSSES WITH BLOWN-IN CELLULOSE
5/8" [16 MM] GYPSUM BOARD

SPRING CLEAT

1 1/2" [38 MM] GAP

VENTED CLOSURE
STRIP

TOP CHORD OF TRUSS

LIQUID APPLIED FLASHING FROM
FIBERBOARD TO PLYWOOD

TAPE SEAMS - WRAP ONTO SIDE OF
TRUSS

WOOD SIDING
2X4 [38X89 MM] VERTICAL FURRING
5/8" [16 MM] WAXED FIBERBOARD WRB
9 1/2" [241 MM] TJI WITH BLOWN-IN FIBERGLASS
1/2" [13 MM] PLYWOOD, ALL SEAMS TAPED
2X6 [38X140 MM] STUDS WITH BLOWN-IN FIBERGLASS
1/2" [13 MM] GYPSUM BOARD

0 ———————— 12"

0 ———————— 300 mm

8.2.7 Shed roof spanned with deep trusses. Air barrier sheathing developed at load-bearing stud walls.

8.2.8 Windows recessed into the depth of the over-framing.
GREEN HAMMER

8.2.9 Completed window surround and rainscreen cladding.
STUDIO-E ARCHITECTURE

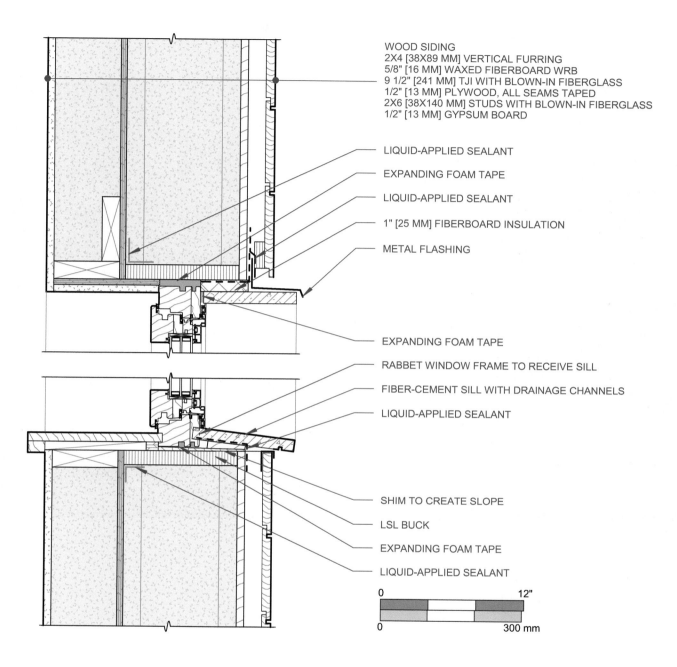

WOOD SIDING
2X4 [38X89 MM] VERTICAL FURRING
5/8" [16 MM] WAXED FIBERBOARD WRB
9 1/2" [241 MM] TJI WITH BLOWN-IN FIBERGLASS
1/2" [13 MM] PLYWOOD, ALL SEAMS TAPED
2X6 [38X140 MM] STUDS WITH BLOWN-IN FIBERGLASS
1/2" [13 MM] GYPSUM BOARD

LIQUID-APPLIED SEALANT

EXPANDING FOAM TAPE

LIQUID-APPLIED SEALANT

1" [25 MM] FIBERBOARD INSULATION

METAL FLASHING

EXPANDING FOAM TAPE

RABBET WINDOW FRAME TO RECEIVE SILL

FIBER-CEMENT SILL WITH DRAINAGE CHANNELS

LIQUID-APPLIED SEALANT

SHIM TO CREATE SLOPE

LSL BUCK

EXPANDING FOAM TAPE

LIQUID-APPLIED SEALANT

0		12"
0		300 mm

8.2.10 Window units mounted to LSL buck within the thickness of the over-framing.

8.2.11 Door sills with level access to exterior paving. GREEN HAMMER

8.2.12 Extended door sill covers concrete foundation wall.
GREEN HAMMER

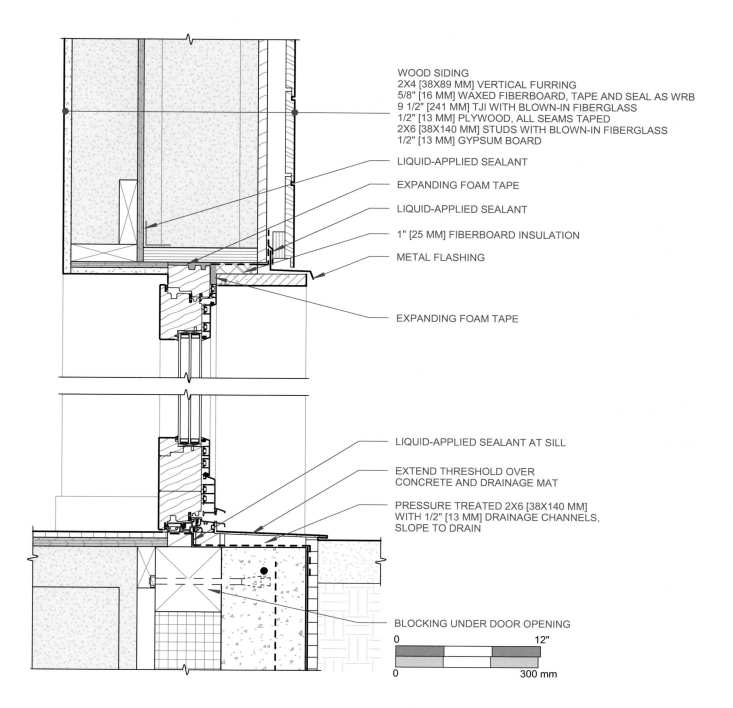

WOOD SIDING
2X4 [38X89 MM] VERTICAL FURRING
5/8" [16 MM] WAXED FIBERBOARD, TAPE AND SEAL AS WRB
9 1/2" [241 MM] TJI WITH BLOWN-IN FIBERGLASS
1/2" [13 MM] PLYWOOD, ALL SEAMS TAPED
2X6 [38X140 MM] STUDS WITH BLOWN-IN FIBERGLASS
1/2" [13 MM] GYPSUM BOARD

LIQUID-APPLIED SEALANT

EXPANDING FOAM TAPE

LIQUID-APPLIED SEALANT

1" [25 MM] FIBERBOARD INSULATION

METAL FLASHING

EXPANDING FOAM TAPE

LIQUID-APPLIED SEALANT AT SILL

EXTEND THRESHOLD OVER
CONCRETE AND DRAINAGE MAT

PRESSURE TREATED 2X6 [38X140 MM]
WITH 1/2" [13 MM] DRAINAGE CHANNELS,
SLOPE TO DRAIN

BLOCKING UNDER DOOR OPENING

0   12"

0   300 mm

8.2.13 Perimeter concrete wall is cut down to permit door sill at the interior floor elevation. Compare with foundation detail.

8.2.14 Development of structural box column within the over-framing. GREEN HAMMER

8.2.15 Steel canopy support attached to box column in the wall. GREEN HAMMER

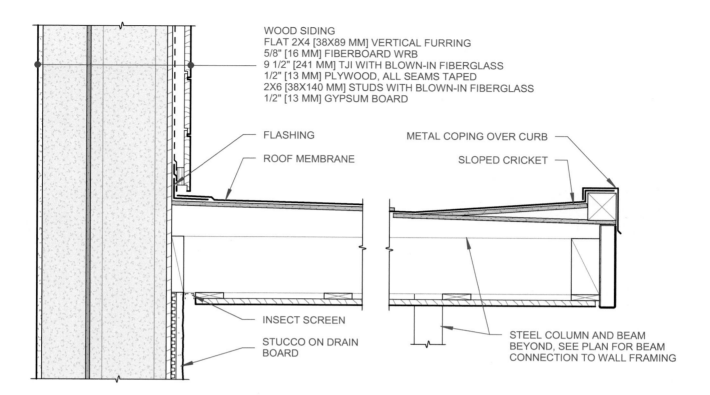

WOOD SIDING
FLAT 2X4 [38X89 MM] VERTICAL FURRING
5/8" [16 MM] FIBERBOARD WRB
9 1/2" [241 MM] TJI WITH BLOWN-IN FIBERGLASS
1/2" [13 MM] PLYWOOD, ALL SEAMS TAPED
2X6 [38X140 MM] STUDS WITH BLOWN-IN FIBERGLASS
1/2" [13 MM] GYPSUM BOARD

FLASHING

ROOF MEMBRANE

METAL COPING OVER CURB

SLOPED CRICKET

INSECT SCREEN

STUCCO ON DRAIN BOARD

STEEL COLUMN AND BEAM BEYOND, SEE PLAN FOR BEAM CONNECTION TO WALL FRAMING

CANOPY SECTION

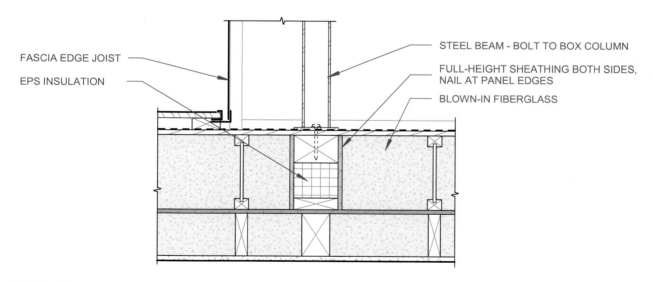

FASCIA EDGE JOIST

EPS INSULATION

STEEL BEAM - BOLT TO BOX COLUMN

FULL-HEIGHT SHEATHING BOTH SIDES, NAIL AT PANEL EDGES

BLOWN-IN FIBERGLASS

BOX COLUMN CONNECTION - PLAN

0   18"
0   400 mm

8.2.16 Canopy roof supported by exterior steel columns and beams. Beams attached to structural box column embedded in the wall.

8.3.1 Earthship Farmstead embedded into the base of an east-facing slope. BRETT WINTER LEMON

Early in the design process, the clients for Earthship Farmstead requested, "We want a house where our sheep can graze on our roof!" They wanted to build a farmstead in the Virginia mountains that would be as self-sufficient as possible. They set performance goals for: net zero energy (or energy positive), passive house standards, and LEED for Homes. Kaplan Thompson Architects sited the house in the hillside, bending the floor plan to carefully fit the contours of the field. The slope faced east, however, and, for the home to be naturally heated, the house needed to capture as much winter sun as possible. The living- and dining-room spaces were extended out onto the crown of the hill, raising a broad bank of carefully shaded windows to the south to scoop in the sun. The clients were looking for a stylish, soft, natural modernism for their house, and the architects chose a palette of white cedar shingles, local fieldstone, and quiet metal accents to harmonize with the colors and tone of the surrounding mountains.

Local, healthy, sustainable materials were specified throughout the project, including strict limits on formaldehydes and VOCs. The building is also insulated with cellulose insulation and water-blown EPS foam. All the flooring is local white oak, the cabinetry is Virginia black walnut, and American Clay paint was used throughout the project. The property is amply supplied by well water, but water pumping can be a large energy draw, and so all pumps and fixtures were carefully evaluated to ensure that the water use wouldn't overtax the energy systems.

The landscape design carefully considered water use as well and included a large cistern that stores and reuses all water from the roof. It is a tough, easy-to-maintain, comfortable, and extremely cost-effective house to live in. The home was built with R-30 slab, R-30 walls, and R-40–R-60 roofs. The windows and doors are by Makrowin, with triple-glazed and thermally broken frames. There is a 12-kW photovoltaic array on the

EARTHSHIP FARMSTEAD

PROJECT INFORMATION

Project title: Earthship Farmstead

Location: Stuart, Virginia

Size: 3,261 ft.^{2} (303 m^2)

Completion: 2013

Recognition: Certified (PHIUS), LEED Platinum, LEED for Homes Award for Outstanding Single Family Home

Type: Single-family house

Architect: Kaplan Thompson Architects

Builder: Structures Design Build

CPHC: Jesse Thompson, Kaplan Thompson Architects

HDD: 3,911 base 65°F (2,173 base 18.3°C)

CDD: 1,143 base 65°F (635 base 18.3°C)

Annual precipitation: 49 in. (1,247 mm)

barn that supplies all the energy the farm needs, making the house fully energy positive, with 100 percent clean production.

8.3.2 Foam-lined formwork for the turned down slab edge. KAPLAN THOMPSON ARCHITECTS

8.3.3 Living-room corner with exterior cmu to support stone wainscot. KAPLAN THOMPSON ARCHITECTS

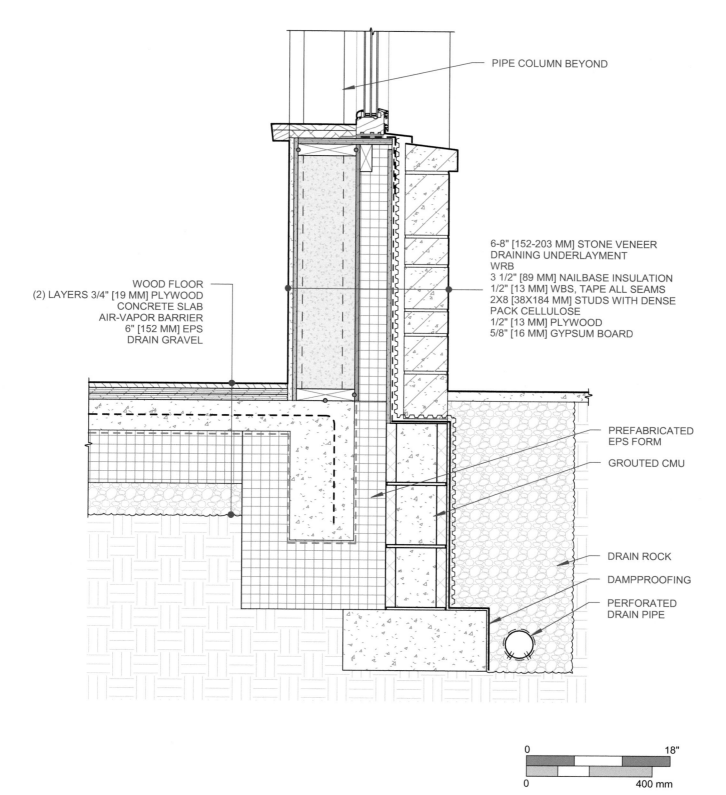

PIPE COLUMN BEYOND

6-8" [152-203 MM] STONE VENEER
DRAINING UNDERLAYMENT
WRB
3 1/2" [89 MM] NAILBASE INSULATION
1/2" [13 MM] WBS, TAPE ALL SEAMS
2X8 [38X184 MM] STUDS WITH DENSE
PACK CELLULOSE
1/2" [13 MM] PLYWOOD
5/8" [16 MM] GYPSUM BOARD

WOOD FLOOR
(2) LAYERS 3/4" [19 MM] PLYWOOD
CONCRETE SLAB
AIR-VAPOR BARRIER
6" [152 MM] EPS
DRAIN GRAVEL

PREFABRICATED
EPS FORM

GROUTED CMU

DRAIN ROCK

DAMPPROOFING

PERFORATED
DRAIN PIPE

0   18"

0   400 mm

8.3.4 Foundation at south-facing window wall. Window is moved to an outward position to make room for a steel pipe column supporting the roof.

8.3.5 Glulam beams span the living room. BRETT WINTER LEMON

8.3.6 Steel pipe supports at southeast corner. KAPLAN THOMPSON ARCHITECTS

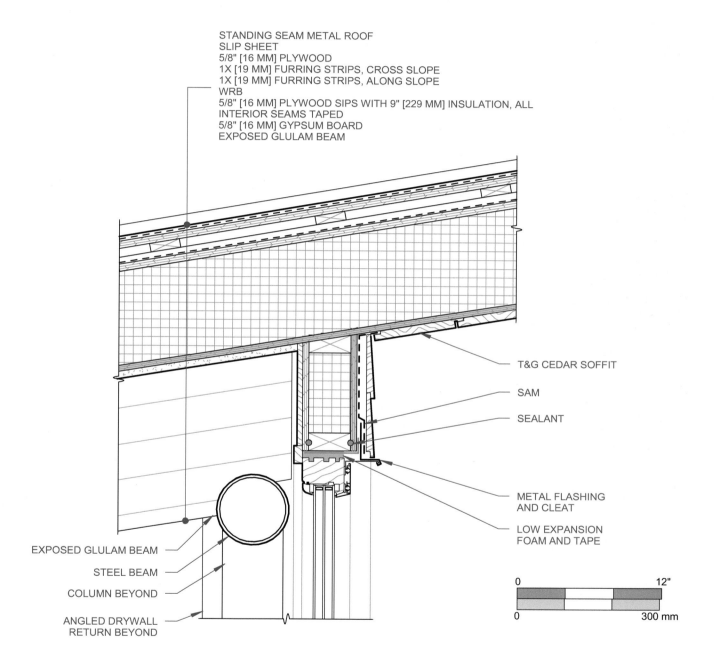

STANDING SEAM METAL ROOF
SLIP SHEET
5/8" [16 MM] PLYWOOD
1X [19 MM] FURRING STRIPS, CROSS SLOPE
1X [19 MM] FURRING STRIPS, ALONG SLOPE
WRB
5/8" [16 MM] PLYWOOD SIPS WITH 9" [229 MM] INSULATION, ALL
INTERIOR SEAMS TAPED
5/8" [16 MM] GYPSUM BOARD
EXPOSED GLULAM BEAM

T&G CEDAR SOFFIT

SAM

SEALANT

METAL FLASHING
AND CLEAT

LOW EXPANSION
FOAM AND TAPE

EXPOSED GLULAM BEAM

STEEL BEAM

COLUMN BEYOND

ANGLED DRYWALL
RETURN BEYOND

0   12"

0   300 mm

8.3.7 Head of south-facing living-room windows. Steel pipes support roof beams at the corner window.

8.3.8 Roof overhang and vented eave at living room.
BRETT WINTER LEMON

8.3.9 Living-room roof using SIPs over glulam beams.
KAPLAN THOMPSON ARCHITECTS

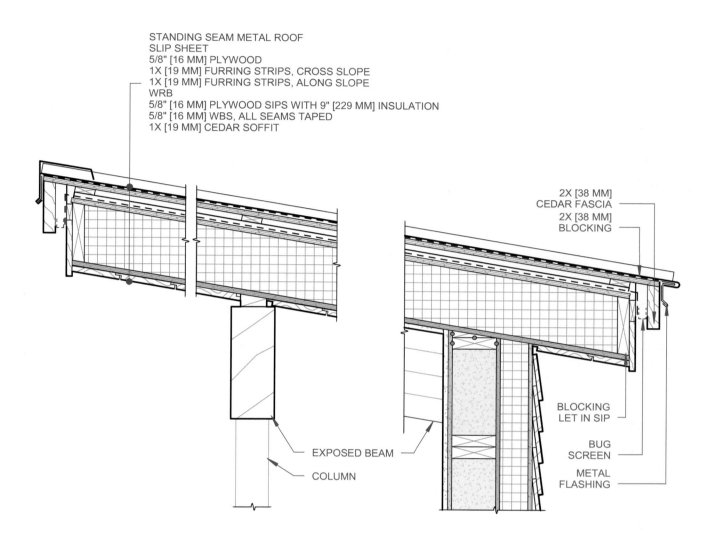

STANDING SEAM METAL ROOF
SLIP SHEET
5/8" [16 MM] PLYWOOD
1X [19 MM] FURRING STRIPS, CROSS SLOPE
1X [19 MM] FURRING STRIPS, ALONG SLOPE
WRB
5/8" [16 MM] PLYWOOD SIPS WITH 9" [229 MM] INSULATION
5/8" [16 MM] WBS, ALL SEAMS TAPED
1X [19 MM] CEDAR SOFFIT

2X [38 MM]
CEDAR FASCIA
2X [38 MM]
BLOCKING

BLOCKING
LET IN SIP

BUG
SCREEN

METAL
FLASHING

EXPOSED BEAM

COLUMN

UPPER EAVE (EXTERIOR)

LOWER EAVE (INTERIOR)

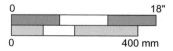

8.3.10 Living-room eaves with SIPs supported by interior and exterior glulam beams. Ventilated sheet metal roof constructed over double furring.

8.3.11 Waterproof membrane and clerestory structure prepared for green roof. KAPLAN THOMPSON ARCHITECTS

8.3.12 Retaining wall and concrete roof slab embedded in hill.
KAPLAN THOMPSON ARCHITECTS

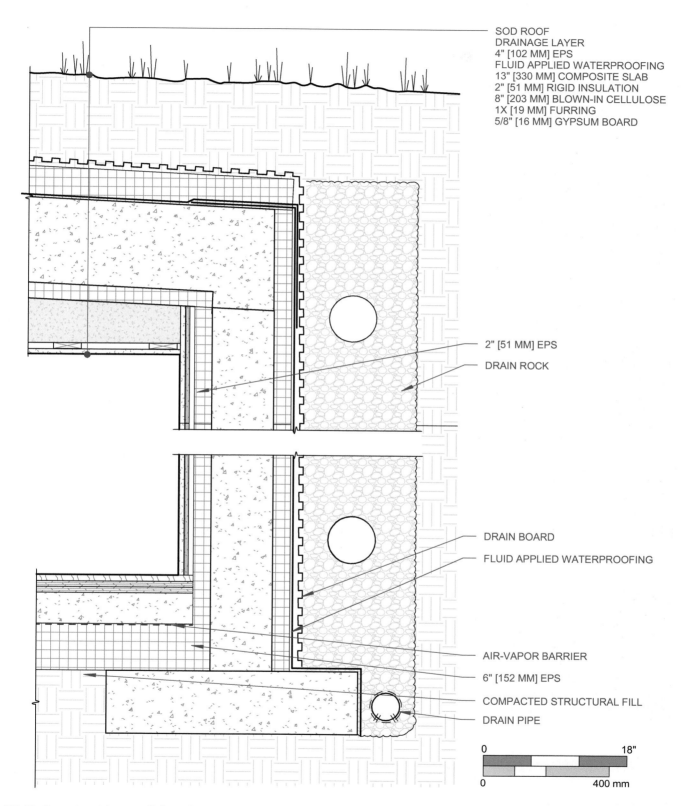

SOD ROOF
DRAINAGE LAYER
4" [102 MM] EPS
FLUID APPLIED WATERPROOFING
13" [330 MM] COMPOSITE SLAB
2" [51 MM] RIGID INSULATION
8" [203 MM] BLOWN-IN CELLULOSE
1X [19 MM] FURRING
5/8" [16 MM] GYPSUM BOARD

2" [51 MM] EPS

DRAIN ROCK

DRAIN BOARD

FLUID APPLIED WATERPROOFING

AIR-VAPOR BARRIER

6" [152 MM] EPS

COMPACTED STRUCTURAL FILL

DRAIN PIPE

0   18"

0   400 mm

8.3.13 Concrete retaining wall, floor slab, and roof slab at bedroom wing. Supports a sod covering that is continuous from the hillside above the building.

8.3.14 Interior view of the clerestory. BRETT WINTER LEMON

8.3.15 Exterior of the clerestory window with solar collector.
BRETT WINTER LEMON

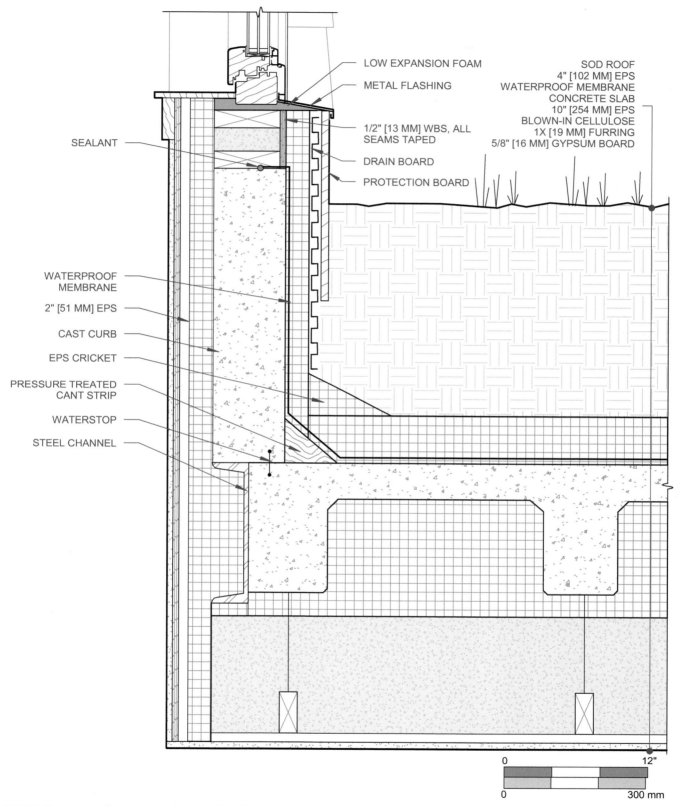

LOW EXPANSION FOAM

METAL FLASHING

1/2" [13 MM] WBS, ALL
SEAMS TAPED

DRAIN BOARD

PROTECTION BOARD

SOD ROOF
4" [102 MM] EPS
WATERPROOF MEMBRANE
CONCRETE SLAB
10" [254 MM] EPS
BLOWN-IN CELLULOSE
1X [19 MM] FURRING
5/8" [16 MM] GYPSUM BOARD

SEALANT

WATERPROOF
MEMBRANE

2" [51 MM] EPS

CAST CURB

EPS CRICKET

PRESSURE TREATED
CANT STRIP

WATERSTOP

STEEL CHANNEL

0   12"

0   300 mm

8.3.16 Concrete roof structure with upstand to lift clerestory window above a thick sod roof.

8.3.17 Recessed window and door at bedrooms.
KAPLAN THOMPSON ARCHITECTS

8.3.18 Recessed window above stone wainscot.
KAPLAN THOMPSON ARCHITECTS

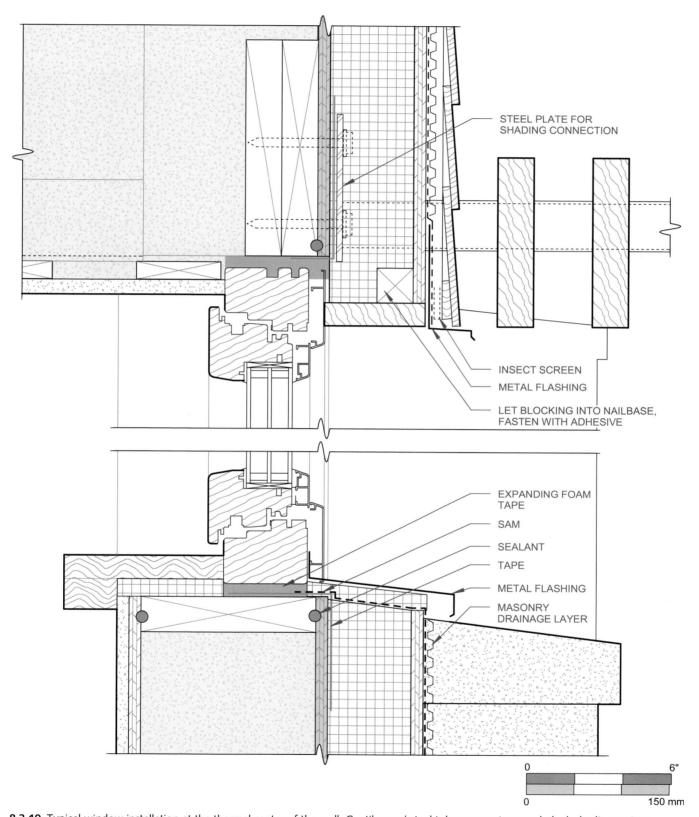

STEEL PLATE FOR
SHADING CONNECTION

INSECT SCREEN

METAL FLASHING

LET BLOCKING INTO NAILBASE,
FASTEN WITH ADHESIVE

EXPANDING FOAM
TAPE

SAM

SEALANT

TAPE

METAL FLASHING

MASONRY
DRAINAGE LAYER

0   6"

0   150 mm

8.3.19 Typical window installation at the thermal center of the wall. Cantilevered steel tubes support a wood plank shading system.

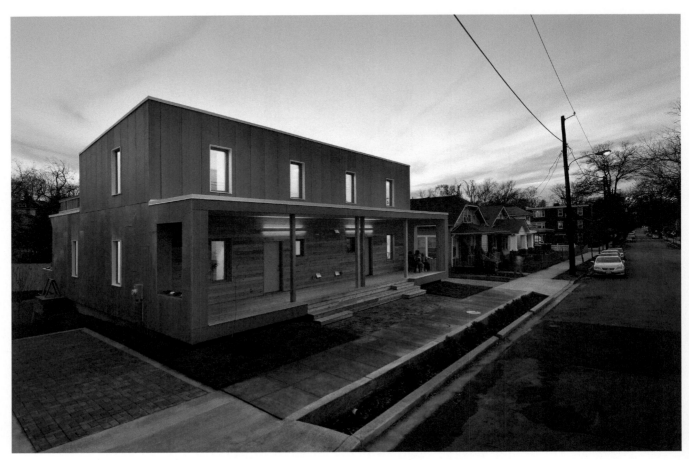

8.4.1 The Empowerhouse modules relocated and expanded to form a two-story duplex. MARTIN SECK

The Empowerhouse is the result of a multiyear, multidisciplinary team approach to the challenges and opportunities of affordable, energy-efficient, and sustainable houses in the United States, all executed under the name of "Empowerhouse," from 2009 to 2015. Empowerhouse began as the competition entry of the team from Parsons The New School for Design, Milano School of International Affairs, Management and Urban Policy at The New School, and Stevens Institute of Technology for the 2011 U.S. Department of Energy Solar Decathlon. More importantly, Empowerhouse took the competition beyond the mall by partnering with Habitat for Humanity of Washington, D.C., and the D.C. Department of Housing and Community Development to create a two-family home in the Deanwood neighborhood of Washington that was occupied by two home owners by 2013.

Unlike the other eighteen entries, Empowerhouse was destined to become a real home for a low-income family, and the home also served as a model of sustainable housing for Habitat for Humanity. The house exhibited during the competition would become the first floor of a two-story duplex home, with Habitat for Humanity of Washington, D.C., completing the second story. Habitat for Humanity would then use the embedded knowledge of the systems and design to build a second home adjacent to the original. The house was based on passive house principles, and Empowerhouse sought to create a home that aligned the energy use with the energy generated by the solar panel array. As a testament to the design, during the Solar Decathlon, Empowerhouse won the first ever Affordability Award.

The exterior envelope is super-insulated and uses deep, engineered wood I-joists sandwiched between two layers of wood sheathing. The cavity is filled with dense-pack cellulose insulation, achieving an R-value above 40. Large, high-gain windows on the south side

EMPOWERHOUSE

PROJECT INFORMATION

Project title: Empowerhouse

Location: Washington, D.C.

Size: 969 ft.^{2} (90 m^2);

Completion: 2013

Recognition: Certified (PHIUS), 2011 Decathlon Affordability Contest First Place Award

Type: Multifamily housing; duplex

Architect: Parsons The New School for Design, Milano School of International Affairs, Management and Urban Policy at The New School, and Stevens Institute of Technology for the 2011 Decathlon house

Builder: Habitat for Humanity

CPHC: Laura Briggs

HDD: 4,001 base 65°F (2,223 base 18.3°C)

CDD: 1,524 base 65°F (847 base 18.3°C)

Annual precipitation: 39.7 in. (1,009 mm)

allow the winter sun to warm the home. Shading was optimized in order to allow maximum sunlight in the winter heating months and avoid overheating in the summer.

8.4.2 The original solar decathalon modules arrive on the temporary site. DAVID J. LEWIS

8.4.3 Completed living room with the module match joint visible in the column and beam. MARTIN SECK

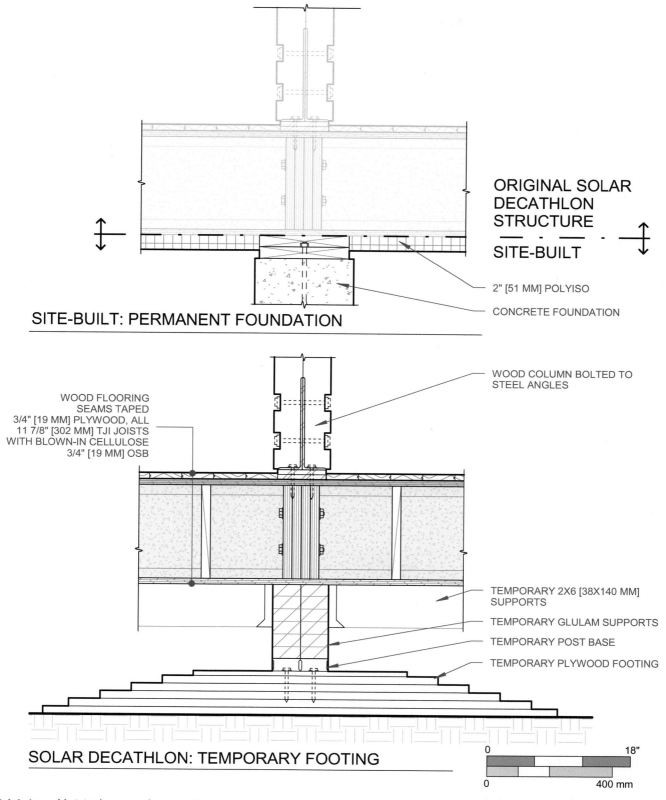

ORIGINAL SOLAR
DECATHLON
STRUCTURE

SITE-BUILT

2" [51 MM] POLYISO

CONCRETE FOUNDATION

SITE-BUILT: PERMANENT FOUNDATION

WOOD COLUMN BOLTED TO
STEEL ANGLES

WOOD FLOORING
SEAMS TAPED
3/4" [19 MM] PLYWOOD, ALL
11 7/8" [302 MM] TJI JOISTS
WITH BLOWN-IN CELLULOSE
3/4" [19 MM] OSB

TEMPORARY 2X6 [38X140 MM]
SUPPORTS

TEMPORARY GLULAM SUPPORTS

TEMPORARY POST BASE

TEMPORARY PLYWOOD FOOTING

SOLAR DECATHLON: TEMPORARY FOOTING

0   18"

0   400 mm

8.4.4 Assembly joint between the two solar decathlon modules. Temporary footing for display and permanent foundation after relocation.

8.4.5 Relocated modules on the left, with the site-built unit on the right. ASHLEY HARTWOOD, HABITAT FOR HUMANITY

8.4.6 Site framing of the second unit with the common wall visible on the right. HABITAT FOR HUMANITY

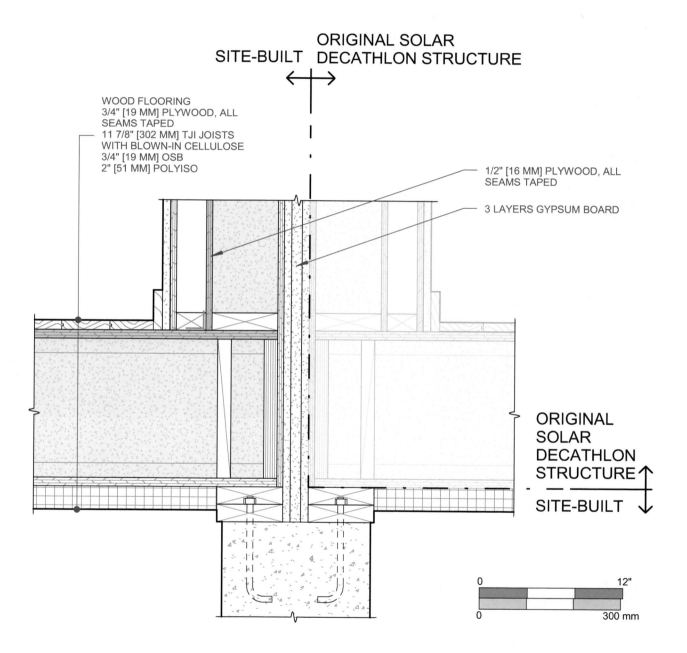

ORIGINAL SOLAR
SITE-BUILT DECATHLON STRUCTURE

WOOD FLOORING
3/4" [19 MM] PLYWOOD, ALL
SEAMS TAPED
11 7/8" [302 MM] TJI JOISTS
WITH BLOWN-IN CELLULOSE
3/4" [19 MM] OSB
2" [51 MM] POLYISO

1/2" [16 MM] PLYWOOD, ALL
SEAMS TAPED

3 LAYERS GYPSUM BOARD

ORIGINAL
SOLAR
DECATHLON
STRUCTURE
SITE-BUILT

0   12"

0   300 mm

8.4.7 Common wall between duplex units. Solar decathlon modules meet the site-built unit.

8.4.8 Original modules as displayed at the solar decathalon. MICHAEL MORAN

8.4.9 Permanent site with vertical expansion of the original modules and foundation for the second unit. LAURA BRIGGS

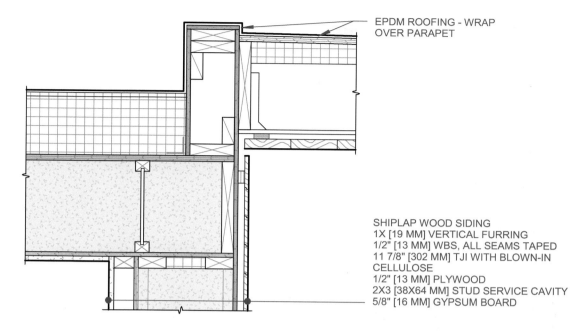

EPDM ROOFING - WRAP
OVER PARAPET

SHIPLAP WOOD SIDING
1X [19 MM] VERTICAL FURRING
1/2" [13 MM] WBS, ALL SEAMS TAPED
11 7/8" [302 MM] TJI WITH BLOWN-IN
CELLULOSE
1/2" [13 MM] PLYWOOD
2X3 [38X64 MM] STUD SERVICE CAVITY
5/8" [16 MM] GYPSUM BOARD

SOLAR DECATHLON: NORTH PORCH

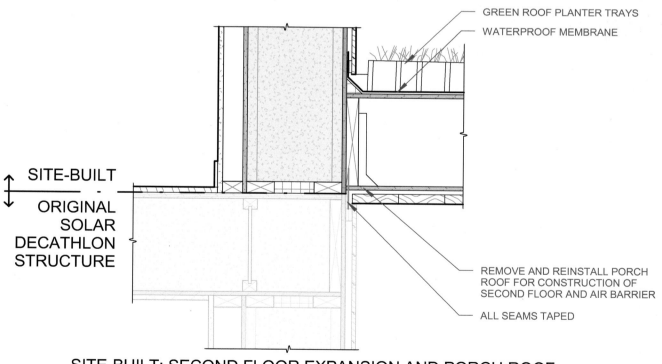

GREEN ROOF PLANTER TRAYS
WATERPROOF MEMBRANE

SITE-BUILT

ORIGINAL
SOLAR
DECATHLON
STRUCTURE

REMOVE AND REINSTALL PORCH
ROOF FOR CONSTRUCTION OF
SECOND FLOOR AND AIR BARRIER

ALL SEAMS TAPED

SITE-BUILT: SECOND FLOOR EXPANSION AND PORCH ROOF

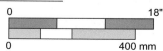

0   18"

0   400 mm

8.4.10 Vertical expansion of the solar decathlon modules at the north wall, creating second-floor living space.

8.4.11 Completed bedroom with splayed window reveals.
MARTIN SECK

8.4.12 Exterior cladding and window casing.
MICHAEL MORAN

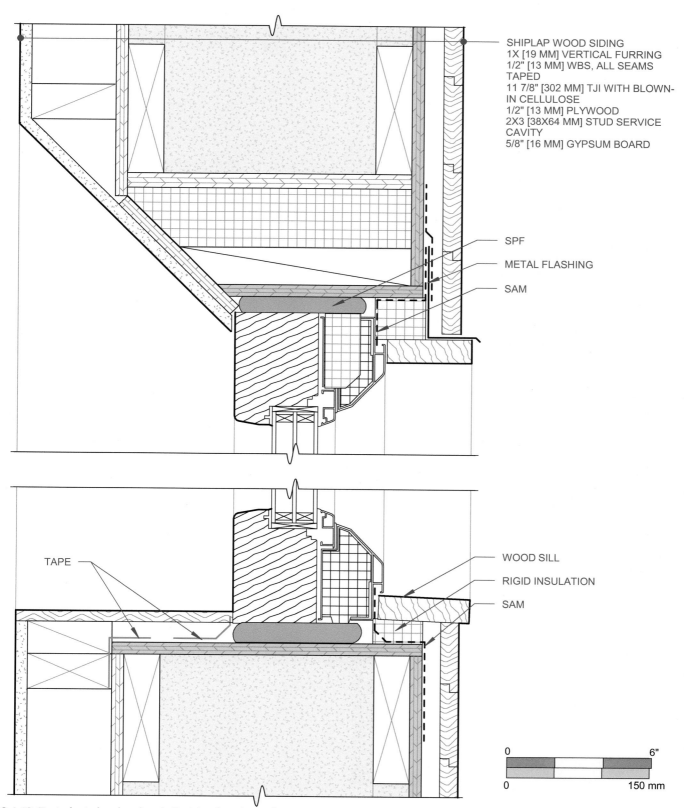

SHIPLAP WOOD SIDING
1X [19 MM] VERTICAL FURRING
1/2" [13 MM] WBS, ALL SEAMS
TAPED
11 7/8" [302 MM] TJI WITH BLOWN-
IN CELLULOSE
1/2" [13 MM] PLYWOOD
2X3 [38X64 MM] STUD SERVICE
CAVITY
5/8" [16 MM] GYPSUM BOARD

SPF

METAL FLASHING

SAM

TAPE

WOOD SILL

RIGID INSULATION

SAM

0   6"

0   150 mm

8.4.13 Typical window head and sill with splayed reveals.

8.4.14 South elevation with parapet, guardrail and roof overhang. MARTIN SECK

8.4.15 Construction of the first-floor roof overhang. HABITAT FOR HUMANITY

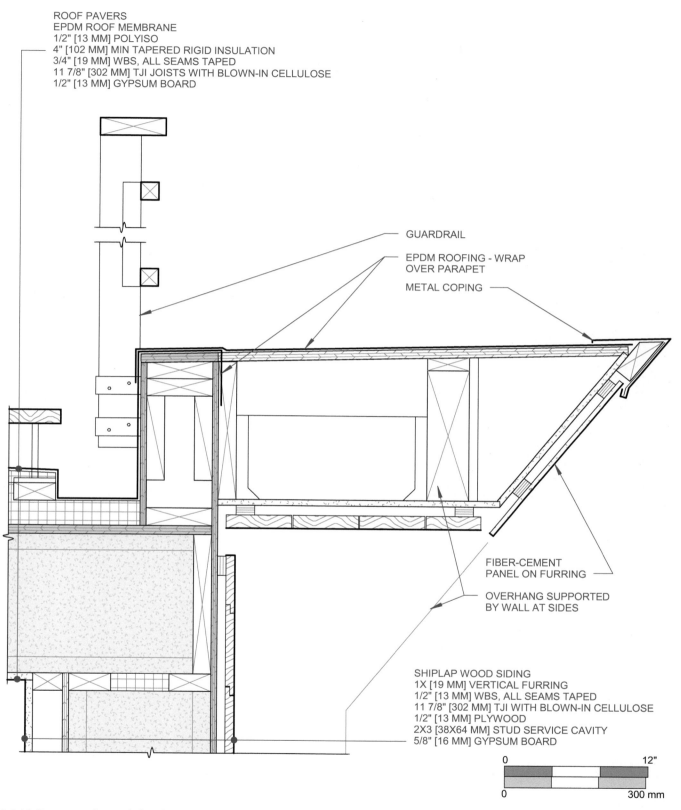

ROOF PAVERS
EPDM ROOF MEMBRANE
1/2" [13 MM] POLYISO
4" [102 MM] MIN TAPERED RIGID INSULATION
3/4" [19 MM] WBS, ALL SEAMS TAPED
11 7/8" [302 MM] TJI JOISTS WITH BLOWN-IN CELLULOSE
1/2" [13 MM] GYPSUM BOARD

GUARDRAIL

EPDM ROOFING - WRAP
OVER PARAPET

METAL COPING

FIBER-CEMENT
PANEL ON FURRING

OVERHANG SUPPORTED
BY WALL AT SIDES

SHIPLAP WOOD SIDING
1X [19 MM] VERTICAL FURRING
1/2" [13 MM] WBS, ALL SEAMS TAPED
11 7/8" [302 MM] TJI WITH BLOWN-IN CELLULOSE
1/2" [13 MM] PLYWOOD
2X3 [38X64 MM] STUD SERVICE CAVITY
5/8" [16 MM] GYPSUM BOARD

0   12"

0   300 mm

8.4.16 Parapet at the south façade, showing overhang for shading and guardrail for upper terrace.

8.4.17 Stairs to the second story and the roof terrace.
MARTIN SECK

8.4.18 Access door to the roof terrace. MARTIN SECK

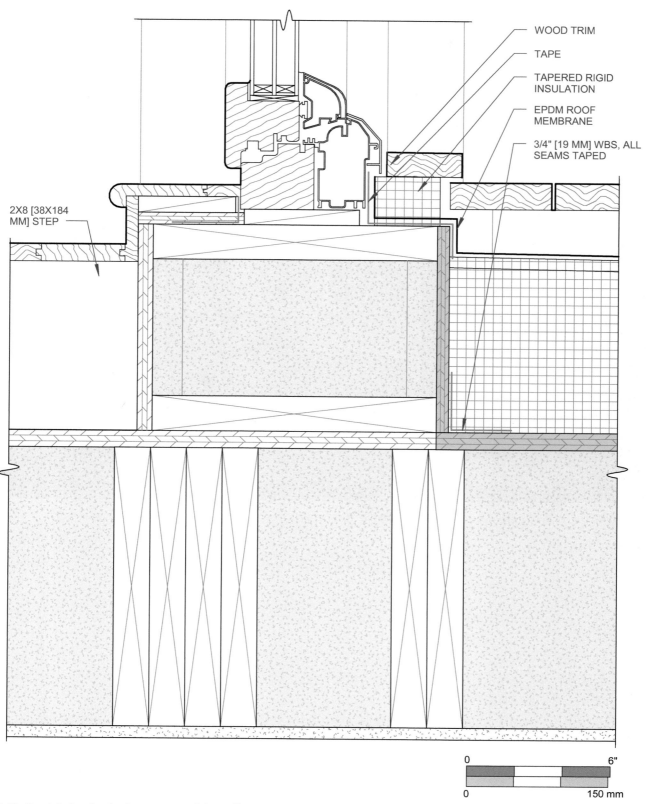

WOOD TRIM

TAPE

TAPERED RIGID INSULATION

EPDM ROOF MEMBRANE

3/4" [19 MM] WBS, ALL SEAMS TAPED

2X8 [38X184 MM] STEP

0 — 6"

0 — 150 mm

8.4.19 One interior step leads over a raised door sill opening onto the south-side roof terrace.

8.5.1 Hayfield House and garage viewed from the southwest. TRENT BELL PHOTOGRAPHY

The Hayfield House in Bolton, Connecticut, is sited on a gently sloping, 3-acre, tree-rimmed hayfield. The Hayfield House is designed for a family with three young children, with the understanding that the home will need to be flexible and adaptable to keep up with the family's changing needs over time. Given the rural surroundings, the clients were interested in building a house that was compatible with the neighboring New England vernacular, but, as their personal tastes were informed by their having lived in cosmopolitan areas, they did not want their home to be completely defined by a country aesthetic. The result is a home with a traditional building form and window openings facing the street, and with larger areas of glass and less traditional detailing facing the field. The interior plan is open, allowing flexible use, with great views out the south- and west-facing floor-to-ceiling triple-glazed windows. The detailing of the interior is also clean and simple, with an exposed wood structure in the living room and white cabinetry contrasted by exposed concrete floors and simple painted surfaces.

The goal of reaching the passive house standard for energy performance was set relatively early in the design process and informed several fundamental design decisions, including the compact massing of the building, south orientation, and large areas of glazing. The building shell is also detailed for energy efficiency, with highly insulated walls, ceiling, and foundation, and includes a ventilation system with heat recovery. In concert, the form, orientation, glazing, and building shell result in a building that uses 90 percent less energy for space heating than standard construction and is comfortable and healthy to live in, with space heating demands on the coldest winter nights satisfied by the equivalent heat output of a hair dryer.

HAYFIELD HOUSE

PROJECT INFORMATION

Project title: Hayfield House

Location: Bolton, Connecticut

Size: 2,200 ft.² (204 m²)

Completion: 2013

Recognition: Certified (PHI)

Type: Single-family home

Architect: GO Logic

Builder: Cooper Lane Builders

CPHC: David White, Right Environments

HDD: 5,622 base 65°F (3,123 base 18.3°C)

CDD: 816 base 65°F (453 base 18.3°C)

Annual precipitation: 50.47 in. (,1,282 mm)

8.5.2 Wall framing installed over slab on grade foundation.
STEVEN TOOMEY AND ANNE DECKER

8.5.3 Slab on grade formed inside proprietary foam shapes.
STEVEN TOOMEY AND ANNE DECKER

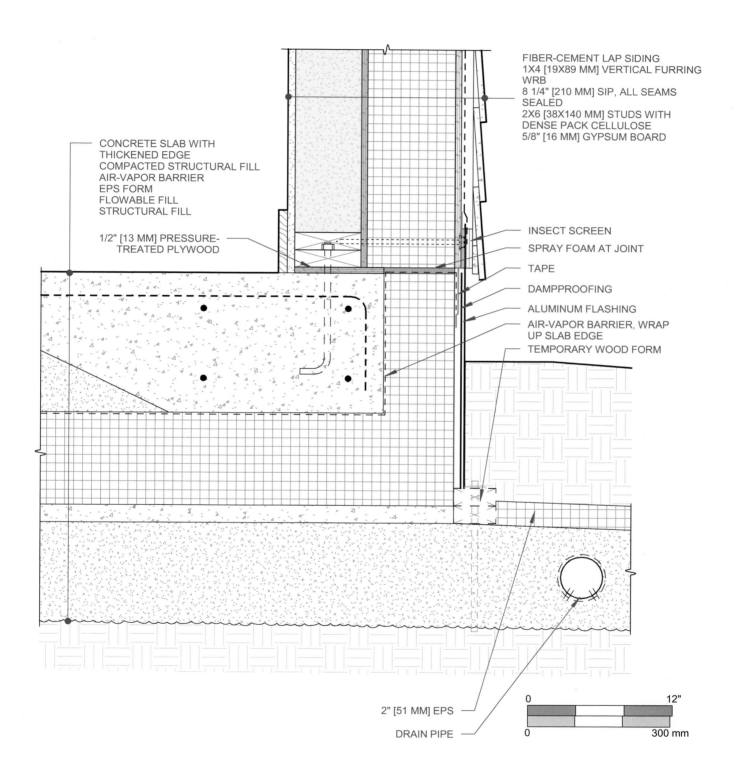

FIBER-CEMENT LAP SIDING
1X4 [19X89 MM] VERTICAL FURRING
WRB
8 1/4" [210 MM] SIP, ALL SEAMS
SEALED
2X6 [38X140 MM] STUDS WITH
DENSE PACK CELLULOSE
5/8" [16 MM] GYPSUM BOARD

CONCRETE SLAB WITH
THICKENED EDGE
COMPACTED STRUCTURAL FILL
AIR-VAPOR BARRIER
EPS FORM
FLOWABLE FILL
STRUCTURAL FILL

1/2" [13 MM] PRESSURE-
TREATED PLYWOOD

INSECT SCREEN
SPRAY FOAM AT JOINT
TAPE
DAMPPROOFING
ALUMINUM FLASHING
AIR-VAPOR BARRIER, WRAP
UP SLAB EDGE
TEMPORARY WOOD FORM

2" [51 MM] EPS

DRAIN PIPE

0   12"

0   300 mm

8.5.4 The slab on grade foundation system is formed inside a custom profile of foam insulation.
GO LOGIC HOLDS A PATENT ON THIS ASSEMBLY.

8.5.5 SIPs installed over wall studs, plates, and rim joist.
STEVEN TOOMEY AND ANNE DECKER

8.5.6 Gable end with SIPs overlaid continuously on two stories.
STEVEN TOOMEY AND ANNE DECKER

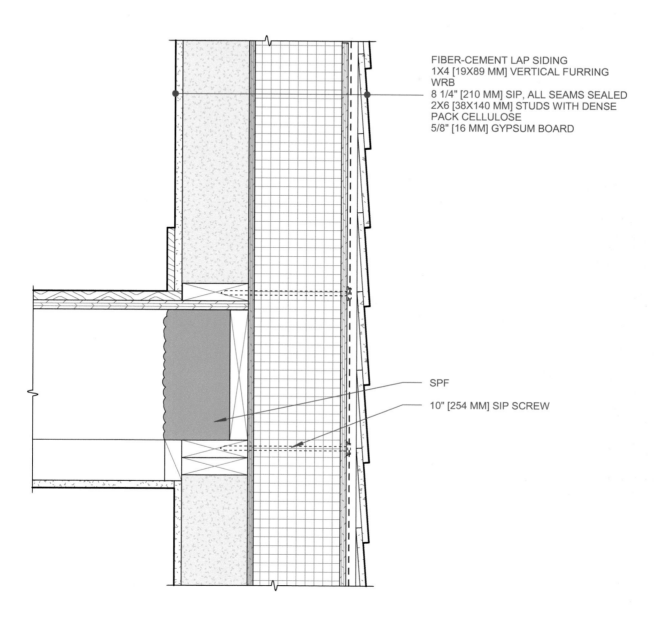

FIBER-CEMENT LAP SIDING
1X4 [19X89 MM] VERTICAL FURRING
WRB
8 1/4" [210 MM] SIP, ALL SEAMS SEALED
2X6 [38X140 MM] STUDS WITH DENSE
PACK CELLULOSE
5/8" [16 MM] GYPSUM BOARD

SPF

10" [254 MM] SIP SCREW

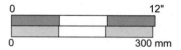

8.5.7 Platform framing of the walls and second floor wrapped with a continuous layer of SIPs as sheathing.

8.5.8 Taping the air barrier sheathing on the underside of roof trusses. STEVEN TOOMEY AND ANNE DECKER

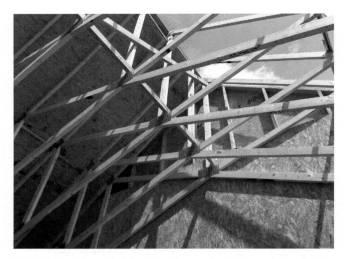

8.5.9 Trusses provide large insulation volume above cathedral ceiling. STEVEN TOOMEY AND ANNE DECKER

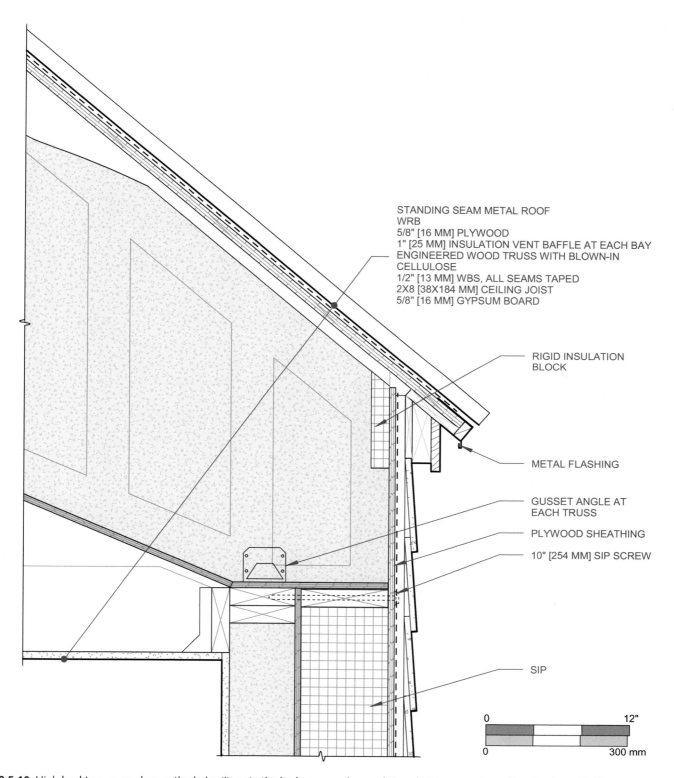

STANDING SEAM METAL ROOF
WRB
5/8" [16 MM] PLYWOOD
1" [25 MM] INSULATION VENT BAFFLE AT EACH BAY
ENGINEERED WOOD TRUSS WITH BLOWN-IN
CELLULOSE
1/2" [13 MM] WBS, ALL SEAMS TAPED
2X8 [38X184 MM] CEILING JOIST
5/8" [16 MM] GYPSUM BOARD

RIGID INSULATION
BLOCK

METAL FLASHING

GUSSET ANGLE AT
EACH TRUSS

PLYWOOD SHEATHING

10" [254 MM] SIP SCREW

SIP

0   12"

0   300 mm

8.5.10 High heel trusses produce cathedral ceilings in the bedrooms and a conditioned attic space above the closets and bathrooms. Siding ventilation is continuous into the roof.

8.5.11 Windows installed in recess with space at the edges to over-insulate the frames. STEVEN TOOMEY AND ANNE DECKER

8.5.12 Siding and window casings installed over furring to create ventilated façade. STEVEN TOOMEY AND ANNE DECKER

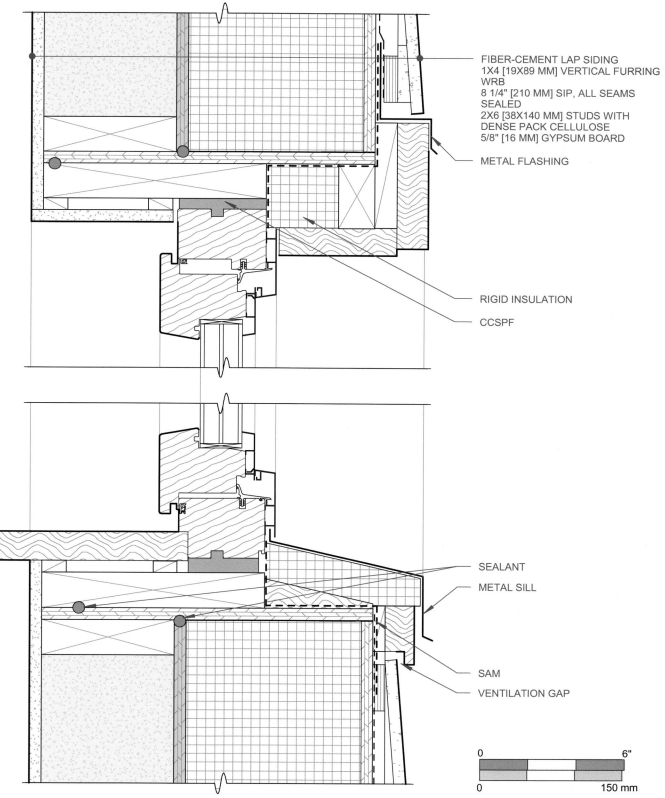

FIBER-CEMENT LAP SIDING
1X4 [19X89 MM] VERTICAL FURRING
WRB
8 1/4" [210 MM] SIP, ALL SEAMS
SEALED
2X6 [38X140 MM] STUDS WITH
DENSE PACK CELLULOSE
5/8" [16 MM] GYPSUM BOARD

METAL FLASHING

RIGID INSULATION

CCSPF

SEALANT

METAL SILL

SAM

VENTILATION GAP

0   6"
0   150 mm

8.5.13 Windows are attached to a recessed buck inside the rough opening. Space at the perimeter allows for over-insulation of the frames.

8.5.14 Exterior sliding screens protect glazing at living room.
STEVEN TOOMEY AND ANNE DECKER

8.5.15 Heavy timber floor framing creates large openings at main living space. STEVEN TOOMEY AND ANNE DECKER

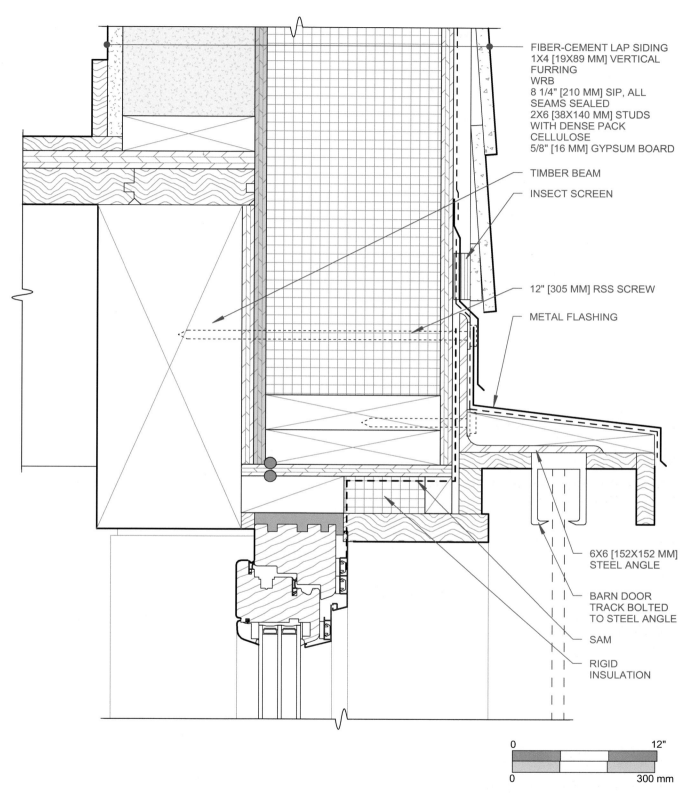

FIBER-CEMENT LAP SIDING
1X4 [19X89 MM] VERTICAL FURRING
WRB
8 1/4" [210 MM] SIP, ALL SEAMS SEALED
2X6 [38X140 MM] STUDS WITH DENSE PACK CELLULOSE
5/8" [16 MM] GYPSUM BOARD

TIMBER BEAM

INSECT SCREEN

12" [305 MM] RSS SCREW

METAL FLASHING

6X6 [152X152 MM] STEEL ANGLE

BARN DOOR TRACK BOLTED TO STEEL ANGLE

SAM

RIGID INSULATION

0   12"

0   300 mm

8.5.16 Heavy timber framing exposed above the living areas. Exterior rolling shutters protect the large window openings.

8.5.17 Air barrier developed above ceiling joists at the one-story portion of the house. STEVEN TOOMEY AND ANNE DECKER

8.5.18 Shed roof with raised heel constructed above the airtight volume. STEVEN TOOMEY AND ANNE DECKER

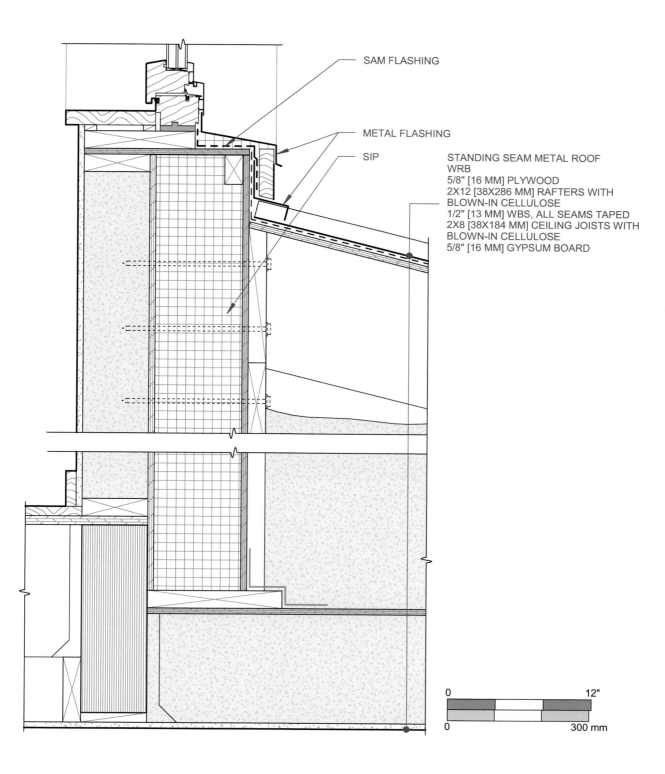

SAM FLASHING

METAL FLASHING

SIP

STANDING SEAM METAL ROOF
WRB
5/8" [16 MM] PLYWOOD
2X12 [38X286 MM] RAFTERS WITH
BLOWN-IN CELLULOSE
1/2" [13 MM] WBS, ALL SEAMS TAPED
2X8 [38X184 MM] CEILING JOISTS WITH
BLOWN-IN CELLULOSE
5/8" [16 MM] GYPSUM BOARD

0   12"

0   300 mm

8.5.19 One-story accessory spaces abut the main volume of the house. A shed roof acts as an umbrella above the airtight volume.

8.6.1 Karuna House viewed from the southeast. JEREMY BITTERMAN PHOTOGRAPHY

The Karuna House sits atop a hillside, at an elevation of approximately 1,050 ft. (320 m), overlooking the Willamette Valley, and it combines a modern and sculptural form with exceptionally high performance. A careful, iterative design process involving the architect, passive house consultant, and builder was essential in meeting the design and performance goals, in particular with respect to site orientation and glazing. The main living spaces are arranged along the south and east and are provided with large windows, taking full advantage of views of the natural surroundings. Through the use of high-performing triple-glazing and an operable shading system, the home is able to achieve a high level of performance without sacrificing views.

All elements of the building's envelope contribute to the energy efficiency of the house. The foundation and floor slab sit on a raft of EPS insulation, completely eliminating thermal bridging at grade. The walls combine thick insulation (R-59 [0.096 W/m²K] at center of cavity) with details that minimize thermal bridging, resulting in a whole-wall value of R-51 (0.111 W/m²K). When a highly insulated roof, airtight walls, and an efficient heat pump and HRV system are added, the home is expected to use 90 percent less heating and cooling energy than the average home.

Because of the exceptionally low energy needs of the home, a 10-kW solar array is enough to make the building net positive and provide a charge for the client's electric car. In addition to low energy use, the simple and non-toxic finishes provide a warm and healthy interior. All of these features together have resulted in making the Karuna House the first in the world to achieve PHIUS+, LEED for Homes Platinum, and Minergie-P-ECO certification.

KARUNA HOUSE

PROJECT INFORMATION

Project title: Karuna House

Location: Newberg, Oregon

Size: 3,261 ft.² (303 m²)

Completion: 2013

Recognition: Certified (PHIUS), LEED for Homes Platinum, Minergie-P-ECO, DOE Zero Energy Ready Home, Earth Advantage Platinum, 2015 First Place—Single Family PHIUS Passive Projects Competition, Beyond Green Award—National Institute of Building Sciences, 2014 Green Home of the Year—*Green Builder Magazine*, 2013 AIA Portland Design Award—2030 Challenge

Type: Single-family house

Architect: Holst Architecture

Builder: Hammer & Hand

CPHC: Dylan Lamar, Green Hammer

HDD: 4,559 base 65°F (2,533 base 18.3°C)

CDD: 300 base 65°F (167 base 18.3°C)

Annual precipitation: 43 in. (1,092 mm)

8.6.2 Foundation at the southeast corner of the living room with insulation at the stem walls. HAMMER & HAND

8.6.3 Footings at the northwest corner cast on top of deep foam base. HAMMER & HAND

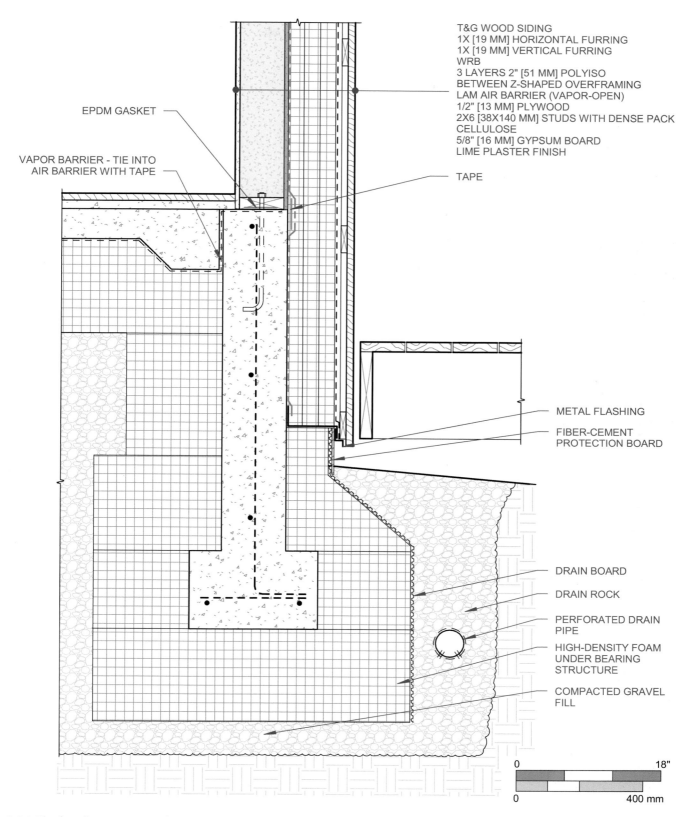

EPDM GASKET

VAPOR BARRIER - TIE INTO
AIR BARRIER WITH TAPE

T&G WOOD SIDING
1X [19 MM] HORIZONTAL FURRING
1X [19 MM] VERTICAL FURRING
WRB
3 LAYERS 2" [51 MM] POLYISO
BETWEEN Z-SHAPED OVERFRAMING
LAM AIR BARRIER (VAPOR-OPEN)
1/2" [13 MM] PLYWOOD
2X6 [38X140 MM] STUDS WITH DENSE PACK
CELLULOSE
5/8" [16 MM] GYPSUM BOARD
LIME PLASTER FINISH

TAPE

METAL FLASHING

FIBER-CEMENT
PROTECTION BOARD

DRAIN BOARD

DRAIN ROCK

PERFORATED DRAIN
PIPE

HIGH-DENSITY FOAM
UNDER BEARING
STRUCTURE

COMPACTED GRAVEL
FILL

0   18"

0   400 mm

8.6.4 The foundation is wrapped on all sides with foam insulation. The footings shown are enlarged under the steel supporting columns.

8.6.5 Combination wood and steel structure spanning the living room. HAMMER & HAND

8.6.6 Second-floor framing looking south through the living space. HAMMER & HAND

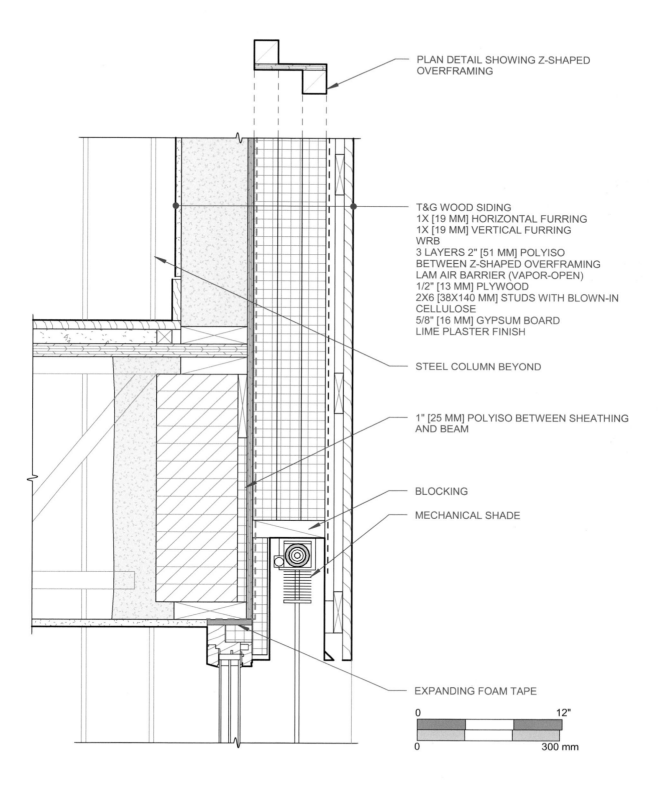

PLAN DETAIL SHOWING Z-SHAPED
OVERFRAMING

T&G WOOD SIDING
1X [19 MM] HORIZONTAL FURRING
1X [19 MM] VERTICAL FURRING
WRB
3 LAYERS 2" [51 MM] POLYISO
BETWEEN Z-SHAPED OVERFRAMING
LAM AIR BARRIER (VAPOR-OPEN)
1/2" [13 MM] PLYWOOD
2X6 [38X140 MM] STUDS WITH BLOWN-IN
CELLULOSE
5/8" [16 MM] GYPSUM BOARD
LIME PLASTER FINISH

STEEL COLUMN BEYOND

1" [25 MM] POLYISO BETWEEN SHEATHING
AND BEAM

BLOCKING

MECHANICAL SHADE

EXPANDING FOAM TAPE

0   12"

0   300 mm

8.6.7 The second-floor framing bears on a continuous perimeter beam that is supported by interior steel columns. This allows large openings in the living room, protected by operable shading.

8.6.8 Roof terrace above the master bedroom wing.
HAMMER & HAND

8.6.9 Parapet and coping at the roof terrace. HAMMER & HAND

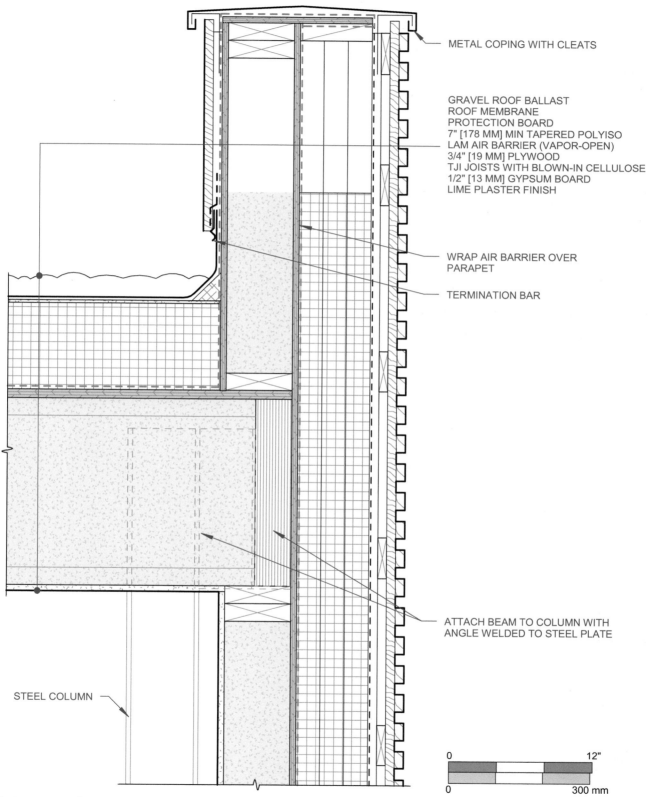

METAL COPING WITH CLEATS

GRAVEL ROOF BALLAST
ROOF MEMBRANE
PROTECTION BOARD
7" [178 MM] MIN TAPERED POLYISO
LAM AIR BARRIER (VAPOR-OPEN)
3/4" [19 MM] PLYWOOD
TJI JOISTS WITH BLOWN-IN CELLULOSE
1/2" [13 MM] GYPSUM BOARD
LIME PLASTER FINISH

WRAP AIR BARRIER OVER
PARAPET

TERMINATION BAR

ATTACH BEAM TO COLUMN WITH
ANGLE WELDED TO STEEL PLATE

STEEL COLUMN

| 0 | | 12" |
| 0 | | 300 mm |

8.6.10 Exterior walls terminate in a parapet that conceals low slope roofs and roof terraces. Insulation continuously wraps the interior framing.

8.6.11 East-facing windows with projecting sheet metal surround at second floor. JEREMY BITTERMAN PHOTOGRAPHY

8.6.12 Operable shading louvers recessed above second-floor window head. HAMMER & HAND

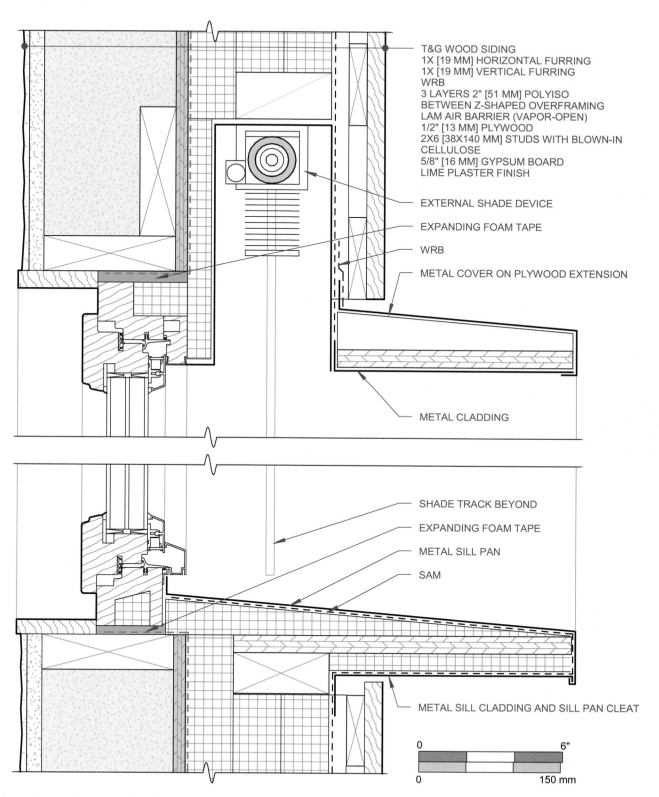

T&G WOOD SIDING
1X [19 MM] HORIZONTAL FURRING
1X [19 MM] VERTICAL FURRING
WRB
3 LAYERS 2" [51 MM] POLYISO
BETWEEN Z-SHAPED OVERFRAMING
LAM AIR BARRIER (VAPOR-OPEN)
1/2" [13 MM] PLYWOOD
2X6 [38X140 MM] STUDS WITH BLOWN-IN
CELLULOSE
5/8" [16 MM] GYPSUM BOARD
LIME PLASTER FINISH

EXTERNAL SHADE DEVICE

EXPANDING FOAM TAPE

WRB

METAL COVER ON PLYWOOD EXTENSION

METAL CLADDING

SHADE TRACK BEYOND

EXPANDING FOAM TAPE

METAL SILL PAN

SAM

METAL SILL CLADDING AND SILL PAN CLEAT

0   6"

0   150 mm

8.6.13 The east-facing window of the master bedroom with projecting elements on all four sides. A custom over-framing system supports the cladding and window trim.

8.6.14 South elevation showing exterior deck at second floor master bedroom. JEREMY BITTERMAN PHOTOGRAPHY

8.6.15 Access door to second-floor deck and cantilevered side wall. HAMMER & HAND

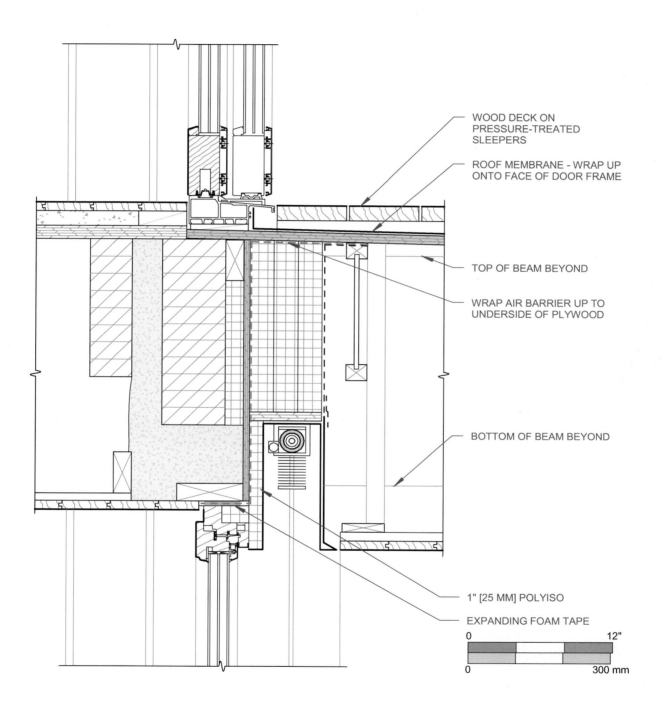

WOOD DECK ON
PRESSURE-TREATED
SLEEPERS

ROOF MEMBRANE - WRAP UP
ONTO FACE OF DOOR FRAME

TOP OF BEAM BEYOND

WRAP AIR BARRIER UP TO
UNDERSIDE OF PLYWOOD

BOTTOM OF BEAM BEYOND

1" [25 MM] POLYISO

EXPANDING FOAM TAPE

0		12"

0		300 mm

8.6.16 At the master bedroom and deck the floor framing systems run parallel to the thermal envelope, both inside and out.

8.6.17 View to south and east from living room with steel columns and window wall. JEREMY BITTERMAN PHOTOGRAPHY

8.6.18 Steel columns inside glazed corner of living room.
HAMMER & HAND

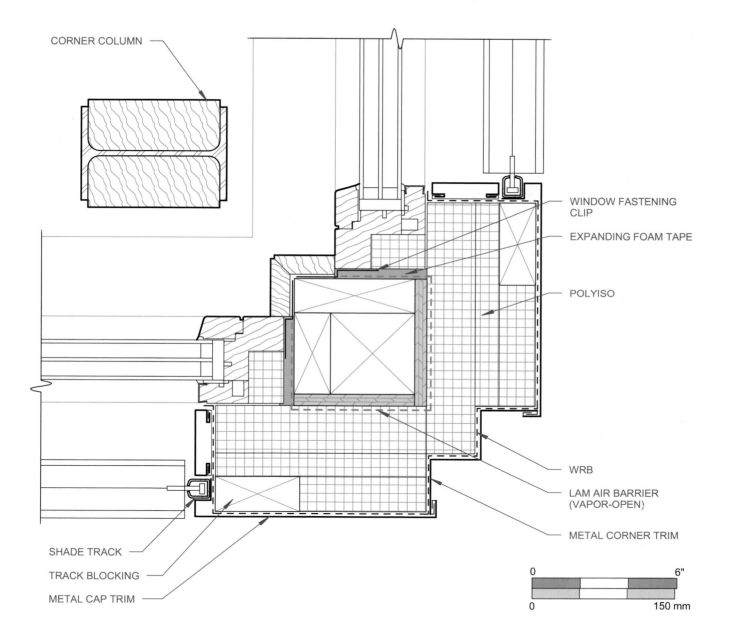

CORNER COLUMN

WINDOW FASTENING CLIP

EXPANDING FOAM TAPE

POLYISO

WRB

LAM AIR BARRIER (VAPOR-OPEN)

METAL CORNER TRIM

SHADE TRACK

TRACK BLOCKING

METAL CAP TRIM

0   6"

0   150 mm

8.6.19 An interior steel column supports the building at the living-room corner. Wood framing connects the windows and supports over-insulation of the frame.

8.7.1 Louisiana House viewed from approach at the street. COREY SAFT

The Louisiana Passive House is located in the humid, subtropical, cooling-dominated climate of south Louisiana, which suffers relentlessly hot and humid summers but relatively benign winters. Because of the humidity, there is a long-established tradition of air conditioning as the only reliable means of achieving comfort, and it is this issue of latent load that makes the application of passive house principles so unique in this project. Corey Saft, architecture professor at the University of Louisiana, designed a house that will stay cool, even in the heat of the bayou, while barely running the air conditioner. Targeting the passive house standard, the project became the first certified building in the South (2010). This three-bedroom, two-bathroom home in Lafayette, Louisiana, has walls filled with open-cell spray foam insulation, on which is layered rigid foam board, which makes the home exceptionally airtight. Daylight is effectively distributed throughout the house with clerestory windows. In the evening, LED and CFL fixtures are used throughout the house. The steel roof system includes a very slick laminated solar electric array that integrates with the aesthetics of the roof plane. The R-28 exterior walls (with a back-vented rainscreen), R-55 roof (also back-vented), R-21 crawl space walls, and R-16.5 crawl space slab create a super-insulated and tight envelope that achieved 0.55 ACH50 airtightness. The project has been monitored and studied since the project was completed, for energy, comfort, and, in particular, the latent issue in ventilation air in a hot humid climate. Both heating (occasionally required) and cooling needs are significantly less than what was predicted by the PHPP. The primary energy demand was higher than predicted, primarily because of the dehumidifier used to manage comfort during the shoulder seasons, where humidity remains an issue, although temperature does not. It is this issue of latent load that has partially driven PHIUS to revolutionize its PH standard to be climate-specific.

LOUISIANA PASSIVE HOUSE

PROJECT INFORMATION

Project title: Louisiana Passive House

Location: Lafayette, Louisiana

Size: 1,600 ft.^{2} (149 m^2); 400 ft.^{2} (37 m^2) basement

Completion: 2010

Recognition: Certification (PHIUS), LEED Platinum

Type: Single-family home

Architect: Corey Saft

Builder: Corey Saft

CPHC: Katrin Klingenberg, PHIUS

HDD: 1,496 base 65°F (831 base 18.3°C)

CDD: 2,763 base 65°F (1,535 base 18.3°C)

Annual precipitation: 30.18 in. (767 mm)

8.7.2 Insulated cores at concrete masonry stem wall.
COREY SAFT

8.7.3 Preparing for concrete slab at insulated crawl space.
COREY SAFT

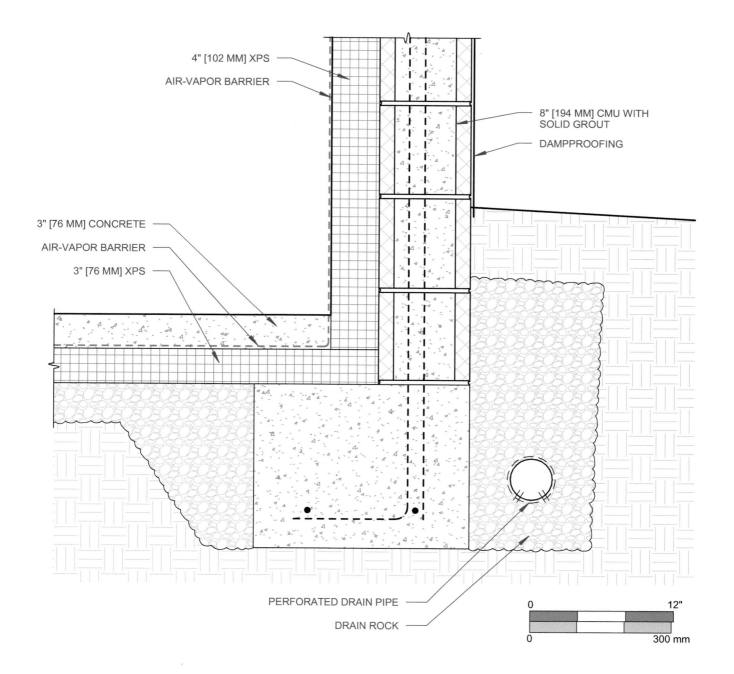

4" [102 MM] XPS

AIR-VAPOR BARRIER

8" [194 MM] CMU WITH SOLID GROUT

DAMPPROOFING

3" [76 MM] CONCRETE

AIR-VAPOR BARRIER

3" [76 MM] XPS

PERFORATED DRAIN PIPE

DRAIN ROCK

0   12"

0   300 mm

8.7.4 A crawl space below the main floor is contained by CMU stem walls insulated on the interior. The space houses the HRV and ductwork.

8.7.5 Floor framing bearing on insulated concrete masonry stem wall. COREY SAFT

8.7.6 Placement of roof rafters at double-height space. COREY SAFT

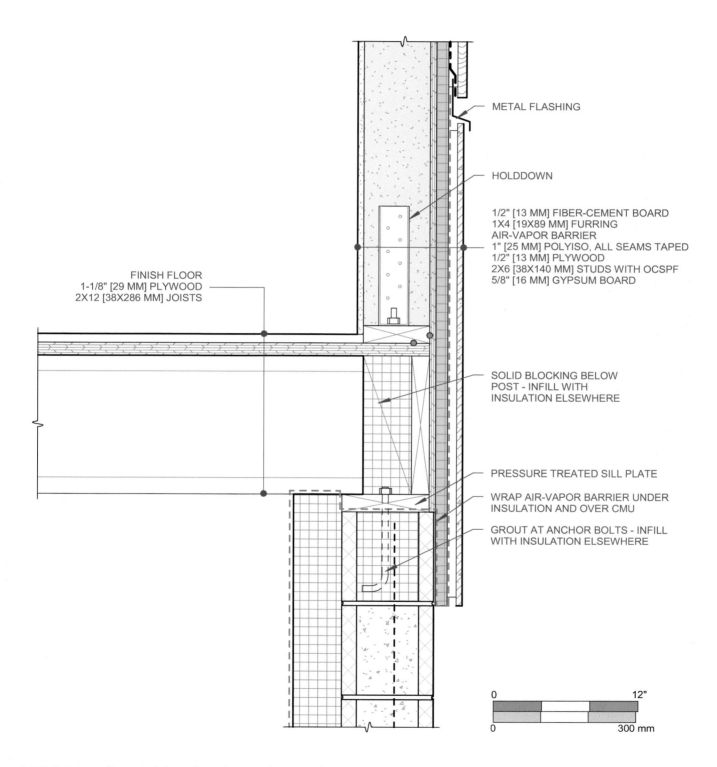

METAL FLASHING

HOLDDOWN

1/2" [13 MM] FIBER-CEMENT BOARD
1X4 [19X89 MM] FURRING
AIR-VAPOR BARRIER
1" [25 MM] POLYISO, ALL SEAMS TAPED
1/2" [13 MM] PLYWOOD
2X6 [38X140 MM] STUDS WITH OCSPF
5/8" [16 MM] GYPSUM BOARD

FINISH FLOOR
1-1/8" [29 MM] PLYWOOD
2X12 [38X286 MM] JOISTS

SOLID BLOCKING BELOW
POST - INFILL WITH
INSULATION ELSEWHERE

PRESSURE TREATED SILL PLATE

WRAP AIR-VAPOR BARRIER UNDER
INSULATION AND OVER CMU

GROUT AT ANCHOR BOLTS - INFILL
WITH INSULATION ELSEWHERE

0 ————————————— 12"
0 ————————————— 300 mm

8.7.7 Exterior walls are tied down through grouted cores in the CMU stem wall. The remaining cores in the top course of block are filled with insulation.

8.7.8 North-side roof overhang supported by struts. COREY SAFT

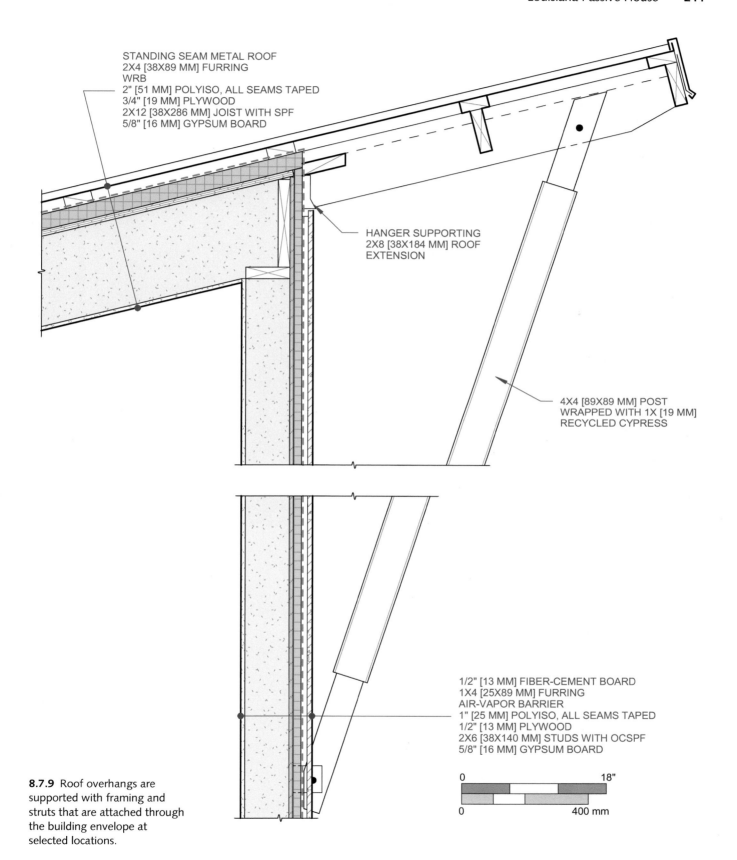

STANDING SEAM METAL ROOF
2X4 [38X89 MM] FURRING
WRB
2" [51 MM] POLYISO, ALL SEAMS TAPED
3/4" [19 MM] PLYWOOD
2X12 [38X286 MM] JOIST WITH SPF
5/8" [16 MM] GYPSUM BOARD

HANGER SUPPORTING
2X8 [38X184 MM] ROOF
EXTENSION

4X4 [89X89 MM] POST
WRAPPED WITH 1X [19 MM]
RECYCLED CYPRESS

1/2" [13 MM] FIBER-CEMENT BOARD
1X4 [25X89 MM] FURRING
AIR-VAPOR BARRIER
1" [25 MM] POLYISO, ALL SEAMS TAPED
1/2" [13 MM] PLYWOOD
2X6 [38X140 MM] STUDS WITH OCSPF
5/8" [16 MM] GYPSUM BOARD

0   18"

0   400 mm

8.7.9 Roof overhangs are supported with framing and struts that are attached through the building envelope at selected locations.

8.7.10 High clerestory windows on north side. COREY SAFT

8.7.11 South elevation with windows taped to rigid insulation.
COREY SAFT

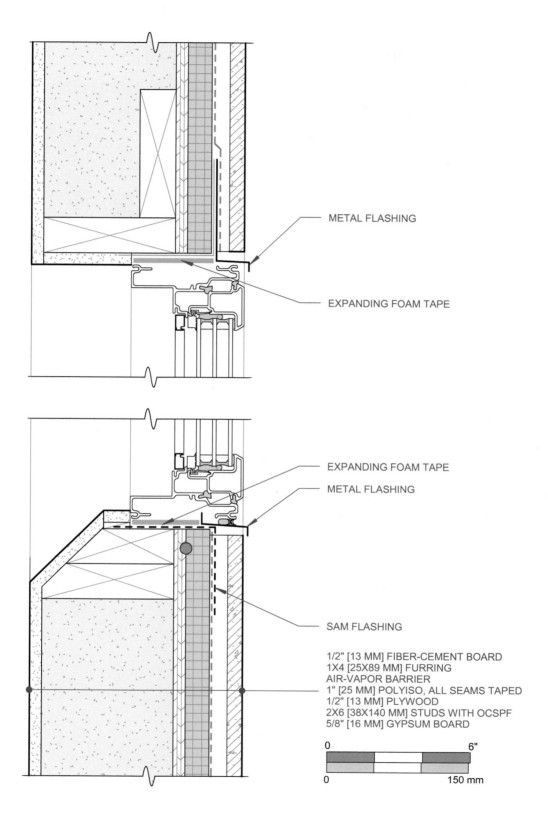

METAL FLASHING

EXPANDING FOAM TAPE

EXPANDING FOAM TAPE

METAL FLASHING

SAM FLASHING

1/2" [13 MM] FIBER-CEMENT BOARD
1X4 [25X89 MM] FURRING
AIR-VAPOR BARRIER
1" [25 MM] POLYISO, ALL SEAMS TAPED
1/2" [13 MM] PLYWOOD
2X6 [38X140 MM] STUDS WITH OCSPF
5/8" [16 MM] GYPSUM BOARD

0   6"

0   150 mm

8.7.12 Clerestory windows on the north elevation have an inclined sill to admit light to the tall living space below.

8.8.1 South elevation of Madrona House with views over Lake Washington to the east. SHED ARCHITECTURE & DESIGN

Long before the design began for the Madrona Passive House, the clients were already deeply involved with environmental philanthropy and advocacy. They wanted to build a home for the family that maximized the positive impact on the climate problem per dollar spent, but also served as an example for others who want to invest in climate solutions. Sitting at the edge of a steep hill in an east-Seattle neighborhood, with commanding views to Lake Washington and the Cascade Mountains, the Madrona house combines contemporary design with high-performance building techniques to create an environmentally responsive and resource-efficient house. Because of the need to negotiate the site's steep slope, a structural slab, supported by twenty-six piles drilled deep into the hillside, effectively "floats" the house above marginal soils on a "platform-on-stilts."

The home's airtight, super-insulated building envelope and passive house design use stained cedar siding as a rainscreen over an advanced framed 2 x 6 (38 x 140-mm) insulated stud wall assembly of high-density cellulose insulation, zip sheathing, and mineral wool exterior insulation at R-34. Large, ZOLA aluminum-clad windows allow daylight and views, and hidden external roll-up shades provide shading to prevent overheating. The roof features high-density cellulose, tapered foam, and thermally isolated stanchions to support the 7-kW solar photovoltaic array that will provide enough energy to offset most, perhaps all, of the home's energy consumption on a net annual basis. So that storm water can be managed, the project employs permeable pavers for site hardscape and one cistern to capture and control rainwater from the home's roof and the green roof on the garage. By investing in sustainable site-development strategies, efficient building systems, and an advanced envelope, the project aims to respect the home's environmentally critical site and achieve the high performance of the passive house energy standard.

MADRONA PASSIVE HOUSE

PROJECT INFORMATION

Project title: Madrona Passive House

Location: Seattle, Washington

Size: 3,766 ft.² (152 m²) treated floor area

Completion: 2015

Recognition: Certified (PHIUS), ILFI Net Zero Energy Building Certification

Type: Single-family house

Architect: SHED Architecture & Design

Builder: Hammer & Hand

CPHC: Daniel Whitmore, Hammer & Hand

HDD: 4,280 base 65°F (2,378 base 18.3°C)

CDD: 279 base 65°F (155 base 18.3°C)

Annual precipitation: 38 in. (965 mm)

8.8.2 Casting grade beams and floor slab over concrete pier foundations. HAMMER & HAND

8.8.3 Retaining walls against the slope, supporting the first floor.
HAMMER & HAND

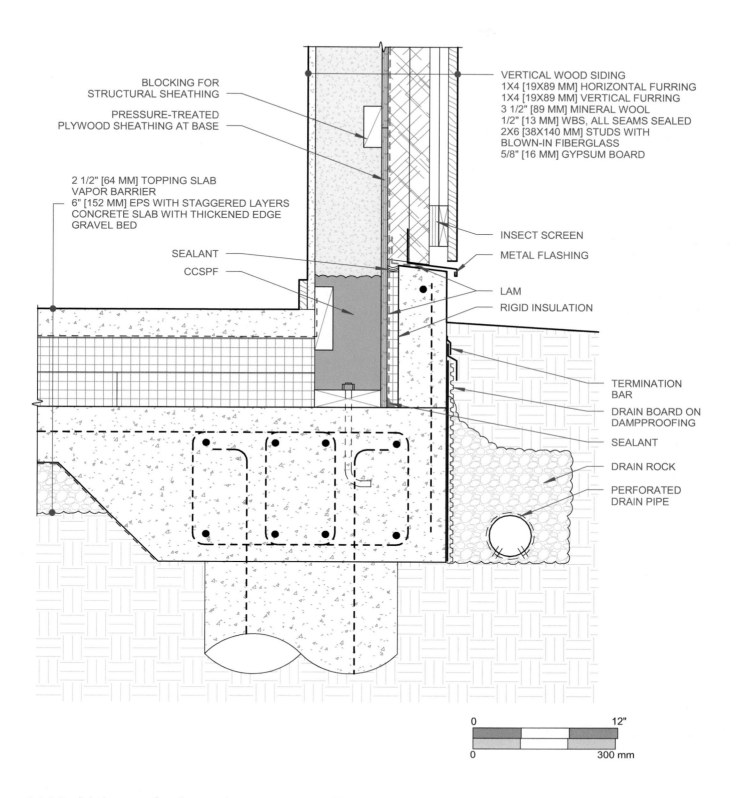

BLOCKING FOR
STRUCTURAL SHEATHING

PRESSURE-TREATED
PLYWOOD SHEATHING AT BASE

2 1/2" [64 MM] TOPPING SLAB
VAPOR BARRIER
6" [152 MM] EPS WITH STAGGERED LAYERS
CONCRETE SLAB WITH THICKENED EDGE
GRAVEL BED

SEALANT

CCSPF

VERTICAL WOOD SIDING
1X4 [19X89 MM] HORIZONTAL FURRING
1X4 [19X89 MM] VERTICAL FURRING
3 1/2" [89 MM] MINERAL WOOL
1/2" [13 MM] WBS, ALL SEAMS SEALED
2X6 [38X140 MM] STUDS WITH
BLOWN-IN FIBERGLASS
5/8" [16 MM] GYPSUM BOARD

INSECT SCREEN

METAL FLASHING

LAM

RIGID INSULATION

TERMINATION
BAR

DRAIN BOARD ON
DAMPPROOFING

SEALANT

DRAIN ROCK

PERFORATED
DRAIN PIPE

0   12"

0   300 mm

8.8.4 Daylight basement foundation with concrete piers to stable soil. Thermally isolated structure stands inside a concrete basin.

8.8.5 First-floor trusses suspended inside the basement retaining wall. HAMMER & HAND

8.8.6 Concrete wall protects deep floor framing at grade.
HAMMER & HAND

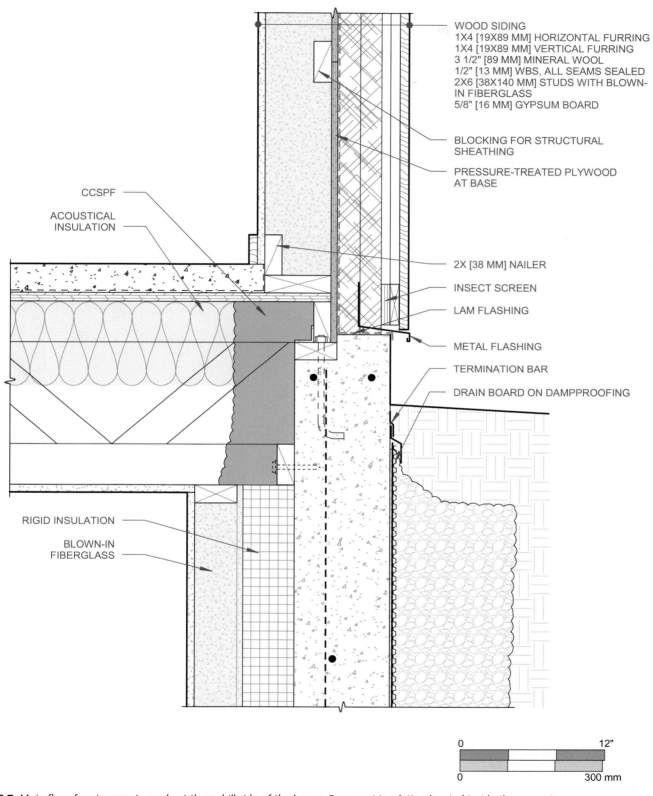

WOOD SIDING
1X4 [19X89 MM] HORIZONTAL FURRING
1X4 [19X89 MM] VERTICAL FURRING
3 1/2" [89 MM] MINERAL WOOL
1/2" [13 MM] WBS, ALL SEAMS SEALED
2X6 [38X140 MM] STUDS WITH BLOWN-IN FIBERGLASS
5/8" [16 MM] GYPSUM BOARD

BLOCKING FOR STRUCTURAL SHEATHING

PRESSURE-TREATED PLYWOOD AT BASE

CCSPF

ACOUSTICAL INSULATION

2X [38 MM] NAILER

INSECT SCREEN

LAM FLASHING

METAL FLASHING

TERMINATION BAR

DRAIN BOARD ON DAMPPROOFING

RIGID INSULATION

BLOWN-IN FIBERGLASS

0   12"

0   300 mm

8.8.7 Main floor framing meets grade at the uphill side of the house. Basement insulation located inside the concrete.

8.8.8 South-side roof deck with finished guardrail and cap. Awaits walk surface. HAMMER & HAND

8.8.9 Main deck guardrail with framing members integrated into the insulation. HAMMER & HAND

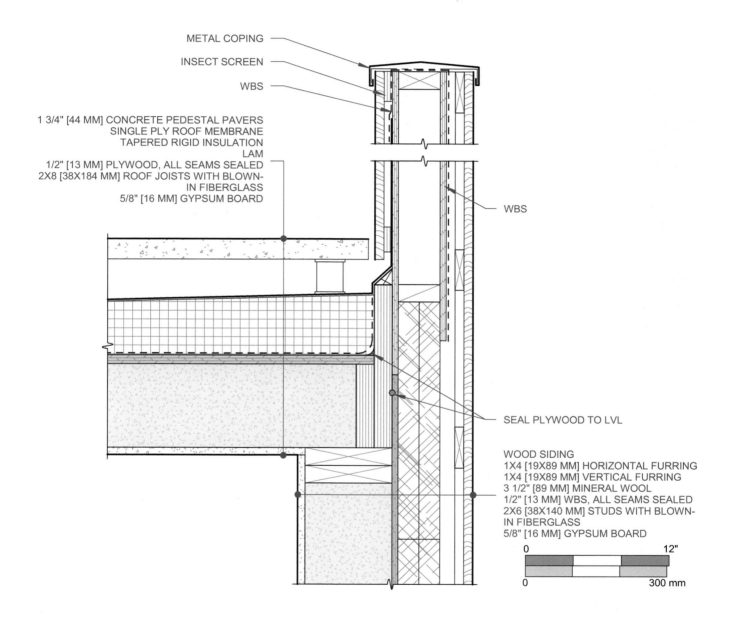

METAL COPING

INSECT SCREEN

WBS

1 3/4" [44 MM] CONCRETE PEDESTAL PAVERS
SINGLE PLY ROOF MEMBRANE
TAPERED RIGID INSULATION
LAM
1/2" [13 MM] PLYWOOD, ALL SEAMS SEALED
2X8 [38X184 MM] ROOF JOISTS WITH BLOWN-
IN FIBERGLASS
5/8" [16 MM] GYPSUM BOARD

WBS

SEAL PLYWOOD TO LVL

WOOD SIDING
1X4 [19X89 MM] HORIZONTAL FURRING
1X4 [19X89 MM] VERTICAL FURRING
3 1/2" [89 MM] MINERAL WOOL
1/2" [13 MM] WBS, ALL SEAMS SEALED
2X6 [38X140 MM] STUDS WITH BLOWN-
IN FIBERGLASS
5/8" [16 MM] GYPSUM BOARD

0   12"

0   300 mm

8.8.10 Main deck guardrail with vertical 2 x 4-in. (51 x 104-mm) framing projecting upward within the insulation layer.

8.8.11 Door to main deck with pedestal pavers under protective cover. HAMMER & HAND

8.8.12 Door to south-side deck from home office. HAMMER & HAND

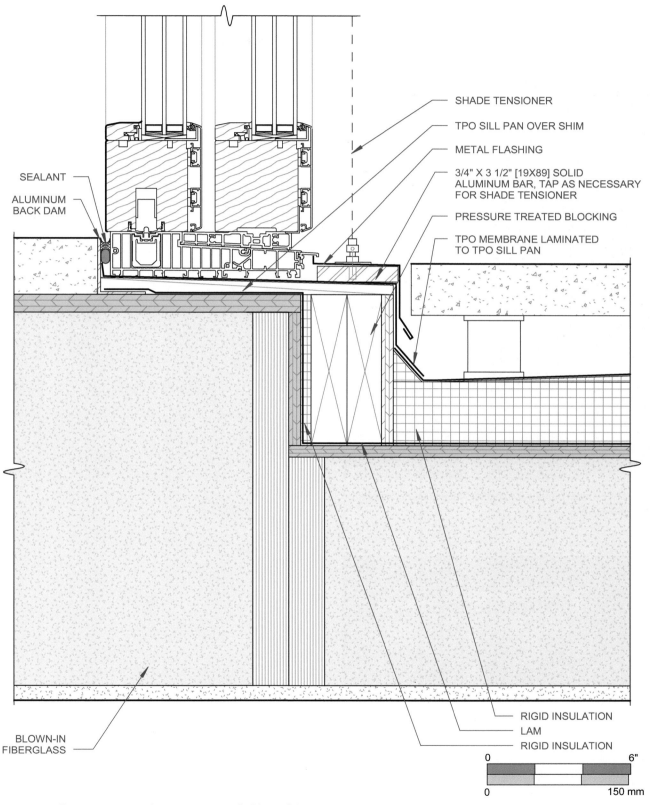

SHADE TENSIONER

TPO SILL PAN OVER SHIM

METAL FLASHING

3/4" X 3 1/2" [19X89] SOLID
ALUMINUM BAR, TAP AS NECESSARY
FOR SHADE TENSIONER

PRESSURE TREATED BLOCKING

TPO MEMBRANE LAMINATED
TO TPO SILL PAN

SEALANT

ALUMINUM
BACK DAM

BLOWN-IN
FIBERGLASS

RIGID INSULATION

LAM

RIGID INSULATION

0 ———————— 6"

0 ———————— 150 mm

8.8.13 Door sill connecting main living space to walkable roof deck.

8.8.14 Sheet metal housing for shading louvers at the door head.
HAMMER & HAND

8.8.15 Main deck door from the interior. HAMMER & HAND

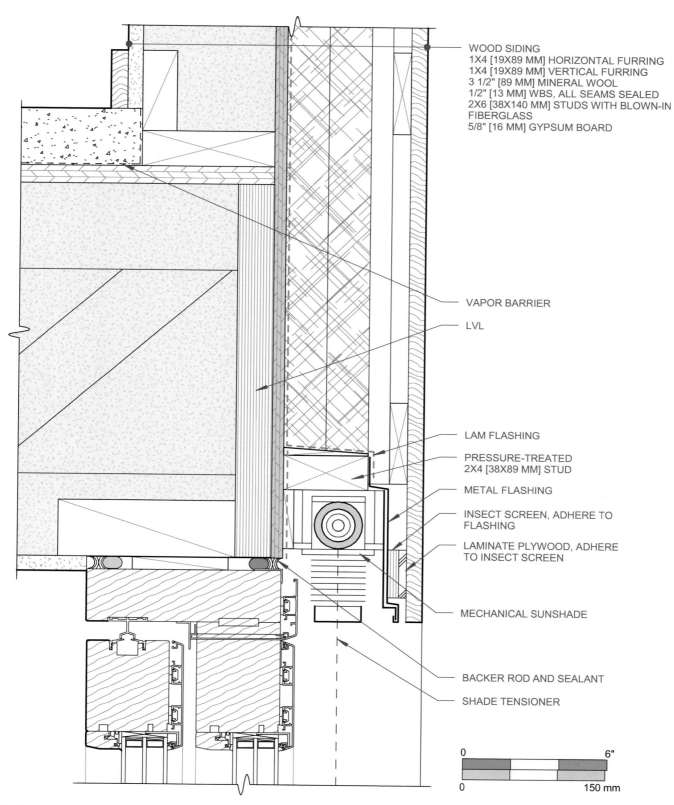

WOOD SIDING
1X4 [19X89 MM] HORIZONTAL FURRING
1X4 [19X89 MM] VERTICAL FURRING
3 1/2" [89 MM] MINERAL WOOL
1/2" [13 MM] WBS, ALL SEAMS SEALED
2X6 [38X140 MM] STUDS WITH BLOWN-IN
FIBERGLASS
5/8" [16 MM] GYPSUM BOARD

VAPOR BARRIER

LVL

LAM FLASHING

PRESSURE-TREATED
2X4 [38X89 MM] STUD

METAL FLASHING

INSECT SCREEN, ADHERE TO
FLASHING

LAMINATE PLYWOOD, ADHERE
TO INSECT SCREEN

MECHANICAL SUNSHADE

BACKER ROD AND SEALANT

SHADE TENSIONER

0   6"

0   150 mm

8.8.16 Door head at main living level with second floor above. Operable shading device tucked into exterior insulation cavity.

8.8.17 Master bedroom view to the southeast. MARK WOODS PHOTOGRAPHY

8.8.18 Corner mullion at living room. HAMMER & HAND

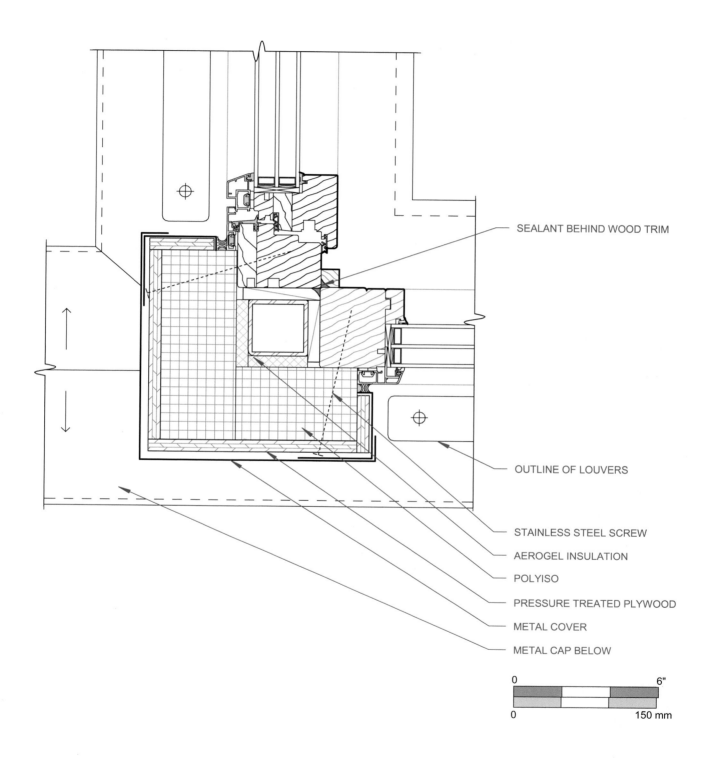

SEALANT BEHIND WOOD TRIM

OUTLINE OF LOUVERS

STAINLESS STEEL SCREW

AEROGEL INSULATION

POLYISO

PRESSURE TREATED PLYWOOD

METAL COVER

METAL CAP BELOW

0   6"

0   150 mm

8.8.19 Abutting windows at corner with over-insulation of the frames on the exterior.

8.9.1 Orchards at Orenco (Hillsboro, Oregon) opened as the largest multifamily passive house building in the United States. It offers fifty-seven apartment units close to retail, restaurants, coffee shops, and grocery stores. CASEY BRAUNGER, ANKROM MOISAN ARCHITECTS, INC.

Orchards at Orenco is a highly efficient, transit-oriented workforce housing project in the Orenco Station neighborhood in Hillsboro, Oregon, for owner/developer REACH Community Development Company. The fifty-seven-unit project, designed by Ankrom Moisan Architects, is the first phase of the Orchards at Orenco development, which, over the course of three phases, will total approximately 150 units. At completion, Orchards was the largest building built to passive house energy standards in North America and one of the first to offer these affordable, sustainable benefits to low-income workers. Tenants will receive unprecedented savings on their energy bills, as compared those of a code-compliant building.

Some key innovative features include: (a) a roof with 12 in. (305 mm) of insulation—that is, approximately quadruple the amount required by code—and a light color that reflects solar radiation and helps moderate the building's temperature; (b) shading devices that allow winter sun but block the sun in the summer; (c) HRVs that use stale air from kitchens and bathrooms (that would otherwise be wasted) to warm fresh, incoming air supplied to bedrooms; (d) PVC–fiberglass hybrid windows throughout that are argon-filled, triple-glazed, and designed to close tighter than most common models; (e) walls with 10-in. (254-mm) stud cavities, compared with 6-in. stud cavities in typical buildings. The building rests on a super-insulated envelope of 4 in. of foam under the ground-floor slab.

The building was completed in June 2015, and the entire team was involved in a comprehensive, integrated design process. Many of the stories and details of the construction process, including successes and challenges encountered, were shared publicly on a blog.

ORCHARDS AT ORENCO

PROJECT INFORMATION

Project title: Orchards at Orenco

Location: Hillsboro, Oregon

Size: 42,584 ft.^{2} (3,956 m^2), fifty-seven units

Completion: 2015

Recognition: Certified (PHIUS)

Type: Multifamily affordable housing

Owner: Reach Community Development, Inc.

Architect: Ankrom Moisan Architects, Inc.

Builder: Walsh Construction Company

CPHC: Dylan Lamar, Green Hammer

HDD: 4,750 base 65°F (2,639 base 18.3°C)

CDD: 280 base 65°F (156 base 18.3°C)

Annual precipitation: 43.5 in. (1,105 mm)

8.9.2 Reinforced concrete footing cast over insulation. WALSH CONSTRUCTION CO.

8.9.3 Brick wainscot support with offset shelf angle.
WALSH CONSTRUCTION CO

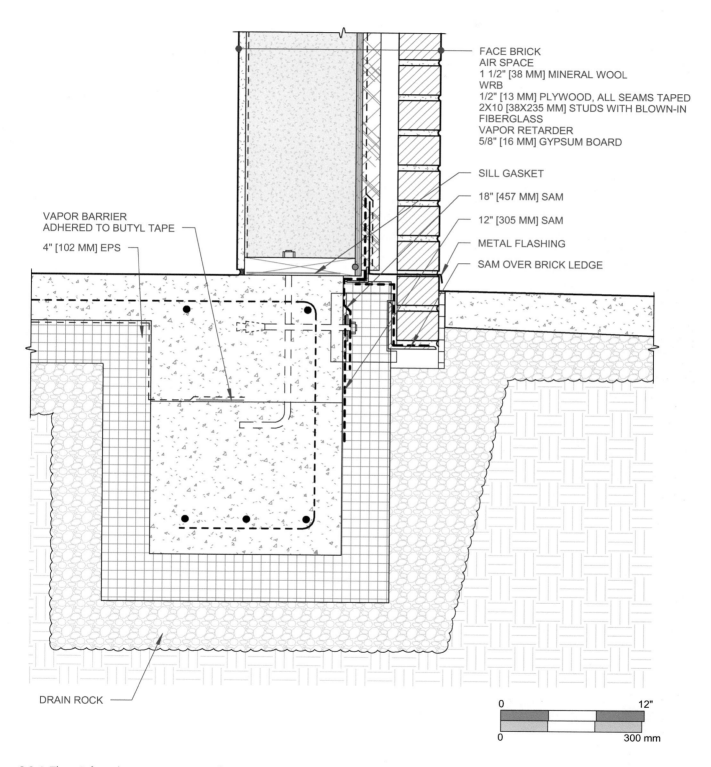

FACE BRICK
AIR SPACE
1 1/2" [38 MM] MINERAL WOOL
WRB
1/2" [13 MM] PLYWOOD, ALL SEAMS TAPED
2X10 [38X235 MM] STUDS WITH BLOWN-IN
FIBERGLASS
VAPOR RETARDER
5/8" [16 MM] GYPSUM BOARD

SILL GASKET

18" [457 MM] SAM

12" [305 MM] SAM

METAL FLASHING

SAM OVER BRICK LEDGE

VAPOR BARRIER
ADHERED TO BUTYL TAPE

4" [102 MM] EPS

DRAIN ROCK

0   12"

0   300 mm

8.9.4 The reinforced concrete perimeter foundation is wrapped with insulation on all sides. An offset steel angle supports the brick wainscot with reduced thermal bridge effects.

8.9.5 Application of fiber cement wall cladding. WALSH CONSTRUCTION CO.

8.9.6 Application of brick veneer with cavity insulation.
WALSH CONSTRUCTION CO.

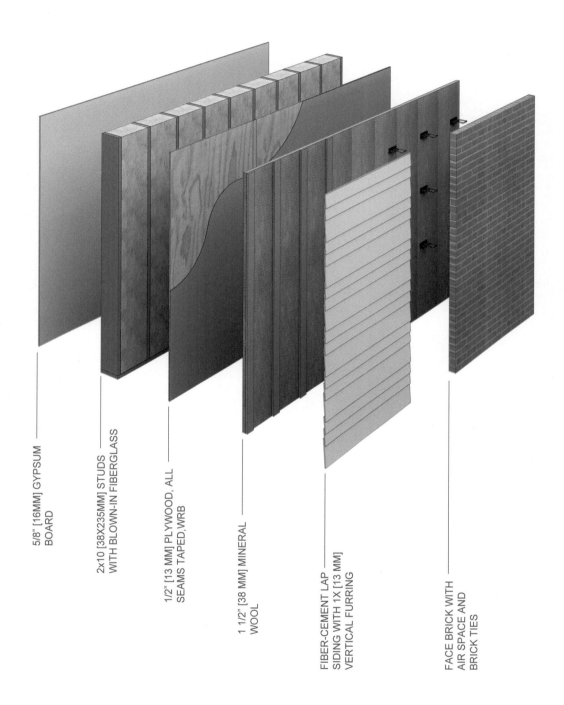

5/8" [16MM] GYPSUM
BOARD

2x10 [38X235MM] STUDS
WITH BLOWN-IN FIBERGLASS

1/2" [13 MM] PLYWOOD, ALL
SEAMS TAPED, WRB

1 1/2" [38 MM] MINERAL
WOOL

FIBER-CEMENT LAP
SIDING WITH 1X [13 MM]
VERTICAL FURRING

FACE BRICK WITH
AIR SPACE AND
BRICK TIES

8.9.7 Wall construction with deep studs and two types of cladding: fiber cement panels and brick veneer.

8.9.8 Overhang and tall parapet expressing thickness of roof assembly. WALSH CONSTRUCTION CO.

8.9.9 Construction of parapet above taped roof sheathing.
WALSH CONSTRUCTION CO.

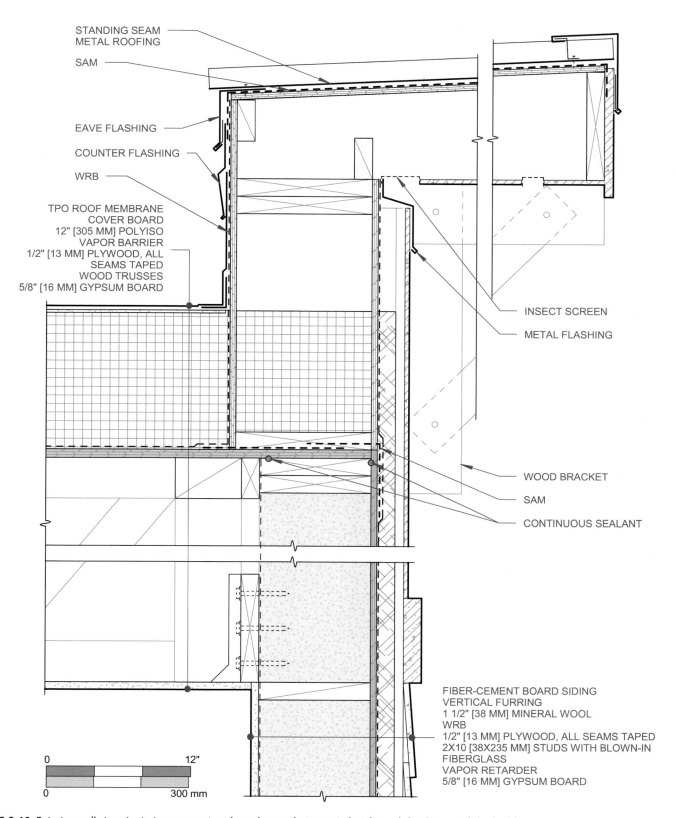

STANDING SEAM
METAL ROOFING

SAM

EAVE FLASHING

COUNTER FLASHING

WRB

TPO ROOF MEMBRANE
COVER BOARD
12" [305 MM] POLYISO
VAPOR BARRIER
1/2" [13 MM] PLYWOOD, ALL
SEAMS TAPED
WOOD TRUSSES
5/8" [16 MM] GYPSUM BOARD

INSECT SCREEN

METAL FLASHING

WOOD BRACKET

SAM

CONTINUOUS SEALANT

FIBER-CEMENT BOARD SIDING
VERTICAL FURRING
1 1/2" [38 MM] MINERAL WOOL
WRB
1/2" [13 MM] PLYWOOD, ALL SEAMS TAPED
2X10 [38X235 MM] STUDS WITH BLOWN-IN
FIBERGLASS
VAPOR RETARDER
5/8" [16 MM] GYPSUM BOARD

0   12"

0   300 mm

8.9.10 Exterior walls terminate in a parapet and overhangs that vary in height and depth around the building.

8.9.11 Preparation of window sill with back dam, sealant, and double shim to support glazing unit and sill flashing.
WALSH CONSTRUCTION CO.

8.9.12 Installed window at brick wainscot prepared for over-insulation at the jambs. WALSH CONSTRUCTION CO.

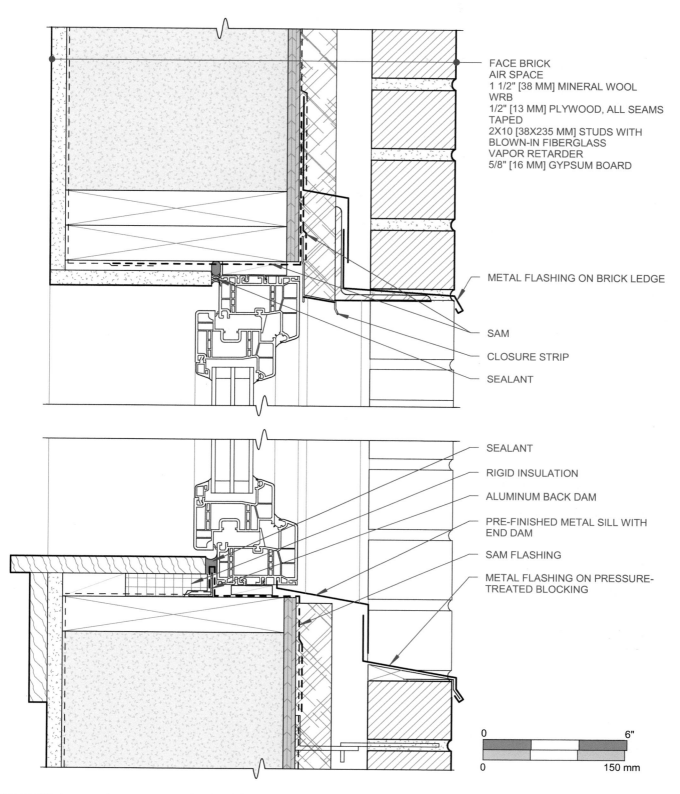

FACE BRICK
AIR SPACE
1 1/2" [38 MM] MINERAL WOOL
WRB
1/2" [13 MM] PLYWOOD, ALL SEAMS
TAPED
2X10 [38X235 MM] STUDS WITH
BLOWN-IN FIBERGLASS
VAPOR RETARDER
5/8" [16 MM] GYPSUM BOARD

METAL FLASHING ON BRICK LEDGE

SAM

CLOSURE STRIP

SEALANT

SEALANT

RIGID INSULATION

ALUMINUM BACK DAM

PRE-FINISHED METAL SILL WITH
END DAM

SAM FLASHING

METAL FLASHING ON PRESSURE-
TREATED BLOCKING

0   6"

0   150 mm

8.9.13 Window openings are protected with a full sill pan and back dam. The space under the window drains freely to the exterior.

8.9.14 Completed cladding prepared for decks and roofs with points of attachment. WALSH CONSTRUCTION CO.

8.9.15 Pressure-treated blocks that are used to attach exterior construction through the cladding and insulation. WALSH CONSTRUCTION CO.

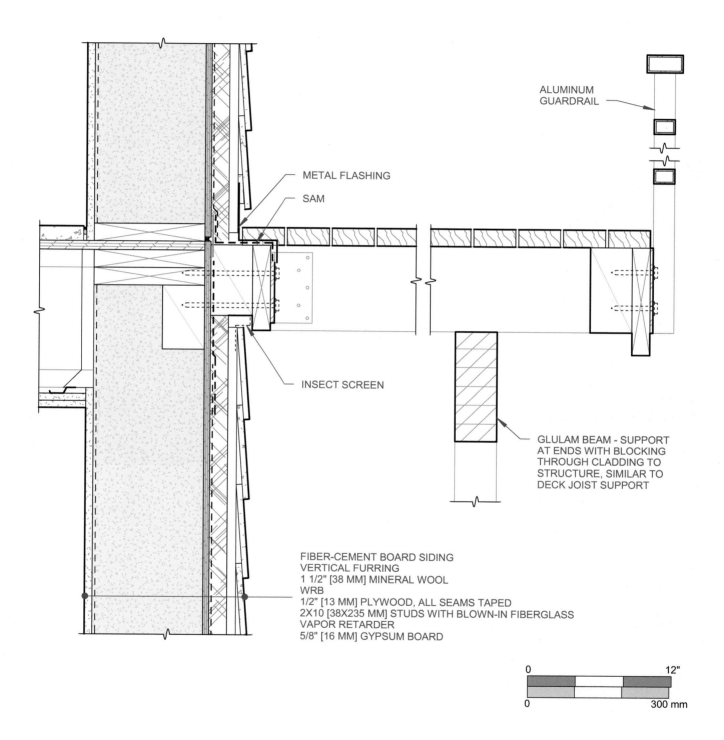

ALUMINUM
GUARDRAIL

METAL FLASHING

SAM

INSECT SCREEN

GLULAM BEAM - SUPPORT
AT ENDS WITH BLOCKING
THROUGH CLADDING TO
STRUCTURE, SIMILAR TO
DECK JOIST SUPPORT

FIBER-CEMENT BOARD SIDING
VERTICAL FURRING
1 1/2" [38 MM] MINERAL WOOL
WRB
1/2" [13 MM] PLYWOOD, ALL SEAMS TAPED
2X10 [38X235 MM] STUDS WITH BLOWN-IN FIBERGLASS
VAPOR RETARDER
5/8" [16 MM] GYPSUM BOARD

0		12"
0		300 mm

8.9.16 Exterior decks are carried by a ledger attached at intervals to the building. A beam under the outside edge is similarly anchored to perpendicular walls.

8.9.17 Overhangs above the windows are aligned with the decks. WALSH CONSTRUCTION CO.

8.9.18 Anchor straps used to develop cantilevered overhangs.
WALSH CONSTRUCTION CO.

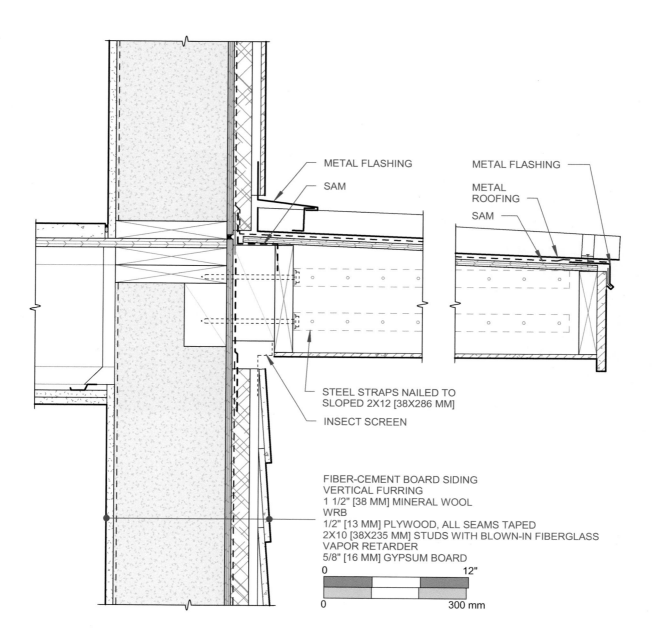

METAL FLASHING

SAM

METAL FLASHING

METAL
ROOFING

SAM

STEEL STRAPS NAILED TO
SLOPED 2X12 [38X286 MM]

INSECT SCREEN

FIBER-CEMENT BOARD SIDING
VERTICAL FURRING
1 1/2" [38 MM] MINERAL WOOL
WRB
1/2" [13 MM] PLYWOOD, ALL SEAMS TAPED
2X10 [38X235 MM] STUDS WITH BLOWN-IN FIBERGLASS
VAPOR RETARDER
5/8" [16 MM] GYPSUM BOARD

0   12"

0   300 mm

8.9.19 Horizontal overhangs above the lower floor windows are developed with cantilevered framing tied back to the structure.

8.10.1 The south side of Prescott Passive House with shaded windows facing the yard. STUDIO 804

Studio 804, who built Prescott Passive House in Kansas City, Kansas, pursued passive house construction to address the current economic situation, where affordability has become a pressing issue in American housing. A focus on passive design strategies, superior envelope construction, and meeting the nascent passive house standard answered the challenge. Affordability was addressed by the targeting of an eventual homeowner earning 80 percent or lower of the area median income. Students worked directly with Community Housing of Wyandotte County and the Prescott Neighborhood Group. A double-height living room connects the main floor with the upper level, where the master bedroom is located. Overlooking the living room and southern array of windows is the flexible loft space. On the main level, the living room is connected to the kitchen and dining spaces, with an exposed concrete thermal mass floor. These living areas are located just off the deck, which also functions as the carport roof. At the west end of the main level are two additional bedrooms, with views to the surrounding double-width lot. Remote-controlled operable skylights create the only break in the northern envelope of the house, and operable glazing stretches the entire length of the southern side to encourage natural ventilation. This façade is protected by louvers optimally angled to allow winter heat gain yet block sunlight from penetrating the house in the summer. Downstairs, a full walkout basement provides ample storage, as well as a finished flex room located directly off the carport. The entire house was framed in engineered lumber. The width of the TJI joists allows for the wall and roof depths needed to enclose the thick cellulose insulation. In addition, the creation of a primary structural system to carry the ridge load through columns to the foundation was accomplished with LVL. This enabled the space to remain open, so that all rooms could be filled with daylight, a principle tenet of the energy-saving concept.

PRESCOTT PASSIVE HOUSE

PROJECT INFORMATION

Project title: Prescott Passive House

Location: Kansas City, Kansas

Size: 1,725 ft.^{2} (160 m^2)

Completion: 2010

Recognition: Certified (PHIUS), LEED Platinum

Type: Single-family house

Architect: Studio 804

Builder: Studio 804

CPHC: Ryan Abenroth

HDD: 5,500 base 65°F (3,056 base 18.3°C)

CDD: 1,288 base 65°F (716 base 18.3°C)

Annual precipitation: 37 in. (938 mm)

8.10.2 Preparing for the basement slab inside ICF walls. STUDIO 804

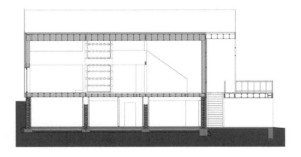

8.10.3 Longitudinal building section looking north.
STUDIO 804

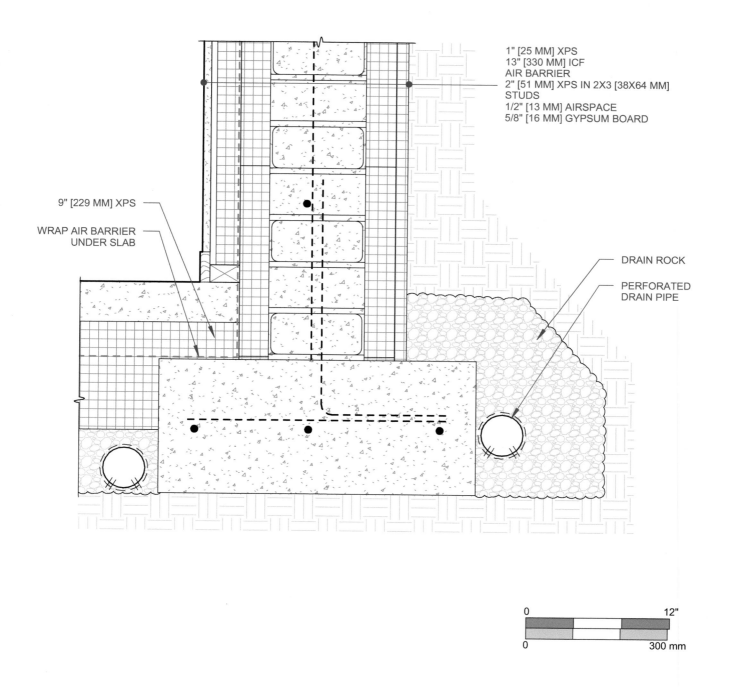

1" [25 MM] XPS
13" [330 MM] ICF
AIR BARRIER
2" [51 MM] XPS IN 2X3 [38X64 MM]
STUDS
1/2" [13 MM] AIRSPACE
5/8" [16 MM] GYPSUM BOARD

9" [229 MM] XPS

WRAP AIR BARRIER
UNDER SLAB

DRAIN ROCK

PERFORATED
DRAIN PIPE

0   12"

0   300 mm

8.10.4 Basement wall constructed with ICF and additional insulation on the interior. Floor slab is cast over bed of rigid insulation.

8.10.5 Main living floor overhangs basement wall.
STUDIO 804

8.10.6 Installing soffit at overhanging floor. STUDIO 804

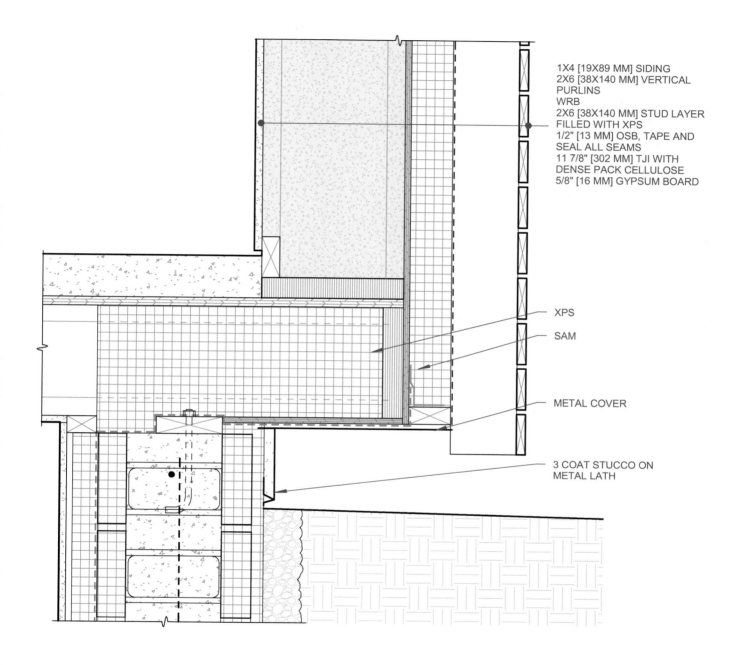

1X4 [19X89 MM] SIDING
2X6 [38X140 MM] VERTICAL
PURLINS
WRB
2X6 [38X140 MM] STUD LAYER
FILLED WITH XPS
1/2" [13 MM] OSB, TAPE AND
SEAL ALL SEAMS
11 7/8" [302 MM] TJI WITH
DENSE PACK CELLULOSE
5/8" [16 MM] GYPSUM BOARD

XPS

SAM

METAL COVER

3 COAT STUCCO ON
METAL LATH

8.10.7 Main floor framed with I-joists cantilevers over the foundation wall.

8.10.8 Inhabited roof volume with supported ridge.
STUDIO 804

8.10.9 Roof framing prepared for insulation. STUDIO 804

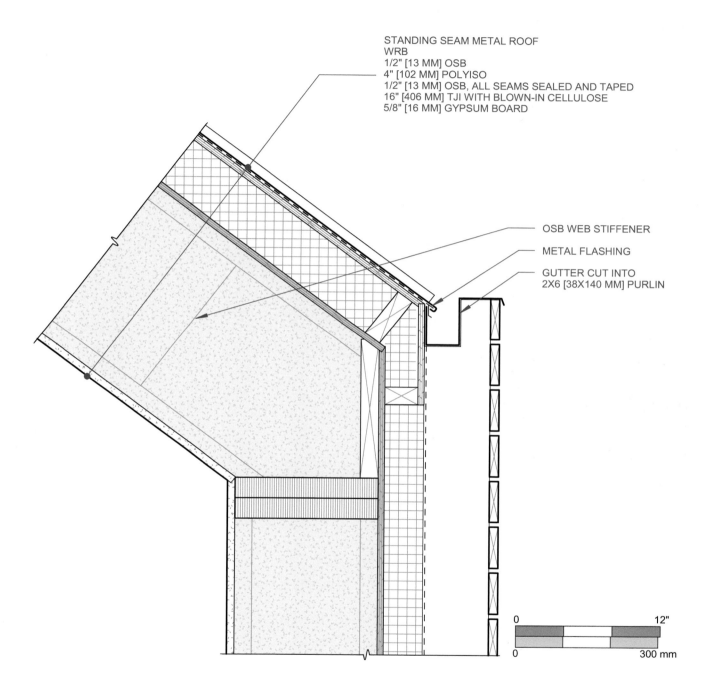

STANDING SEAM METAL ROOF
WRB
1/2" [13 MM] OSB
4" [102 MM] POLYISO
1/2" [13 MM] OSB, ALL SEAMS SEALED AND TAPED
16" [406 MM] TJI WITH BLOWN-IN CELLULOSE
5/8" [16 MM] GYPSUM BOARD

OSB WEB STIFFENER

METAL FLASHING

GUTTER CUT INTO
2X6 [38X140 MM] PURLIN

0   12"

0   300 mm

8.10.10 Roof constructed with deep I-joists and a rigid insulation overlay. Gutter integrated behind rainscreen wall. Wall and roof planes meet with no overhang or eaves.

8.10.11 Living room with shaded south window wall.
STUDIO 804

8.10.12 Window wall prior to installation of louvers.
STUDIO 804

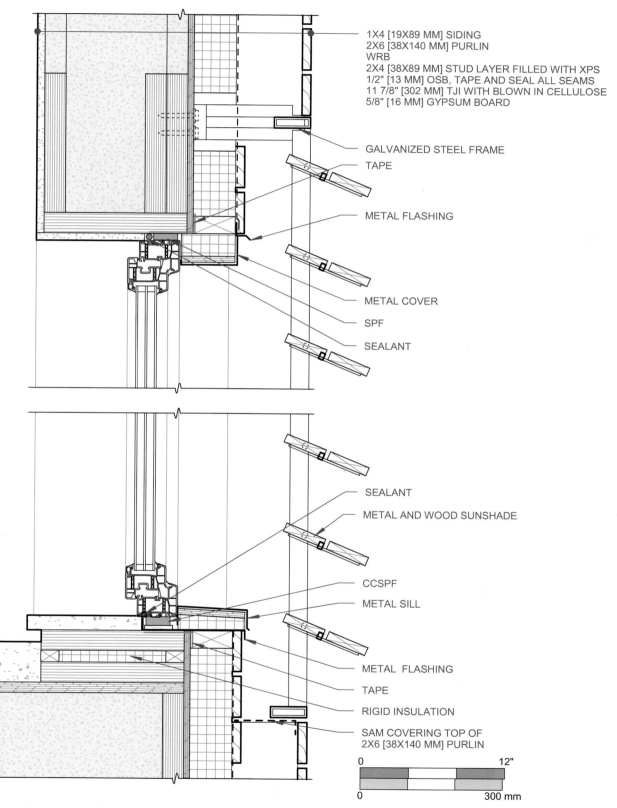

1X4 [19X89 MM] SIDING
2X6 [38X140 MM] PURLIN
WRB
2X4 [38X89 MM] STUD LAYER FILLED WITH XPS
1/2" [13 MM] OSB, TAPE AND SEAL ALL SEAMS
11 7/8" [302 MM] TJI WITH BLOWN IN CELLULOSE
5/8" [16 MM] GYPSUM BOARD

GALVANIZED STEEL FRAME

TAPE

METAL FLASHING

METAL COVER

SPF

SEALANT

SEALANT

METAL AND WOOD SUNSHADE

CCSPF

METAL SILL

METAL FLASHING

TAPE

RIGID INSULATION

SAM COVERING TOP OF
2X6 [38X140 MM] PURLIN

0   12"

0   300 mm

8.10.13 South-facing window wall protected by rotating louvers that are adjustable by season.

8.10.14 East-facing porch and deck at main living level. STUDIO 804

8.10.15 East elevation with detached deck above parking.
STUDIO 804

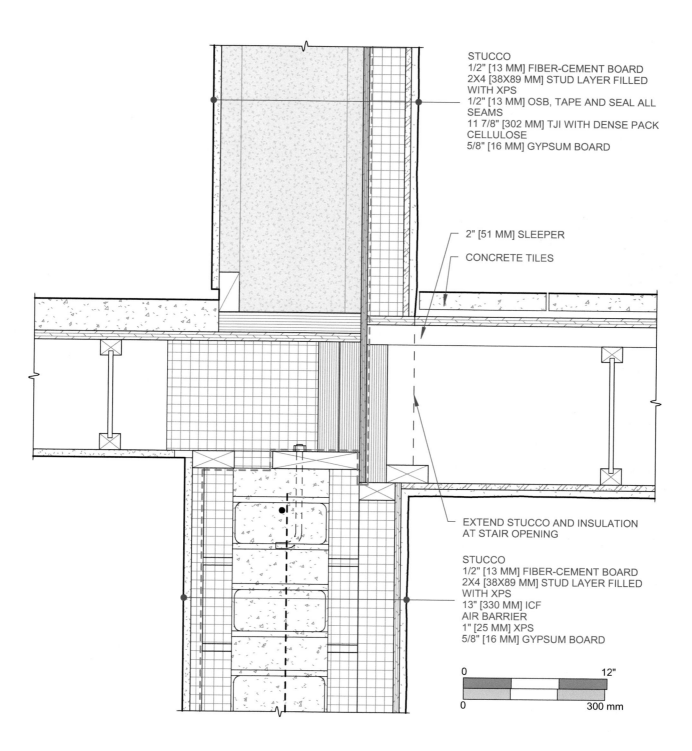

STUCCO
1/2" [13 MM] FIBER-CEMENT BOARD
2X4 [38X89 MM] STUD LAYER FILLED
WITH XPS
1/2" [13 MM] OSB, TAPE AND SEAL ALL
SEAMS
11 7/8" [302 MM] TJI WITH DENSE PACK
CELLULOSE
5/8" [16 MM] GYPSUM BOARD

2" [51 MM] SLEEPER

CONCRETE TILES

EXTEND STUCCO AND INSULATION
AT STAIR OPENING

STUCCO
1/2" [13 MM] FIBER-CEMENT BOARD
2X4 [38X89 MM] STUD LAYER FILLED
WITH XPS
13" [330 MM] ICF
AIR BARRIER
1" [25 MM] XPS
5/8" [16 MM] GYPSUM BOARD

0   12"

0   300 mm

8.10.16 Exterior deck and porch are isolated from the house by a stair opening. Floor bridging to zone of access is shown. STUDIO 804

8.11.1 Prefabricated San Juan Passive House assembled on Shaw Island, Washington. ART GRAY PHOTOGRAPHY

This prefabricated 1,800-ft.² (167-m²) certified passive house is located in the rugged central highlands in the San Juan Islands. It was the first certified project in the San Juans, and the fourth in Washington State. The home was built for $330 per square foot, whereas construction costs for residential projects in the San Juan market often exceed $600 per square foot. The home was largely prefabricated in a Washington facility that was originally intended to be a nuclear power plant. The exterior walls were installed as completed panels. The kitchen, two bathrooms, and most of the mechanicals of the home were preconstructed as a central "pod" and craned into place on site. The home was "weathered in" 17 days after the start of construction. The clients are retired teachers who desired a low-maintenance, cost-effective, energy-efficient house in which they could age in peace; a restful shelter from clutter, stress, and overstimulation. The floor plan centers on the prefabricated pod. Radiating from the pod, cabinetry and a minimum of walls define the functions, with a series of sliding and concealable doors providing flexible privacy to the peripheral spaces. The interior palette consists of windfallen light maple floors, locally made, custom FSC-certified cabinets, low-flow water fixtures, stainless-steel hardware, and all LED lighting. The exterior materials are painted concrete fiberboard lap siding, ipe wood slats, and galvanized metal. The freestanding covered entry sculpture provides a unique focal point for the building without compromising the building envelope. The envelope achieved 0.58 ACH50 in its final test.

SAN JUAN PASSIVE HOUSE

PROJECT INFORMATION

Project title: San Juan Passive House

Location: Shaw Island, Washington

Size: 1,800 ft.² (167 m²)

Completion: 2014

Recognition: Certified (PHIUS)

Type: Single-family home

Architect: Artisans Group

Builder: Artisans Group

CPHC: Tessa Smith, Artisans Group

HDD: 5,541 base 65°F (3,078 base 18.3°C)

CDD: 18 base 65°F (10 base 18.3°C)

Annual precipitation: 46 in. (1,168 mm)

8.11.2 Concrete retaining wall creates crawl space. ARTISANS GROUP

8.11.3 Ventilated wood construction inside perimeter wall.
ARTISANS GROUP

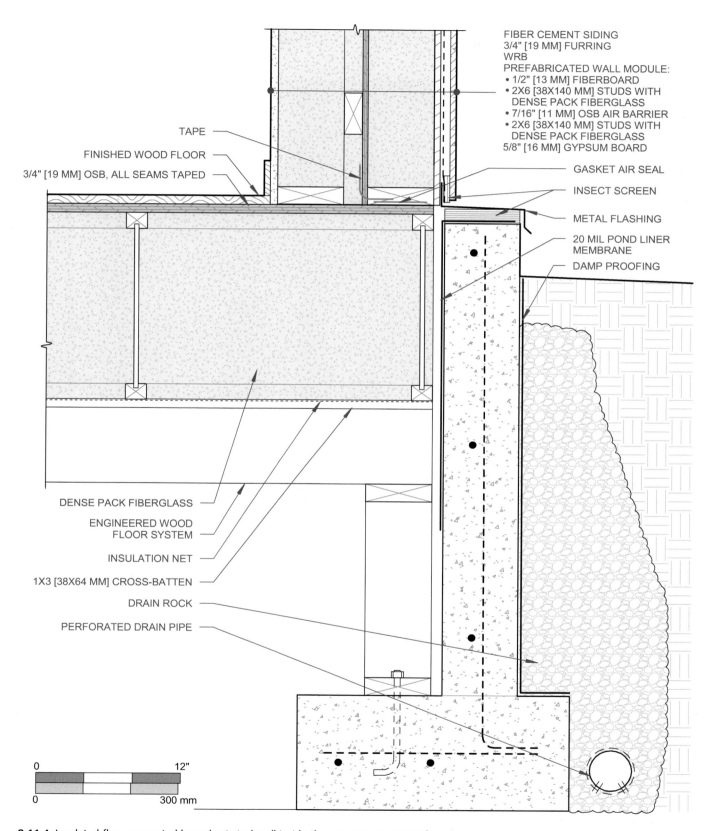

FIBER CEMENT SIDING
3/4" [19 MM] FURRING
WRB
PREFABRICATED WALL MODULE:
• 1/2" [13 MM] FIBERBOARD
• 2X6 [38X140 MM] STUDS WITH
  DENSE PACK FIBERGLASS
• 7/16" [11 MM] OSB AIR BARRIER
• 2X6 [38X140 MM] STUDS WITH
  DENSE PACK FIBERGLASS
5/8" [16 MM] GYPSUM BOARD

TAPE

FINISHED WOOD FLOOR

3/4" [19 MM] OSB, ALL SEAMS TAPED

GASKET AIR SEAL

INSECT SCREEN

METAL FLASHING

20 MIL POND LINER
MEMBRANE

DAMP PROOFING

DENSE PACK FIBERGLASS

ENGINEERED WOOD
FLOOR SYSTEM

INSULATION NET

1X3 [38X64 MM] CROSS-BATTEN

DRAIN ROCK

PERFORATED DRAIN PIPE

0   12"

0   300 mm

8.11.4 Insulated floor supported by a short stud wall inside the concrete perimeter foundation.

8.11.5 Placing the panelized double stud walls. ARTISANS GROUP

8.11.6 Open stud cavity inside the air barrier sheathing.
ARTISANS GROUP

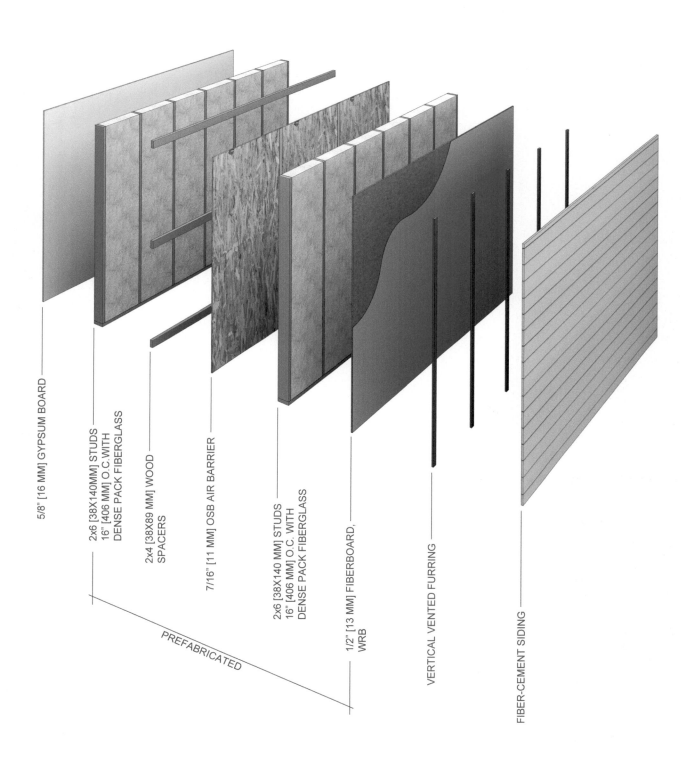

5/8" [16 MM] GYPSUM BOARD

2x6 [38X140MM] STUDS 16" [406 MM] O.C. WITH DENSE PACK FIBERGLASS

2x4 [38X89 MM] WOOD SPACERS

7/16" [11 MM] OSB AIR BARRIER

2x6 [38X140 MM] STUDS 16" [406 MM] O.C. WITH DENSE PACK FIBERGLASS

1/2" [13 MM] FIBERBOARD, WRB

VERTICAL VENTED FURRING

FIBER-CEMENT SIDING

PREFABRICATED

8.11.7 Panelized double stud walls with air barrier sheathing that subdivides the cavity.

8.11.8 Two-way cantilevered roof plate created with trusses. ARTISANS GROUP

8.11.9 Thickened truss chords and outlookers frame the overhangs. ARTISANS GROUP

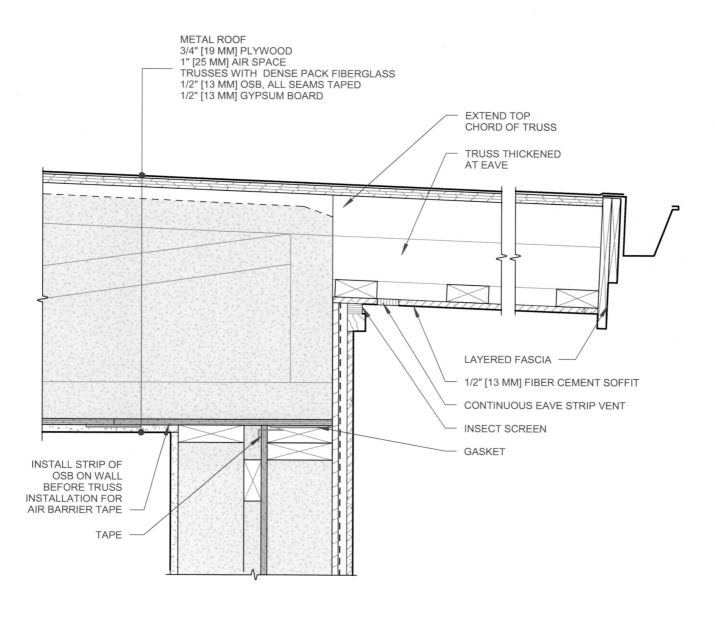

METAL ROOF
3/4" [19 MM] PLYWOOD
1" [25 MM] AIR SPACE
TRUSSES WITH DENSE PACK FIBERGLASS
1/2" [13 MM] OSB, ALL SEAMS TAPED
1/2" [13 MM] GYPSUM BOARD

EXTEND TOP
CHORD OF TRUSS

TRUSS THICKENED
AT EAVE

LAYERED FASCIA

1/2" [13 MM] FIBER CEMENT SOFFIT

CONTINUOUS EAVE STRIP VENT

INSECT SCREEN

GASKET

INSTALL STRIP OF
OSB ON WALL
BEFORE TRUSS
INSTALLATION FOR
AIR BARRIER TAPE

TAPE

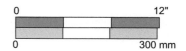

0   12"

0   300 mm

8.11.10 Plywood buck provides mounting surface for window units. Trim and over-insulation at the head and jambs.

8.11.11 Window and door openings in panelized walls. ARTISANS GROUP

8.11.12 Sheet metal flashing pan at window sill. ARTISANS GROUP

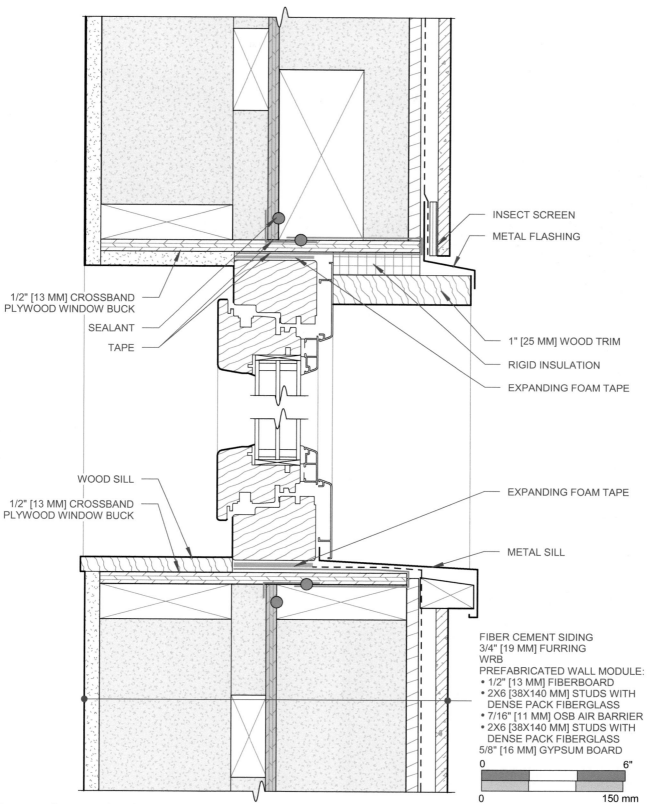

1/2" [13 MM] CROSSBAND
PLYWOOD WINDOW BUCK

SEALANT

TAPE

INSECT SCREEN

METAL FLASHING

1" [25 MM] WOOD TRIM

RIGID INSULATION

EXPANDING FOAM TAPE

WOOD SILL

1/2" [13 MM] CROSSBAND
PLYWOOD WINDOW BUCK

EXPANDING FOAM TAPE

METAL SILL

FIBER CEMENT SIDING
3/4" [19 MM] FURRING
WRB
PREFABRICATED WALL MODULE:
• 1/2" [13 MM] FIBERBOARD
• 2X6 [38X140 MM] STUDS WITH
  DENSE PACK FIBERGLASS
• 7/16" [11 MM] OSB AIR BARRIER
• 2X6 [38X140 MM] STUDS WITH
  DENSE PACK FIBERGLASS
5/8" [16 MM] GYPSUM BOARD

0   6"

0   150 mm

8.11.13 Roof trusses with air barrier sheathing attached to the bottom chord. Overhangs are outside the controlled envelope.

8.11.14 Kitchen counter constructed against central service pod. ART GRAY PHOTOGRAPHY

8.11.15 Service pod installed and covered with a tarp. Flanked by panelized walls. ARTISANS GROUP

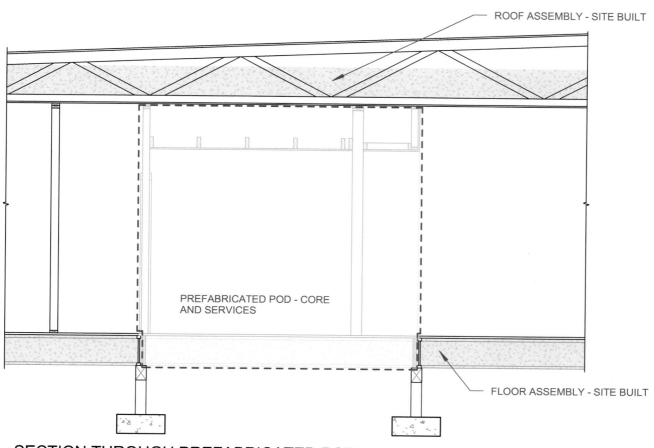

ROOF ASSEMBLY - SITE BUILT

PREFABRICATED POD - CORE AND SERVICES

FLOOR ASSEMBLY - SITE BUILT

SECTION THROUGH PREFABRICATED POD

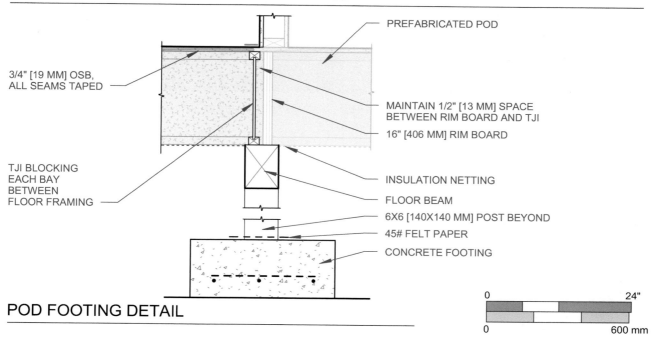

3/4" [19 MM] OSB, ALL SEAMS TAPED

PREFABRICATED POD

MAINTAIN 1/2" [13 MM] SPACE BETWEEN RIM BOARD AND TJI

16" [406 MM] RIM BOARD

TJI BLOCKING EACH BAY BETWEEN FLOOR FRAMING

INSULATION NETTING

FLOOR BEAM

6X6 [140X140 MM] POST BEYOND

45# FELT PAPER

CONCRETE FOOTING

POD FOOTING DETAIL

0   24"

0   600 mm

8.11.16 Prefabricated kitchen and bathroom pod supported on floor beams at the center of the house.

8.12.1 Seen from the northwest, the living areas follow the ridge. BRIGGSKNOWLES ARCHITECTURE+DESIGN

The Saugerties Residence is strategically sited on a wooded lot in the Hudson River Valley of New York. The project combines passive house design with the efficiency and innovation of CNC-cut and factory-produced wall and ceiling panels. BriggsKnowles Architecture+Design collaborated with Bensonwood to develop an energy-efficient, high-performance wood frame. Through an innovative parametric design and analysis process the panels accommodated the curved walls and the complex, compound roof pitches needed to realize this contemporary design. The striking three-bedroom, two-and-a-half-bath house reimagines the traditional home, with its own unique curvilinear aesthetic, open space plan, and multilevel views. The first-floor plan includes a living area with a wood stove and screened porch, a separate kitchen and dining area, two bedrooms, one-and-a-half baths, a mechanical room, and a polished concrete floor. The dining area and one of the bedrooms are built into the curvature of the outer-wall design, creating interesting interior spaces and angled wall partitions. The second floor has a generous, curved main suite complete with a large walk-in closet, sauna, sustainable wool carpet, balcony, and dramatic, cantilevered porch. The second floor also has a large playroom, open at one end to the living area below. The house was constructed during the winter, and Bensonwood built the panels of the shell in the shop and transported them for assembly by the on-site builder. The house uses R-49 roof panels and R-35 wall panels that were prepared for Zola triple-glazed windows. On site, additional layers of insulation were added to the exterior to bring the house up to passive house performance levels.

SAUGERTIES RESIDENCE

PROJECT INFORMATION

Project title: Saugerties Residence

Location: Saugerties, New York

Size: 2,148 ft.^{2} (200 m^2) treated floor area

Completion: 2015

Recognition: Certified (PHIUS)

Type: Single-family home

Architect: BriggsKnowles Architecture+Design

Builder: Bensonwood and John Hommel, Ashley Homes, Inc.

CPHC: Jonathan Knowles

HDD: 6,212 base 65°F (3,451 base 18.3°C)

CDD: 678 base 65°F (377 base 18.3°C)

Annual precipitation: 46 in. (1,168 mm)

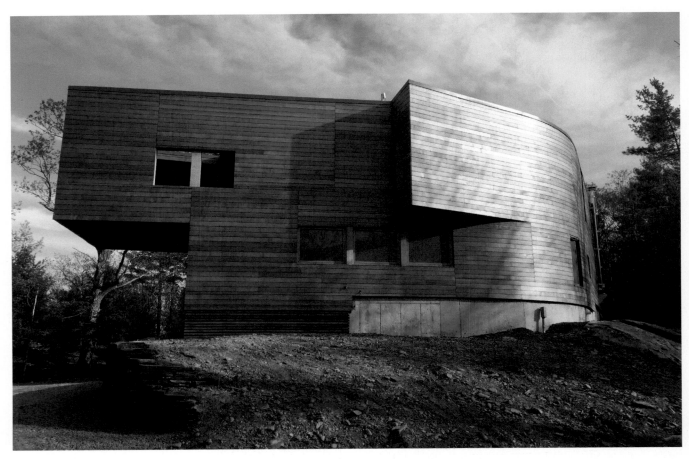

8.12.2 The foundation bears directly on the rock ledge. BRIGGSKNOWLES ARCHITECTURE+DESIGN

8.12.3 The rock ledge is cleared for construction.
BRIGGSKNOWLES ARCHITECTURE+DESIGN

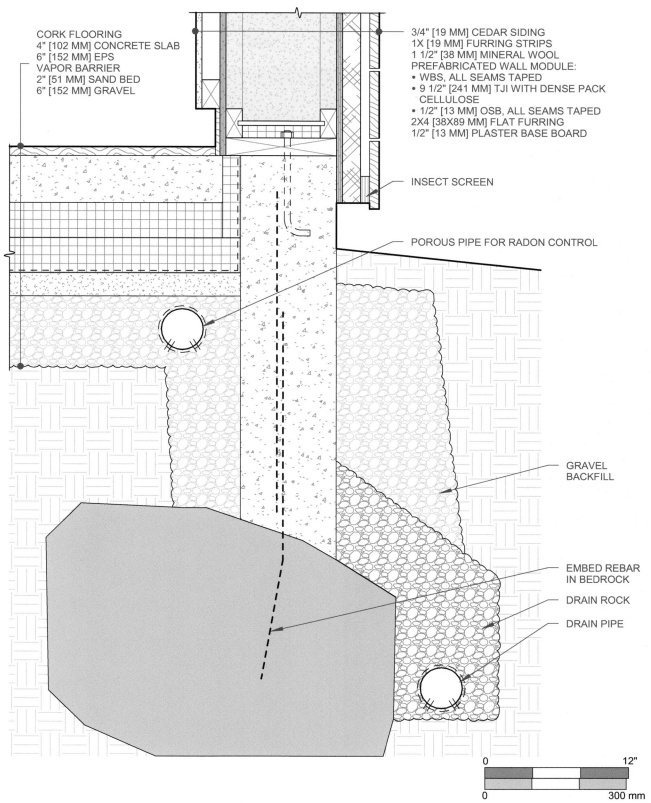

CORK FLOORING
4" [102 MM] CONCRETE SLAB
6" [152 MM] EPS
VAPOR BARRIER
2" [51 MM] SAND BED
6" [152 MM] GRAVEL

3/4" [19 MM] CEDAR SIDING
1X [19 MM] FURRING STRIPS
1 1/2" [38 MM] MINERAL WOOL
PREFABRICATED WALL MODULE:
• WBS, ALL SEAMS TAPED
• 9 1/2" [241 MM] TJI WITH DENSE PACK
  CELLULOSE
• 1/2" [13 MM] OSB, ALL SEAMS TAPED
2X4 [38X89 MM] FLAT FURRING
1/2" [13 MM] PLASTER BASE BOARD

INSECT SCREEN

POROUS PIPE FOR RADON CONTROL

GRAVEL
BACKFILL

EMBED REBAR
IN BEDROCK

DRAIN ROCK

DRAIN PIPE

0 _____ 12"

0 _____ 300 mm

8.12.4 Concrete stem wall dowelled directly to rock ledge. Interior floor slab cast over rigid insulation.

8.12.5 Placement of a panelized wall component. BRIGGSKNOWLES ARCHITECTURE+DESIGN

8.12.6 Wall going up. Looking into the living room from the ridge. BRIGGSKNOWLES ARCHITECTURE+DESIGN

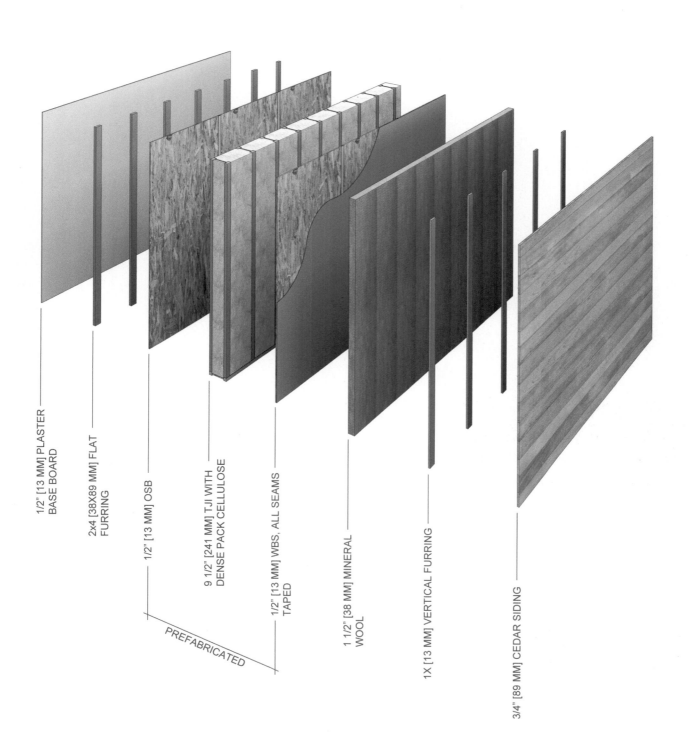

1/2" [13 MM] PLASTER BASE BOARD

2x4 [38X89 MM] FLAT FURRING

1/2" [13 MM] OSB

9 1/2" [241 MM] TJI WITH DENSE PACK CELLULOSE

1/2" [13 MM] WBS, ALL SEAMS TAPED

PREFABRICATED

1 1/2" [38 MM] MINERAL WOOL

1X [13 MM] VERTICAL FURRING

3/4" [89 MM] CEDAR SIDING

8.12.7 Panelized wall assembly composed of I-joists and sheathing. Interior service cavity and exterior insulation added on site.

8.12.8 Prefabricated curved wall segment craned into position.
BRIGGSKNOWLES ARCHITECTURE+DESIGN

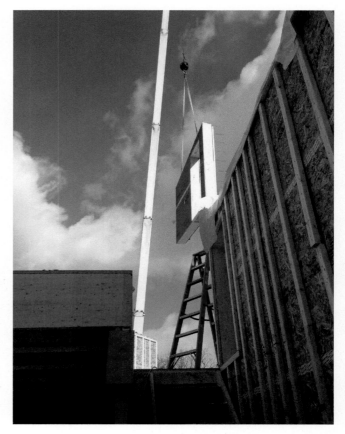

8.12.9 Wall panel with window opening lowered into place.
BRIGGSKNOWLES ARCHITECTURE+DESIGN

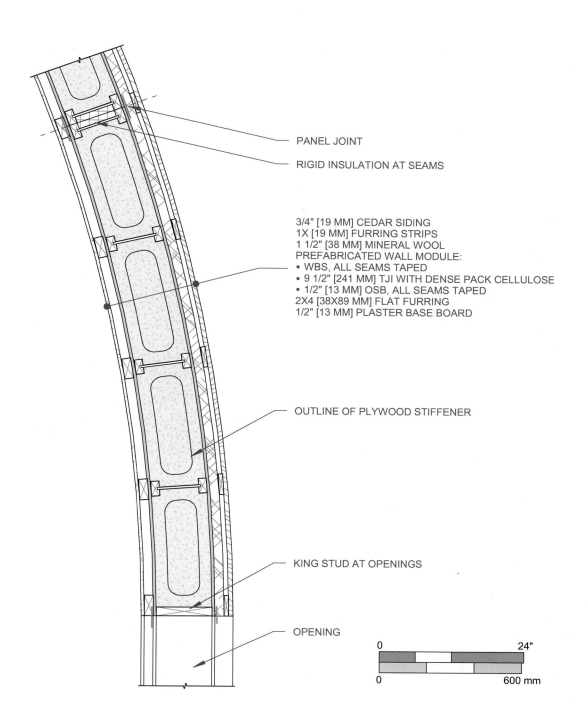

PANEL JOINT

RIGID INSULATION AT SEAMS

3/4" [19 MM] CEDAR SIDING
1X [19 MM] FURRING STRIPS
1 1/2" [38 MM] MINERAL WOOL
PREFABRICATED WALL MODULE:
• WBS, ALL SEAMS TAPED
• 9 1/2" [241 MM] TJI WITH DENSE PACK CELLULOSE
• 1/2" [13 MM] OSB, ALL SEAMS TAPED
2X4 [38X89 MM] FLAT FURRING
1/2" [13 MM] PLASTER BASE BOARD

OUTLINE OF PLYWOOD STIFFENER

KING STUD AT OPENINGS

OPENING

| 0 | | 24" |
| 0 | | 600 mm |

8.12.10 Curved wall segment formed in shop with custom-cut bridging and two layers of sheathing to retain the shape.

8.12.11 Placement of a prefabricated roof panel. BRIGGSKNOWLES ARCHITECTURE+DESIGN

8.12.12 Interior volume looking toward the living room.
BRIGGSKNOWLES ARCHITECTURE+DESIGN

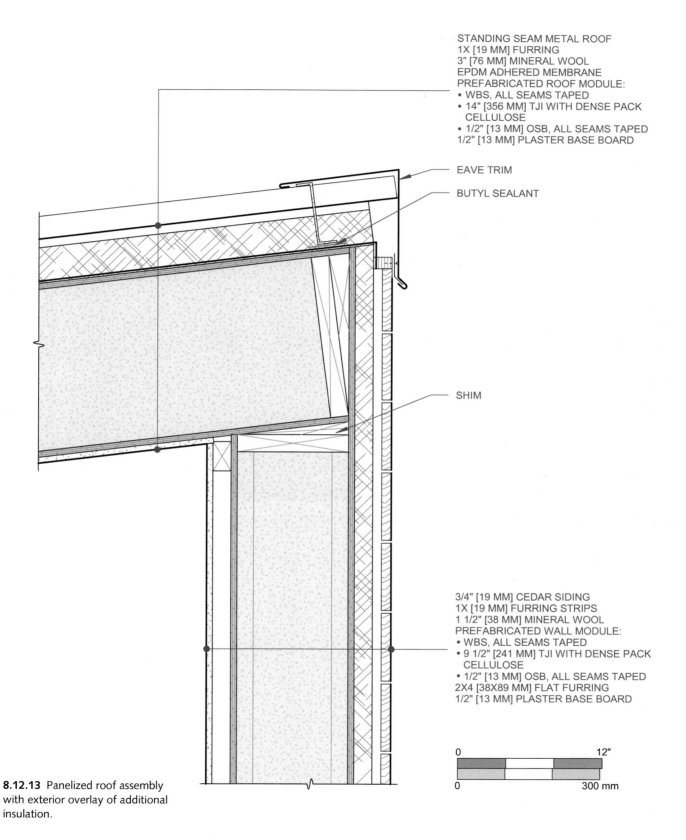

STANDING SEAM METAL ROOF
1X [19 MM] FURRING
3" [76 MM] MINERAL WOOL
EPDM ADHERED MEMBRANE
PREFABRICATED ROOF MODULE:
• WBS, ALL SEAMS TAPED
• 14" [356 MM] TJI WITH DENSE PACK
  CELLULOSE
• 1/2" [13 MM] OSB, ALL SEAMS TAPED
1/2" [13 MM] PLASTER BASE BOARD

EAVE TRIM

BUTYL SEALANT

SHIM

3/4" [19 MM] CEDAR SIDING
1X [19 MM] FURRING STRIPS
1 1/2" [38 MM] MINERAL WOOL
PREFABRICATED WALL MODULE:
• WBS, ALL SEAMS TAPED
• 9 1/2" [241 MM] TJI WITH DENSE PACK
  CELLULOSE
• 1/2" [13 MM] OSB, ALL SEAMS TAPED
2X4 [38X89 MM] FLAT FURRING
1/2" [13 MM] PLASTER BASE BOARD

0   12"

0   300 mm

8.12.13 Panelized roof assembly
with exterior overlay of additional
insulation.

8.12.14 Living-room windows and entry sequence. BRIGGSKNOWLES ARCHITECTURE+DESIGN

8.12.15 Framed window opening in side wall panel.
BRIGGSKNOWLES ARCHITECTURE+DESIGN

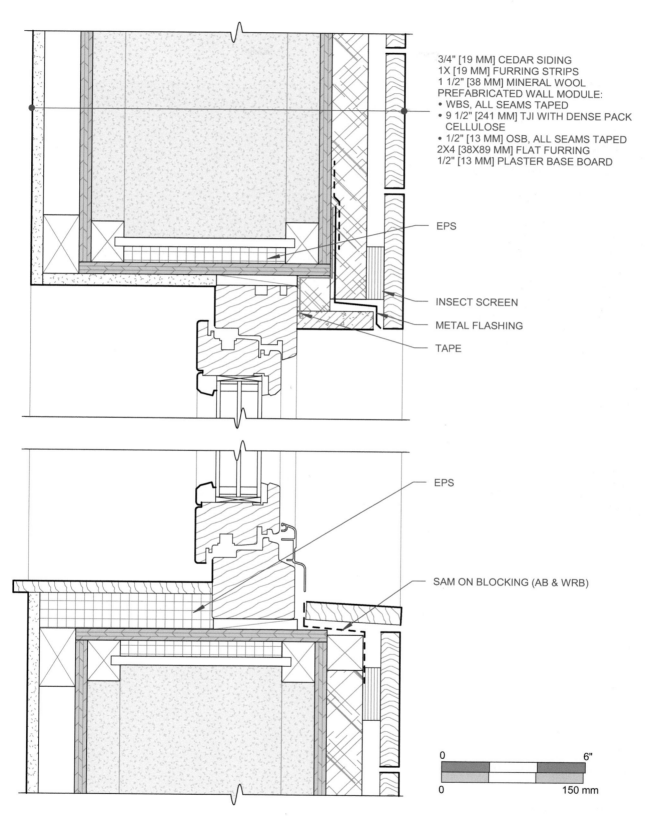

3/4" [19 MM] CEDAR SIDING
1X [19 MM] FURRING STRIPS
1 1/2" [38 MM] MINERAL WOOL
PREFABRICATED WALL MODULE:
• WBS, ALL SEAMS TAPED
• 9 1/2" [241 MM] TJI WITH DENSE PACK
  CELLULOSE
• 1/2" [13 MM] OSB, ALL SEAMS TAPED
2X4 [38X89 MM] FLAT FURRING
1/2" [13 MM] PLASTER BASE BOARD

EPS

INSECT SCREEN

METAL FLASHING

TAPE

EPS

SAM ON BLOCKING (AB & WRB)

0   6"

0   150 mm

8.12.16 Window units fastened to a plywood buck. Exterior surround flush with rainscreen wall.

8.12.17 Side wall cantilevers support outdoor deck over parking. BRIGGSKNOWLES ARCHITECTURE+DESIGN

8.12.18 View through open end of cantilevered deck.
BRIGGSKNOWLES ARCHITECTURE+DESIGN

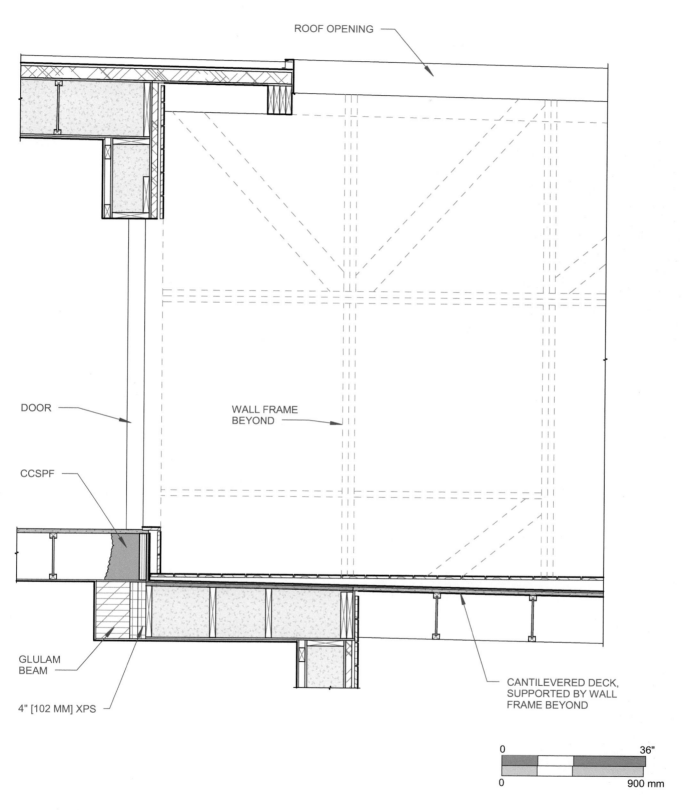

ROOF OPENING

DOOR

WALL FRAME
BEYOND

CCSPF

GLULAM
BEAM

4" [102 MM] XPS

CANTILEVERED DECK,
SUPPORTED BY WALL
FRAME BEYOND

0   36"

0   900 mm

8.12.19 Truss framing in side walls supports cantilevered deck. Floor framing and deck framing run parallel, inside and out.

8.13.1 South façade facing onto Fifth Avenue. KENT SUHRBIER, FORTYEIGHTY ARCHITECTURE

Designed and developed by FortyEighty Architecture and Action Housing, the Uptown Lofts on Fifth offer twenty-four units of transitional housing for youth who have aged out of foster care. The first floor combines common tenant spaces with offices for program coordinators. The Pennsylvania Housing Finance Authority mandated energy conservation and green building criteria for this project including: meeting Energy Star® Certified Homes (3.0) and reaching envelope U-values that exceed the 2009 IECC requirements by 10 percent. The design/development team concurrently constructed a low-income apartment building across the street, meeting the same energy targets. Both buildings are being monitored so that the payback period for this type of innovative construction can be established.

A rainscreen cladding assembly is utilized to articulate the building façades while allowing the airtight building enclosure to remain uncomplicated. The cement board cladding is supported by thermally broken brackets and rails of varying depths. The masonry veneer anchors are thermally broken, with thermal-isolation joints where structural steel extends through the building enclosure.

The dew point is moved outside of the structural cavity by the application of foam board insulation outboard of the spray-applied weather resistant barrier and roof sheathing. Batt insulation fills the advanced wood framing, further reducing the thermal transmittance. There is continuous foundation insulation, under slabs, columns, and elevator bases. The windows are insulated, thermally broken fiberglass frames, with triple-glazed (suspended film), argon-filled glazing. Careful detailing ensures airtight, thermally isolated enclosure at grade transitions, roof lines, wall openings, and soffits.

Space-conditioning energy is minimized, and occupant comfort is maximized, by the VRF system, with heat recovery and branch circuit controllers. Programmable thermostats are available to each tenant, with the fresh

UPTOWN LOFTS ON FIFTH

PROJECT INFORMATION

Project title: Uptown Lofts on Fifth

Location: Pittsburgh, Pennsylvania

Size: 29,672 ft.^{2} (2,757 m^2); 24 units

Completion: 2015

Recognition: Certified (PHIUS+); Honor Award, Pittsburgh Chapter, American Institute of Architects; Innovation in Design Award, Pennsylvania Housing Finance Agency

Type: Multifamily housing

Architect: FortyEighty Architecture

Builder: Mosites Construction

CPHC: Kaplan Thompson Architects, Morgan Law

HDD: 5,624 base 65°F (3,124 base 18.3°C)

CDD: 751 base 65°F (417 base 18.3°C)

Annual precipitation: 37 in. (940 mm)

air delivered to each unit independent of the operable windows. Exhaust air streams are routed through energy recovery units on each floor.

The project demonstrates the viability and benefits of passive house design for affordable, mid-rise, multifamily construction. In a neighborhood fighting to recover from years of neglect, the success and vibrancy of this project reflect and raise aspirations.

8.13.2 Construction of the foundation and planter. FORTYEIGHTY ARCHITECTURE & MOSITES CONSTRUCTION

8.13.3 Foundation conditions along Fifth Avenue.
KENT SUHRBIER, FORTYEIGHTY ARCHITECTURE

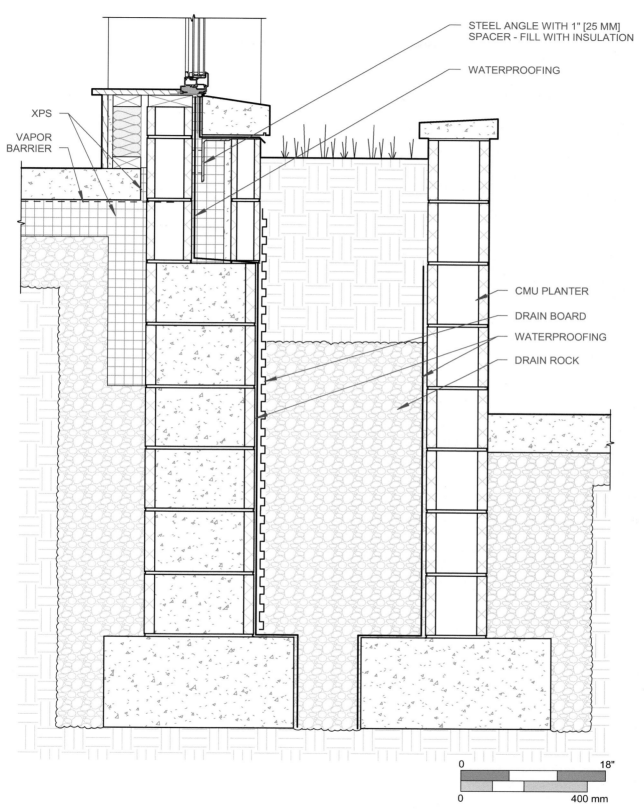

STEEL ANGLE WITH 1" [25 MM]
SPACER - FILL WITH INSULATION

WATERPROOFING

XPS

VAPOR
BARRIER

CMU PLANTER

DRAIN BOARD

WATERPROOFING

DRAIN ROCK

0   18"

0   400 mm

8.13.4 Foundation under recessed window wall at the street façade. Planter at sidewalk edge.

8.13.5 Finished soffit detail at the west end. KENT SUHRBIER, FORTYEIGHTY ARCHITECTURE

8.13.6 Construction of recessed wall and soffit at south side. FORTYEIGHTY ARCHITECTURE & MOSITES CONSTRUCTION

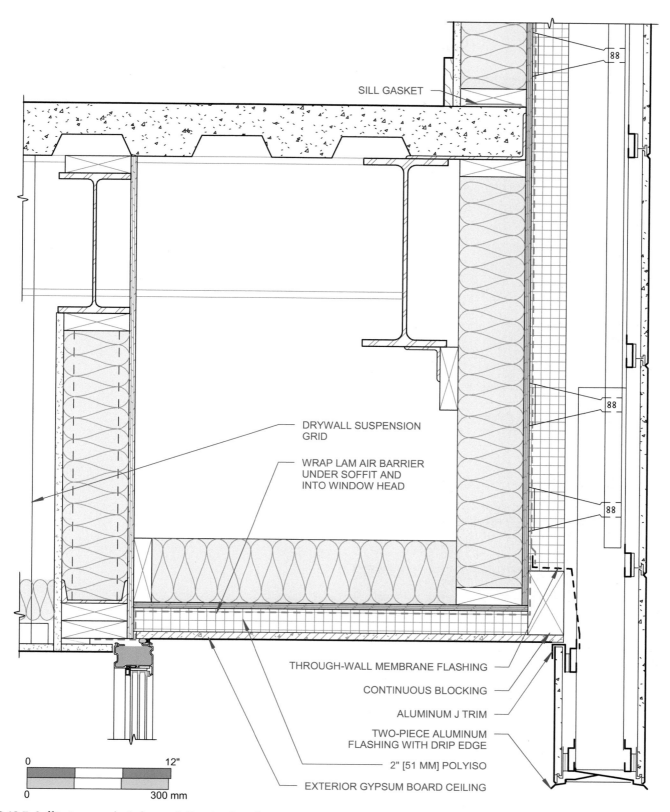

SILL GASKET

88

DRYWALL SUSPENSION
GRID

WRAP LAM AIR BARRIER
UNDER SOFFIT AND
INTO WINDOW HEAD

88

88

THROUGH-WALL MEMBRANE FLASHING

CONTINUOUS BLOCKING

ALUMINUM J TRIM

TWO-PIECE ALUMINUM
FLASHING WITH DRIP EDGE

2" [51 MM] POLYISO

EXTERIOR GYPSUM BOARD CEILING

0   12"

0   300 mm

8.13.7 Soffit at recessed window wall. Termination of rainscreen cladding from floors above.

8.13.8 Continuous sheet metal eave passes over a variety of wall types. KENT SUHRBIER, FORTYEIGHTY ARCHITECTURE

8.13.9 Framing of the roof parapet and overhang.
FORTYEIGHTY ARCHITECTURE & MOSITES CONSTRUCTION

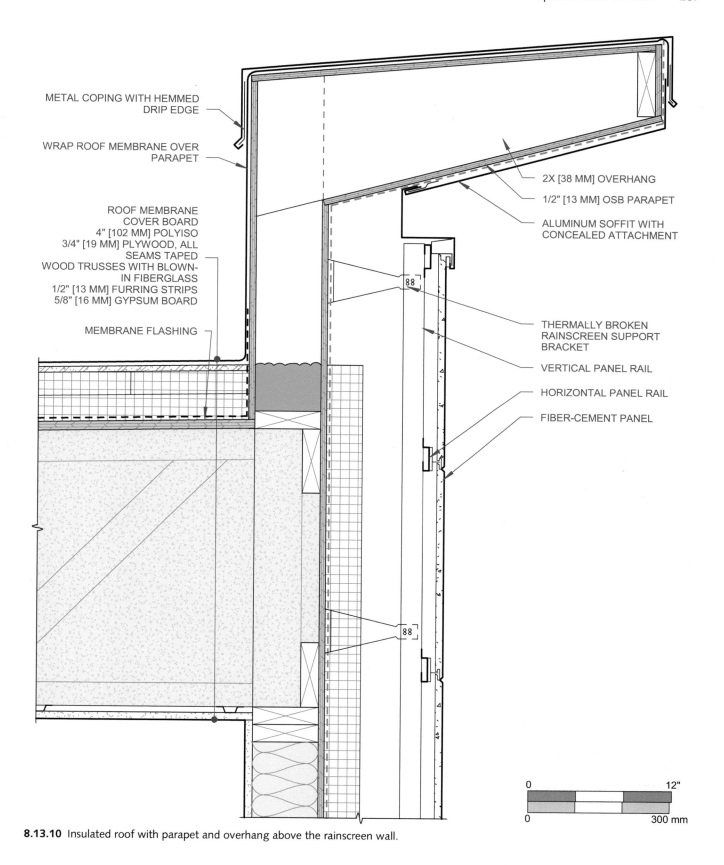

METAL COPING WITH HEMMED
DRIP EDGE

WRAP ROOF MEMBRANE OVER
PARAPET

ROOF MEMBRANE
COVER BOARD
4" [102 MM] POLYISO
3/4" [19 MM] PLYWOOD, ALL
SEAMS TAPED
WOOD TRUSSES WITH BLOWN-
IN FIBERGLASS
1/2" [13 MM] FURRING STRIPS
5/8" [16 MM] GYPSUM BOARD

MEMBRANE FLASHING

2X [38 MM] OVERHANG

1/2" [13 MM] OSB PARAPET

ALUMINUM SOFFIT WITH
CONCEALED ATTACHMENT

88

THERMALLY BROKEN
RAINSCREEN SUPPORT
BRACKET

VERTICAL PANEL RAIL

HORIZONTAL PANEL RAIL

FIBER-CEMENT PANEL

88

0   12"

0   300 mm

8.13.10 Insulated roof with parapet and overhang above the rainscreen wall.

8.13.11 Window surrounds at rainscreen wall. FORTYEIGHTY ARCHITECTURE & MOSITES CONSTRUCTION

8.13.12 Rails for attachment of rainscreen panels. FORTYEIGHTY ARCHITECTURE & MOSITES CONSTRUCTION

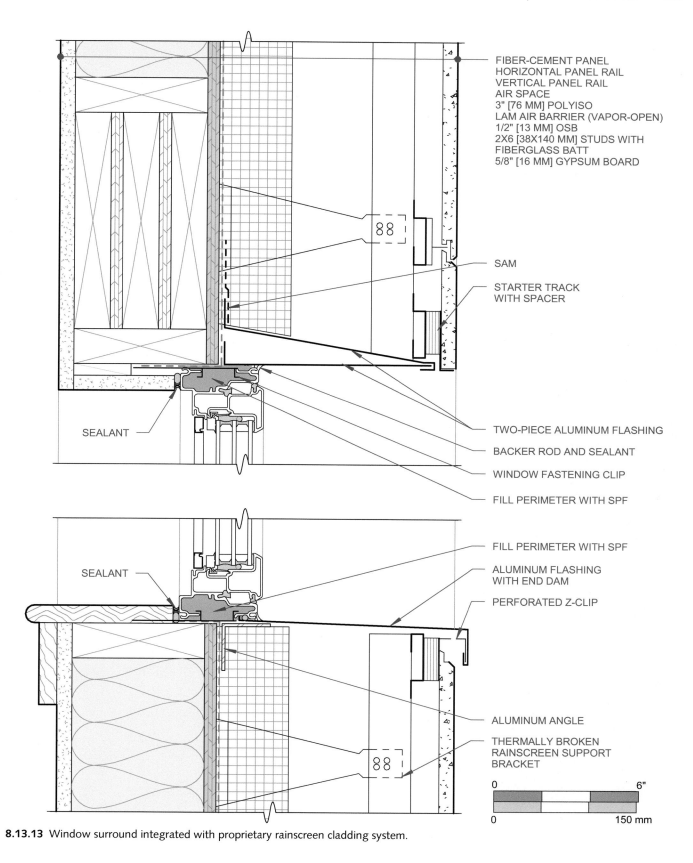

FIBER-CEMENT PANEL
HORIZONTAL PANEL RAIL
VERTICAL PANEL RAIL
AIR SPACE
3" [76 MM] POLYISO
LAM AIR BARRIER (VAPOR-OPEN)
1/2" [13 MM] OSB
2X6 [38X140 MM] STUDS WITH
FIBERGLASS BATT
5/8" [16 MM] GYPSUM BOARD

SAM

STARTER TRACK
WITH SPACER

SEALANT

TWO-PIECE ALUMINUM FLASHING

BACKER ROD AND SEALANT

WINDOW FASTENING CLIP

FILL PERIMETER WITH SPF

FILL PERIMETER WITH SPF

ALUMINUM FLASHING
WITH END DAM

PERFORATED Z-CLIP

SEALANT

ALUMINUM ANGLE

THERMALLY BROKEN
RAINSCREEN SUPPORT
BRACKET

0   6"
0   150 mm

8.13.13 Window surround integrated with proprietary rainscreen cladding system.

8.13.14 Window openings at masonry veneer.
FORTYEIGHTY ARCHITECTURE & MOSITES CONSTRUCTION

8.13.15 Placement of the masonry veneer.
FORTYEIGHTY ARCHITECTURE & MOSITES CONSTRUCTION

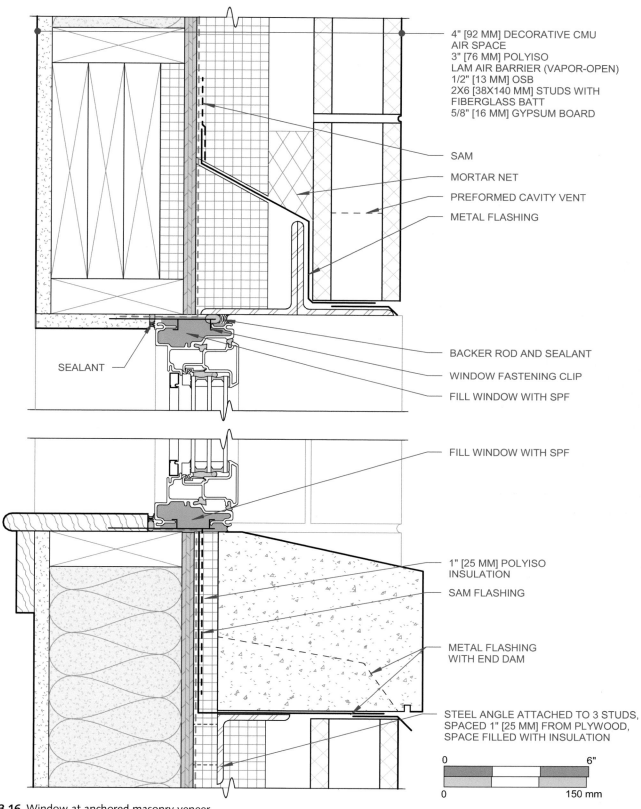

4" [92 MM] DECORATIVE CMU
AIR SPACE
3" [76 MM] POLYISO
LAM AIR BARRIER (VAPOR-OPEN)
1/2" [13 MM] OSB
2X6 [38X140 MM] STUDS WITH
FIBERGLASS BATT
5/8" [16 MM] GYPSUM BOARD

SAM

MORTAR NET

PREFORMED CAVITY VENT

METAL FLASHING

SEALANT

BACKER ROD AND SEALANT

WINDOW FASTENING CLIP

FILL WINDOW WITH SPF

FILL WINDOW WITH SPF

1" [25 MM] POLYISO
INSULATION

SAM FLASHING

METAL FLASHING
WITH END DAM

STEEL ANGLE ATTACHED TO 3 STUDS,
SPACED 1" [25 MM] FROM PLYWOOD,
SPACE FILLED WITH INSULATION

0   6"

0   150 mm

8.13.16 Window at anchored masonry veneer.

8.14.1 View of the approach from the parking to the southeast. TRENT BELL PHOTOGRAPHY

The Viridescent Building in Falmouth, Maine, is located on one corner of a much larger, eco-friendly commercial campus operated by TideSmart Global. The structure replaces a house in an area rezoned for commercial activities. Materials from the house were salvaged and donated to Maine Building Materials Exchange, a non-profit in Lisbon. The new building was intentionally designed to be flexible as either a house or as an office building, so that, with a few modifications, the building could revert to a home at some point in the future. Viridescent is the first net positive, certified passive house building in the state of Maine. It is expected to produce twice the amount of energy required to meet its needs. In planning for the future, the strategies include: radiant heat, a 19.4-kW photovoltaic array, low-flush toilets, 100 percent LED lighting, and non-toxic finished materials and products. Locally sourced FSC oak flooring is finished with vinegar and steel wool or Black Magic and Polywhey. There are electric car charging stations in the parking lot, available to visitors and the public free of charge.

The building has a concrete slab foundation for thermal mass. The insulation was fabricated offsite, dramatically reducing waste. Elements were cut from Type IX EPS polystyrene based on the architect's CAD files and were assembled in place and became the formwork for the slab. The walls were constructed with a vapor-open over-framing system. The walls were first constructed as traditional stud walls with Zip System sheathing. The sheathing serves as both the primary air sealing layer and the vapor control layer. Wood I-joists are fastened on the outside vertically and wrapped with Homasote and a water-resistive barrier that act as the building's secondary air control layer. A ventilated rainscreen cladding system completes the exterior. Airtightness of 0.54 ACH50 was verified by blower door testing. There is an extensive monitoring system to provide the owner and design team with real-time and historic data on energy usage.

VIRIDESCENT BUILDING

PROJECT INFORMATION

Project title: Viridescent Building

Location: Falmouth, Maine

Size: 1,470 ft.² (137 m²)

Completion: 2015

Recognition: Pre-certified (PHIUS)

Type: Commercial office

Architect: BRIBURN, Inc.

Builder: R&G Bilodeau Carpentry and Electrical

CPHC: Edward Pais

HDD: 7,082 base 65°F (3,934 base 18.3°C)

CDD: 365 base 65°F (203 base 18.3°C)

Annual precipitation: 47.33 in. (1,202 mm)

8.14.2 Perimeter foam blocks used to form the slab on grade. BRIBURN LLC

8.14.3 Slab reinforcement at the edge band. BRIBURN LLC

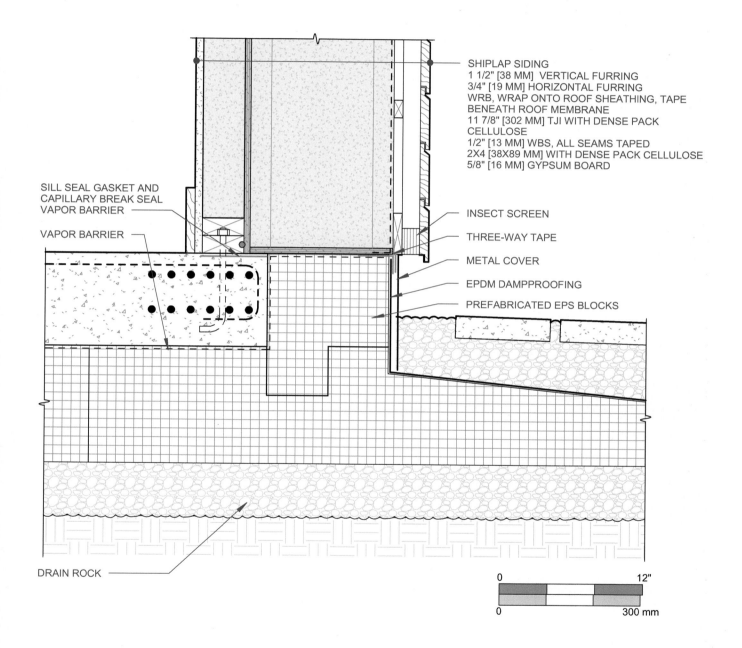

SHIPLAP SIDING
1 1/2" [38 MM] VERTICAL FURRING
3/4" [19 MM] HORIZONTAL FURRING
WRB, WRAP ONTO ROOF SHEATHING, TAPE
BENEATH ROOF MEMBRANE
11 7/8" [302 MM] TJI WITH DENSE PACK
CELLULOSE
1/2" [13 MM] WBS, ALL SEAMS TAPED
2X4 [38X89 MM] WITH DENSE PACK CELLULOSE
5/8" [16 MM] GYPSUM BOARD

INSECT SCREEN

THREE-WAY TAPE

METAL COVER

EPDM DAMPPROOFING

PREFABRICATED EPS BLOCKS

SILL SEAL GASKET AND
CAPILLARY BREAK SEAL
VAPOR BARRIER

VAPOR BARRIER

DRAIN ROCK

0   12"

0   300 mm

8.14.4 Reinforced concrete slab foundation cast over insulation that extends beyond the building footprint.

8.14.5 Overhangs generated by top chord of roof trusses. BRIBURN LLC

8.14.6 Finished eaves and soffit. BRIBURN LLC

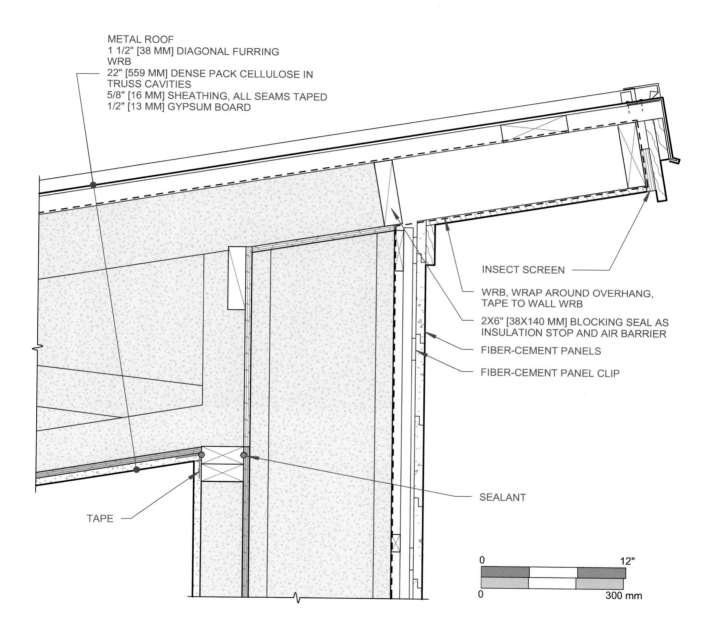

METAL ROOF
1 1/2" [38 MM] DIAGONAL FURRING
WRB
22" [559 MM] DENSE PACK CELLULOSE IN
TRUSS CAVITIES
5/8" [16 MM] SHEATHING, ALL SEAMS TAPED
1/2" [13 MM] GYPSUM BOARD

INSECT SCREEN

WRB, WRAP AROUND OVERHANG,
TAPE TO WALL WRB

2X6" [38X140 MM] BLOCKING SEAL AS
INSULATION STOP AND AIR BARRIER

FIBER-CEMENT PANELS

FIBER-CEMENT PANEL CLIP

SEALANT

TAPE

0 ———— 12"
0 ———— 300 mm

8.14.7 Deep truss roof at north elevation. Air barrier attached to lower chord. Roof overhang outside the control boundary.

8.14.8 Framing of the double cantilever at roof corner. BRIBURN LLC

8.14.9 Preparing for perpendicular roof framing at corner.
BRIBURN LLC

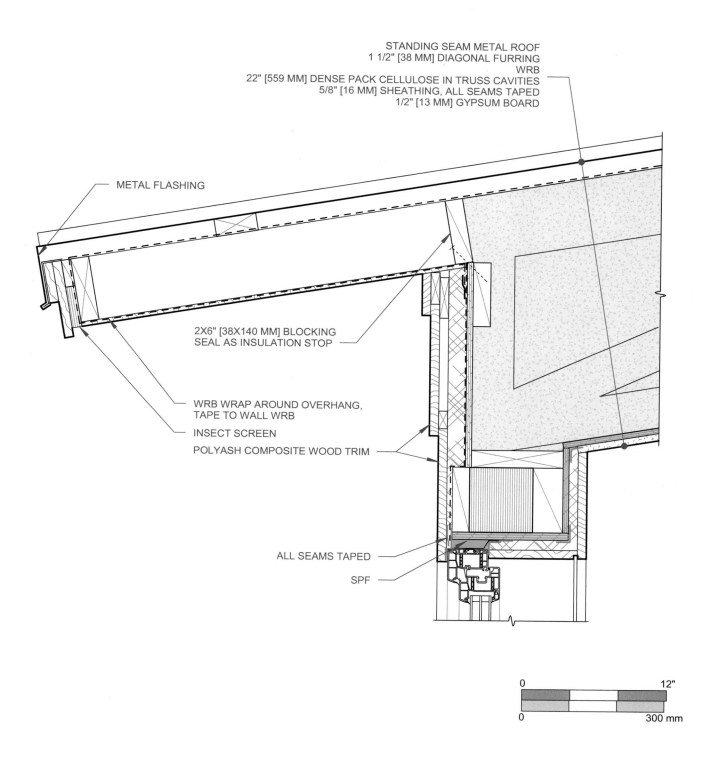

STANDING SEAM METAL ROOF
1 1/2" [38 MM] DIAGONAL FURRING
WRB
22" [559 MM] DENSE PACK CELLULOSE IN TRUSS CAVITIES
5/8" [16 MM] SHEATHING, ALL SEAMS TAPED
1/2" [13 MM] GYPSUM BOARD

METAL FLASHING

2X6" [38X140 MM] BLOCKING
SEAL AS INSULATION STOP

WRB WRAP AROUND OVERHANG,
TAPE TO WALL WRB

INSECT SCREEN

POLYASH COMPOSITE WOOD TRIM

ALL SEAMS TAPED

SPF

0   12"
0   300 mm

8.14.10 Overhang and eaves at south elevation. Roof trusses supported directly above window head.

8.14.11 Entry vestibule in one-story element at the left. BRIBURN LLC

8.14.12 Framing of the porch and entry vestibule.
BRIBURN LLC

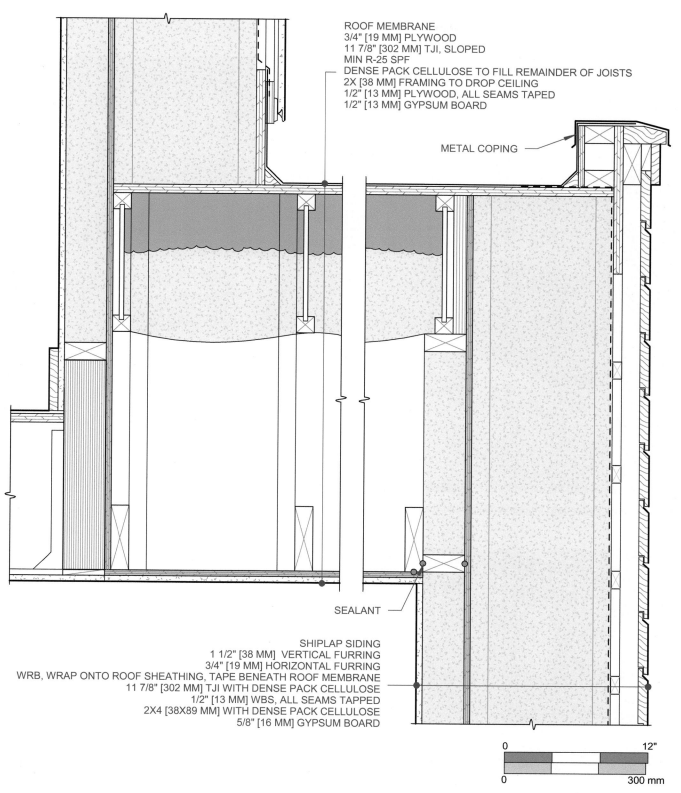

ROOF MEMBRANE
3/4" [19 MM] PLYWOOD
11 7/8" [302 MM] TJI, SLOPED
MIN R-25 SPF
DENSE PACK CELLULOSE TO FILL REMAINDER OF JOISTS
2X [38 MM] FRAMING TO DROP CEILING
1/2" [13 MM] PLYWOOD, ALL SEAMS TAPED
1/2" [13 MM] GYPSUM BOARD

METAL COPING

SEALANT

SHIPLAP SIDING
1 1/2" [38 MM] VERTICAL FURRING
3/4" [19 MM] HORIZONTAL FURRING
WRB, WRAP ONTO ROOF SHEATHING, TAPE BENEATH ROOF MEMBRANE
11 7/8" [302 MM] TJI WITH DENSE PACK CELLULOSE
1/2" [13 MM] WBS, ALL SEAMS TAPPED
2X4 [38X89 MM] WITH DENSE PACK CELLULOSE
5/8" [16 MM] GYPSUM BOARD

0   12"

0   300 mm

8.14.13 Flat roof at entry vestibule. Air barrier follows suspended ceiling.

8.14.14 South façade with typical punched windows at the left. BRIBURN LLC

8.14.15 Installation of a window in the rainscreen wall.
BRIBURN LLC

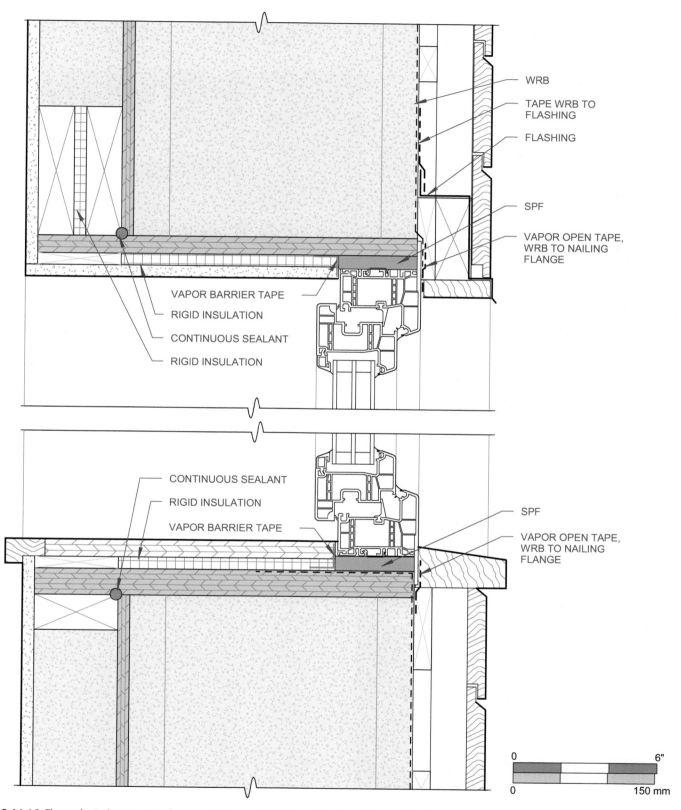

WRB

TAPE WRB TO
FLASHING

FLASHING

SPF

VAPOR OPEN TAPE,
WRB TO NAILING
FLANGE

VAPOR BARRIER TAPE

RIGID INSULATION

CONTINUOUS SEALANT

RIGID INSULATION

CONTINUOUS SEALANT

RIGID INSULATION

VAPOR BARRIER TAPE

SPF

VAPOR OPEN TAPE,
WRB TO NAILING
FLANGE

0   6"

0   150 mm

8.14.16 Flanged window mounted to outside face of I-joist over-framing. Plywood buck.

8.14.17 Curtain wall openings at southeast corner. BRIBURN LLC

8.14.18 Structural mullions and curtain wall from the interior.
BRIBURN LLC

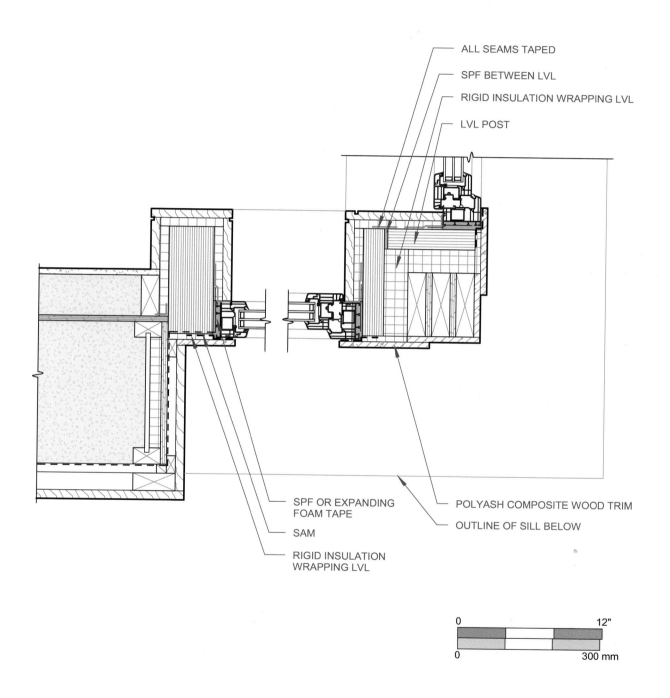

ALL SEAMS TAPED

SPF BETWEEN LVL

RIGID INSULATION WRAPPING LVL

LVL POST

SPF OR EXPANDING
FOAM TAPE

SAM

RIGID INSULATION
WRAPPING LVL

POLYASH COMPOSITE WOOD TRIM

OUTLINE OF SILL BELOW

0   12"

0   300 mm

8.14.19 Wall terminus and corner mullion at glazed curtain wall. Insulation surrounds the LVL mullions.

APPENDIX A

Abbreviations and Graphic Symbols Used in Detail Drawings

Table A.1 Legend for Selected Materials Used in the Construction Detail Drawings

CCSPF	Closed-cell spray foam insulation
CMU	Concrete masonry unit
EPS	Expanded polystyrene insulation
ICF	Insulated concrete form
LAM	Liquid-applied membrane
LVL	Laminated veneer lumber
OCSPF	Open-cell spray foam insulation
SAM	Self-adhered membrane
SIP	Structural insulated panel
T&G	Tongue and groove
TPO	Thermoplastic polyolefin
XPS	Extruded polystyrene insulation
WBS	Water-barrier sheathing
WRB	Water-resistive barrier

SHEATHING / CLADDING

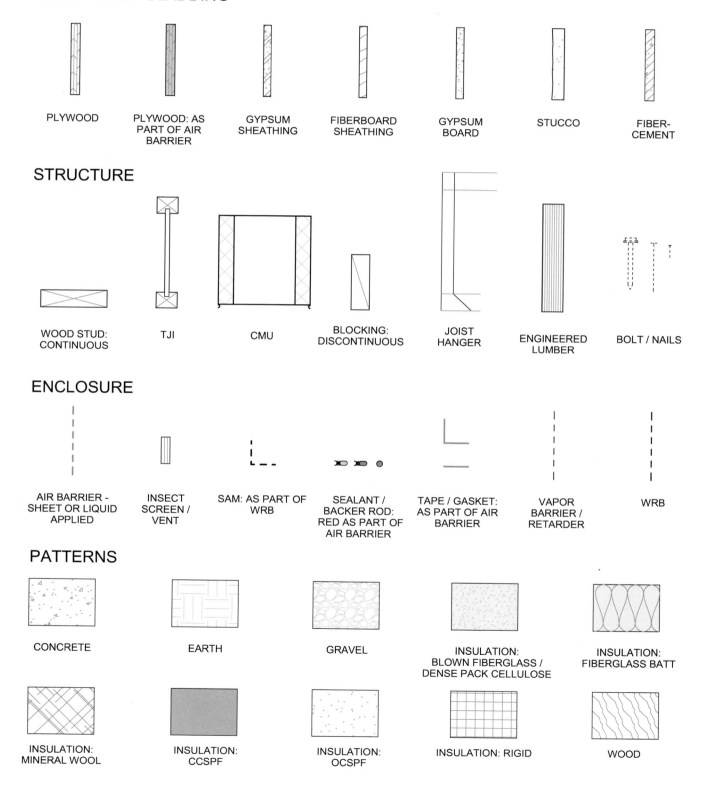

PLYWOOD

PLYWOOD: AS PART OF AIR BARRIER

GYPSUM SHEATHING

FIBERBOARD SHEATHING

GYPSUM BOARD

STUCCO

FIBER-CEMENT

STRUCTURE

WOOD STUD: CONTINUOUS

TJI

CMU

BLOCKING: DISCONTINUOUS

JOIST HANGER

ENGINEERED LUMBER

BOLT / NAILS

ENCLOSURE

AIR BARRIER - SHEET OR LIQUID APPLIED

INSECT SCREEN / VENT

SAM: AS PART OF WRB

SEALANT / BACKER ROD: RED AS PART OF AIR BARRIER

TAPE / GASKET: AS PART OF AIR BARRIER

VAPOR BARRIER / RETARDER

WRB

PATTERNS

CONCRETE

EARTH

GRAVEL

INSULATION: BLOWN FIBERGLASS / DENSE PACK CELLULOSE

INSULATION: FIBERGLASS BATT

INSULATION: MINERAL WOOL

INSULATION: CCSPF

INSULATION: OCSPF

INSULATION: RIGID

WOOD

Project Information

The details described in this this book are listed here, with their location and primary design architect, builder, and certified passive house consultant.

Table B.1 Project Information

Project Name	Location	Architect	Builder	CPHC
Ankeny Row Net Zero Community*	Portland, Oregon	Daryl Rantis and Dylan Lamar	Green Hammer	Dylan Lamar
Arlington House	Arlington, Virginia	Kaplan Thompson Architects	Metro Green, LLC	Jesse Thompson, Kaplan Thompson Architects
Balance Project	Santa Fe, New Mexico	Jonah Stanford, NEEDBASED Inc.	Buck Construction	Jonah Stanford, NEEDBASED Inc.
Bayside Anchor	Portland, Maine	Kaplan Thompson Architects	Wright-Ryan Construction	Kaplan Thompson Architects, Jesse Thompson
CH2	Portland, Oregon	Robert Hawthorne, PDX Living, LLC	PDX Living, LLC	PDX Living, LLC
Cowhorn Vineyard House*	Jacksonville, Oregon	Jan Fillinger	Green Hammer	Dylan Lamar
Earthship Farmstead*	Stuart, Virginia	Kaplan Thompson Architects	Structures Design Build	Jesse Thompson, Kaplan Thompson Architects
Empowerhouse*	Washington, D.C.	Parsons The New School for Design, Milano School of International Affairs, Management and Urban Policy at The New School, and Stevens Institute of Technology for the 2011 Decathlon house	Habitat for Humanity	Laura Briggs
Fineline House	Ashland, Oregon	Jan Fillinger	Green Hammer	Alex Boetzel
Freeman House	Freeman, Maine	BriggsKnowles Architecture+Design	Sebastian Tooker Construction	Jonathan Knowles, BKAD

Table B.1 *continued*

Project Name	Location	Architect	Builder	CPHC
Full Plane Residence	Portland, Oregon	Michelle Jeresek, while partner at Departure Architecture, now at Ivon Street Studio	JRA Green Building, Inc.	Eric Storm, James Ray Arnold
Hayfield House*	Bolton, Connecticut	GO Logic	Cooper Lane Builders	David White, Right Environments
Hollis Montessori School	Hollis, New Hampshire	Windy Hill Associates	TMD Construction Services, LLC	ZeroEnergy Design
Jung Haus	Holly, Michigan	GO Logic	Energy Wise Homes	Think Little
Karuna House*	Newberg, Oregon	Holst Architecture	Hammer & Hand	Dylan Lamar, Green Hammer
Lone Fir Residence	Portland, Oregon	Owner	Owner & Green Hammer (core & shell)	Owner
Louisiana Passive House*	Lafayette, Louisiana	Corey Saft	Corey Saft	Katrin Klingenberg, PHIUS
Madrona Passive House*	Seattle, Washington	SHED Architecture & Design	Hammer & Hand	Daniel Whitmore, Hammer & Hand
MARTak Rest/ Work Space	Masonville, Colorado	Andrew Michler, Baosol	John Parr, Parr Custom Builders Inc.	Andrew Michler, Baosol
Midorihaus	Santa Cruz, California	Essential Habitat Architecture	Santa Cruz Green Builders	Graham Irwin, Essential Habitat Architecture
New York Street Passive House	Lawrence, Kansas	Studio 804	Studio 804	Studio 804
Orchard Street House	Eugene, Oregon	STUDIO-E Architecture	EcoBuilding Collaborative of Oregon	Jan Fillinger and Win Swafford
Orchards at Orenco*	Hillsboro, Oregon	Ankrom Moisan Architects, Inc.	Walsh Construction Company	Dylan Lamar, Green Hammer
Portola Valley Passive House	Portola Valley, California	EHDD Architecture	DeSmidt Builders	Graham Irwin, Essential Habitat Architecture
Prescott Passive House*	Kansas City, Kansas	Studio 804	Studio 804	Ryan Abenroth
Project Green Home	Palo Alto, California	Arkin Tilt Architects	Josh Moore, Red Company	Dan Johnson
Pumpkin Ridge Passive House	North Plains, Oregon	Scott | Edwards Architecture	Hammer & Hand	Skylar Swinford, Hammer & Hand
San Juan Passive House*	Shaw Island, Washington	Artisans Group	Artisans Group	Tessa Smith, Artisans Group
Saugerties Residence*	Saugerties, New York	BriggsKnowles Architecture+Design	Bensonwood and John Hommel, Ashley Homes, Inc.	Jonathan Knowles

Table B.1 *continued*

Project Name	Location	Architect	Builder	CPHC
Skidmore House	Portland, Oregon	Jeff Stern, In Situ Architecture	Jeff Stern, In Situ Architecture	Jeff Stern, In Situ Architecture
Specht Residence	Thaxton, Virginia	Adam Cohen	Structures Design/ Build	Adam Cohen
Stellar Apartments Passive House	Eugene, Oregon	Bergsund DeLaney Architecture and Planning	Meili Construction Co.	Win Swafford, Jan Fillinger
Tighthouse Brownstone	Brooklyn, New York	FNA/Fete Nature Architecture, PLLC	WM Dorvillier & Co.	ZeroEnergy Design
Uptown Lofts on Fifth*	Pittsburgh, Pennsylvania	FortyEighty Architecture	Mosites Construction	Kaplan Thompson Architects, Morgan Law
Viridescent Building*	Falmouth, Maine	BRIBURN, Inc.	R&G Bilodeau Carpentry and Electrical	Edward Pais
VOLKsHouse 1.0	Santa Fe, New Mexico	Vahid Mojarrab, WAMO Studio, LLC	Justin Young, August Construction	Graham Irwin, Essential Habitat
Warren Woods Ecological Field Station	Berrien County, Michigan	GO Logic	GO Logic and Ebels Construction	GO Logic
Windy View Passive House	Philomath, Oregon	Concept by Nathan Good Architects; plans by Bilyeu Homes, Inc.	Bilyeu Homes, Inc.	Blake Bilyeu
Zero Cottage	San Francisco, California	David Baker Architects	Falcon Five Design Build, Jon Landon	Prudence Ferreira, Integral Impact

Note: * Chapter 8 case studies

Bibliography

Alexander, C., Ishikawa, S., Silverstein, M., with Jacobsen, M., Fiksdahl-King, I., and Angel, S. 1977. *A Pattern Language: Towns, Buildings, Construction*, Oxford, UK: Oxford University Press.

Architecture2030: http://Architecture 2030.org/2030_challenges/2030-challenge (accessed January 10, 2017).

Canada Mortgage and Housing Corporation. 2005. "Wood-frame Envelopes in the Coastal Climate of British Columbia," www.tboake.com/guides/BC_wood.pdf (accessed January 11, 2017).

Christensen, C., Horowitz, S., Givler, T., Courtney, A., and Barker, G. 2005. "BEopt: Software for Identifying Optimal Building Designs on the Path to Zero Net Energy." Conference Paper Golden, CO: National Renewable Energy Laboratory, NREL/CP-550-37733. ISES 2005 Solar World Congress, Orlando, FL, August 2005.

Fraunhofer Institute for Building Physics. 2016. "What is WUFI?" https://wufi.de/en/software/what-is-wufi/ (accessed January 11, 2017).

Fraunhofer Institute for Building Physics. WUFI® Passive software: https://wufi.de/en/software/wufi-passive/ (accessed January 11, 2017).

International Living Future Institute: http//living-future.org/lbc (accessed January 10, 2017).

Lamar, D., and Everhart, T. (n.d.). "Kitchen Exhaust Ventilation with HRV at Ankeny Row," Northwest Eco-Building Guild, www.ecobuilding.org/code-innovations/case-studies/kitchen-exhaust-by-continuous-ventilation-with-hrv-at-ankeny-row (accessed January 22, 2017).

Lstiburek, Joseph. 2010. "BSI-001: The Perfect Wall." Building Science Corporation, http://buildingscience.com/documents/insights/bsi-001-the-perfect-wall (accessed January 11, 2017).

Passive House Institute United States (PHIUS): www.passivehouse.us/ (accessed January 10, 2017).

Passivhaus Institute (PHI): www.passiv.de/ (accessed January 10, 2017).

PHIUS+ 2015: Passive Building Standard North America: www.phius.org/phius-2015-new-passive-building-standard-summary (accessed January 10, 2017).

Shick, Wayne L., and Rudard A. Jones. 1976. "Illinois and Lo-Cal House, C2.3," *Small Homes Council-Building Research Council*, University of Illinois at Urbana-Champaign, Vol. 1, Number 4, Spring 1976.

TenWolde, A., and M. Bomberg. "Design Tools," Chapter 10, *Moisture Control in Buildings: The Key Factor in Mold Prevention*, 2nd ed. H. Trechsel and M. Bomberg, eds. West Conshohocken, PA: ASTM International, 2009. www.fpl.fs.fed.us/documnts/pdf2009/fpl_2009_tenwolde001.pdf (accessed January 11, 2017).

The Carbon Reality Project: www.climaterealityproject.org/blog/idea-whose-time-has-come-why-net-zero-emissions-way-future (accessed January 10, 2017).

Torcellini, P.A., Pless, S., Deru, M., and Crawley, D.B. 2006. "Zero Energy Buildings: A Critical Look at the Definition," ACEEE Summer Study on Energy Efficiency in Buildings, Pacific Grove, CA, August 2006.

U.S. Department of Energy/National Renewable Energy Laboratory. 2015. *Climate-Specific Passive Building Standards*, prepared by G.S. Wright and K. Klingenberg (PHIUS) and Building Science Corporation. NREL: DE-AC36–08GO28308.

WARM blog. 2012. "10 most common PHPP mistakes," www.peterwarm.co.uk/10-most-common-phpp-mistakes/ October 25, 2012 (accessed January 11, 2017).

West, Cornel. 1993. "An Abiding Sense of History," Wesleyan University, Middletown CT, May 30, 1993.

SELECTED PASSIVE HOUSE PUBLICATIONS AND RESOURCES

Bere, J. 2014. *An Introduction to Passive House*, London: RIBA.

Cotterell, J. 2012. *The Passivhaus Handbook: A Practical Guide to Constructing and Retrofitting Buildings for Ultra-Low Energy Performance (Sustainable Building)*, Cambridge, UK: UIT Cambridge.

Hopfe, C.J., and McLeod, R.S. (eds.). 2015. *Passivhaus Designer's Manual: A Technical Guide to Low and Zero Energy Buildings*, Abingdon, UK: Routledge.

Ibo Österreichisches Institut für Baubiologie und Bauökologie (ed.). 2016. *Details for Passive Houses: Renovation: A Catalogue of Ecologically Rated Constructions for Renovations*, Basel: Birkhauser.

James, M. 2010. *Recreating the American Home: The Passive House Approach*, Low Carbon Productions.

James, M., and James, B. 2016. *Passive House in Different Climates: The Path to Net Zero*, New York and Abingdon, UK: Routledge.

Klingenberg, K., Kernagis, M., and James. M. 2009. *Homes for a Changing Climate: Passive Houses in the United State*s, White River Junction, VT: Chelsea Green.

Maclay, B. 2014. *The New Net Zero: Leading-Edge Design and Construction of Homes and Buildings for a Renewable Energy Future*, White River Junction, VT: Chelsea Green.

Moskovitz, J.T. 2013. *The Greenest Home: Superinsulated and Passive Design*, New York: Princeton Architectural Press.

Pokorny, W. (ed.). 2009. *Passivhaus-Bauteilkatalog: Ökologisch bewertete Konstruktionen [Details for Passive Houses: A Catalogue of Ecologically Rated Constructions]*, Vienna: Springer Vienna Architecture.

Roberto, G., and Vallentin, R. 2014. *Passive House Design: A Compendium for Architects*, Munich: Detail Green Books.

van Ufflelen, C. 2012. *Passive Houses: Energy Efficient Homes*, Salenstein, Switzerland: Braun.

Index

affordable housing *see* Orchards at Orenco; Stellar Apartments
airtight construction 42–47, 62–63, 108–109, 134–135
Alexander, Christopher, *A Pattern Language* 7
American Society of Heating, Refrigerating and Air-Conditioning Engineers (ASHRAE) x
Ankeny Row Net Zero Community, Portland, Oregon 21, 73, 114, 122–135
apartments *see* multifamily housing
Architecture 2030 Challenge 1
Arlington House, Arlington, Virginia 54, 58–59
Artisans Group (architects and builders) 255
Ashley Homes, Inc. (builders) 267
August Construction 24, 80

Balance Project, Santa Fe, New Mexico 40–41
balconies 50–51, 134–135
balloon framing 26–27, 42–43, 56–57
Baosol (architects) 66
basements 12, 30–35, 216–219, 244–245
Bayside Anchor, Portland, Maine 54, 94, 104–105
Bensonwood (builders) 267
Bergsund DeLaney Architecture and Planning 38, 96
Bilyeu Homes, Inc. (builders) 44, 120
box columns 146–147
brackets 84–85, 134–135
BRIBURN, Inc. (architects) 293
BriggsKnowles Architecture+Design 26, 106, 267
Buck Construction 40
Building Science Corporation 16
building information modelling (BIM) 15

California *see* Midorihaus, Santa Cruz; Portola Valley Passive House, Portola Valley; Project Green Home, Palo Alto; Zero Cottage, San Francisco

casement windows 96–97
case studies 121–305; project information 308–310; *see also* Ankeny Row Net Zero Community; Cowhorn Vineyard House; Earthship Farmstead; Empower-house; Hayfield House; Karuna House; Louisiana Passive House; Madrona Passive House; Orchards at Orenco; Prescott House; San Juan Passive House; Saugerties Residence; Uptown Lofts on Fifth; Viridescent Building
cathedral ceilings 86–87, 182–183
ceilings 74–75; cathedral 86–87, 182–183
cellulose insulation 26–27, 40–41, 74–77
CH2 Passive House, Portland, Oregon 54, 64–65
cladding, wall 12–13, 48–49, 56–57; rainscreen 98–99, 142–143, 288–289
clerestory windows 90–91, 212–213
climate 7–8
CMUs (concrete masonry units) 206–209, 290–291
code requirements 82–83, 113–114
Cohen, Adam (architect) 34
co-housing *see* multifamily housing
Colorado, MARTak Rest/Work Space, Masonville 66–67, 114
commercial offices, Viridescent Building 20, 94, 115, 292–305
concrete masonry units (CMUs) 206–209, 290–291
Connecticut, Hayfield House, Bolton 20, 38, 72, 94, 95, 115, 116, 176–189
Cooper Lane Builders 177
corner windows 106–107, 226–227
Cowhorn Vineyard House, Jacksonville, Oregon 21, 73, 136–147
crawl space 44–45, 206–207
curtain walls 60–61, 98–99, 304–305

David Baker Architects 90
decks 130–133, 200–201, 220–225, 238–241, 252–253, 278–279; *see also* terraces

design 1, 5–17; for activities within the house 6–7; for complete system performance 8–10; components 10–14; development concepts and methods 14–17; site and climate 7–8
DeSmidt Builders 62
doors 92–95; Cowhorn Vineyard House 144–145; Earthship Farmstead 160–161; entry vestibules 300–301; Hayfield House 186–187; Jung Haus 94, 102–103; Madrona Passive House 222–225; pet 120; San Juan Passive House 262–263; screens 110–111; Viridescent Building 300–301; Warren Woods Ecological Field Station 95, 110–111
dormers, shed 88–89
double stud walls 58–59, 104–105
drainage 95–97
duplexes, Empowerhouse 39, 162–175

Earth Advantage Certification 28, 96
Earthship Farmstead, Stuart, Virginia 21, 73, 94, 148–161
Ebels Construction 68, 110
EcoBuilding Collaborative of Oregon 50, 84
EHDD Architecture 62
electrical openings 113–120
Empowerhouse, Washington, D.C. 39, 162–175
energy modeling 14–15
energy recovery ventilators (ERV) 104
Energy Wise Homes (builders) 32, 102
entry vestibules 300–301
EPS (expanded polystyrene) insulation 22–25, 40–46, 149–150, 178–179, 192–193, 293–295
Essential Habitat Architecture 46, 74

Falcon Five Design Build 90
Fete Nature Architecture 108
Fillinger, Jan (architect) 30, 137
Fineline House, Ashland, Oregon 21, 30–31

fireplaces 113, 119

floors 12, 37–39; Balance Project 40–41; Cowhorn Vineyard House 138–139; Karuna House 39, 48–49; Madrona Passive House 218–219; Midorihaus 38, 46–47; Orchard Street House 39, 50–51; Prescott House 246–247; Skidmore House 38, 42–43; Windy View Passive House 38, 44–45; see also decks

Forest Stewardship Council (FSC) 60, 98, 255, 293

FortyEighty Architecture 281

foundations 12, 19–21; Ankeny Row Net Zero Community 124–125; Earthship Farmstead 150–151; Fineline House 21, 30–31; Freeman House 21, 26–27; Hayfield House 178–179; Jung Haus 21, 32–33; Karuna House 192–193; Louisiana Passive House 206–207; Madrona Passive House 216–217; Orchards at Orenco 230–231; Pumpkin Ridge Passive House 20, 22–23; San Juan Passive House 256–257; Saugerties Residence 268–269; Specht Residence 21, 34–35; Stellar Apartments 21, 28–29; Uptown Lofts on Fifth 282–283; Viridescent Building 294–295; VOLKsHouse 1.0 20, 24–25; see also basements

framing 40–41, 62–63, 194–195, 208–209, 218–219; balloon 26–27, 42–43, 56–57; steel 48–49; platform 37, 41, 181

Freeman House, Freeman, Maine 21, 26–27, 54, 94–95, 106–107

Full Plane Residence, Portland, Oregon 21, 60–61, 115

furring strips 56–57

gable roofs 78–79, 84–85

geofoam EPS 22–23

glazing 56–57, 60–63, 66–67

GO Logic (architects and builders) 32, 68, 102, 110, 177

Green Hammer (builders) 30, 82, 98, 123, 137

Habitat for Humanity (builders) 163

Hammer & Hand Inc. (builders) 22, 48, 86, 100, 191, 215

Hawthorne, Robert (architect) 64

Hayfield House 184–187

Hayfield House, Bolton, Connecticut 20, 38, 72, 94, 95, 115, 116, 176–189

heat recovery ventilation (HRV) 42–44, 64–65, 108–109, 116, 119

high-density insulation 58–60, 86–87

Hollis Montessori School, Hollis, New Hampshire 71, 76–77

Holst Architecture 48, 191

Hommel, John (builder) 267

HRV (heat recovery ventilation) 42–44, 64–65, 108–109, 116, 119

hygrothermal analysis 17

ICFs (insulating concrete forms) 32–33

i-joists 64–65, 102–103

In Situ Architecture 42, 56

insulating concrete forms (ICFs) 32–33

insulation: cellulose 26–27, 40–41, 74–77; expanded polystyrene (EPS) 22–25, 40–46, 149–150, 178–179, 192–193, 293–295; high-density 58–60, 86–87; mineral wool 108–109; over-insulation 14, 94, 95, 135, 185, 227, 261; super-insulation 9–10, 62–63, 76–77

infiltration x, 2, 19, 68, 76, 96

Jeresek, Michelle (architect) 60

JRA Green Building, Inc. 60

Jung Haus, Holly, Michigan 21, 32–33, 94, 102–103

Kansas see New York Street Passive House, Lawrence; Prescott House, Kansas City

Kaplan Thompson Architects 58, 104, 149

Karuna House, Newberg, Oregon 20, 39, 48–49, 94, 190–203

kitchens 264–265

laboratories, Warren Woods Ecological Field Station 54, 68–69, 95, 110–111, 115

Lamar, Dylan (architect) 123

laminated veneer lumber (LVL) 304–305

Landon, Jon (builder) 90

Larsen trusses 40–41, 66–67

Living Building Challenge 1

"Lo Cal" house 9, 14

loft space 78–79

Lone Fir Residence, Portland, Oregon 72, 73, 82–83, 94, 98–99, 115

Louisiana Passive House, Lafayette, Louisiana 20, 73, 204–213

louvers 250–251

Lstiburek, Joseph 16, 55

LVL (laminated veneer lumber) 304–305

Madrona Passive House, Seattle, Washington 20, 38, 94–95, 100–101, 214–227

Maine see Bayside Anchor, Portland; Freeman House, Freeman; Viridescent Building, Falmouth

MARTak Rest/Work Space, Masonville, Colorado 66–67, 114

mechanical openings 113–120

Meili Construction Co. 38, 96

Metro Green (builders) 58

Michigan see Jung Haus, Holly; Warren Woods Ecological Field Station, Berrien County

Michler, Andrew (architect) 66

Midorihaus, Santa Cruz, California 38, 46–47, 71, 74–75

mineral wool insulation 108–109

mixed-use building, Zero Cottage 73, 90–91

modules 164–169

moisture management 16–17; see also ventilation

Mojarrab, Vahid (architect) 24, 80

Moore, Josh (builder) 88

Mosites Construction 281

multifamily housing see Ankeny Row Net Zero Community; Bayside Anchor; Uptown Lofts on Fifth; Stella Apartments

Nathan Good Architects 44

NEEDBASE Inc. (architects) 40

net zero emissions 1

net zero source energy 1

New Hampshire, Hollis Montessori School, Hollis 71, 76–77

New Mexico see Balance Project, Santa Fe; VOLKsHouse 1.0, Santa Fe

New York see Saugerties Residence, Saugerties; Tighthouse Brownstone, Brooklyn

New York Street Passive House, Lawrence, Kansas 72, 73, 78–79

Orchards at Orenco, Hillsboro, Oregon 21, 39, 72, 95, 228–241

Orchard Street House, Eugene, Oregon 39, 50–51, 73, 84–85

Oregon see Ankeny Row New Zero Community, Portland; CH2 Passive House, Portland; Cowhorn Vineyard House, Jacksonville; Fineline House, Ashland; Full Place Residence, Portland; Karuna House, Newberg; Lone Fir Residence, Portland; Orchards at Orenco, Hillsboro; Orchard Street House, Eugene; Pumpkin Ridge Passive House, North Plains; Skidmore House, Portland; Stellar Apartments,

Eugene; Windy View Passive House, Philomath

Parr Custom Builders Inc. 66
passive house building principles 1–3
PDX Living (architects and builders) 64
Pennsylvania, Uptown Lofts on Fifth, Pittsburgh 21, 280–291
"perfect wall" 16, 55, 114–115
pet doors 120
photovoltaic 50, 62, 79, 90, 108, 123, 149, 215, 293
planters 124–125, 282–283
plumbing openings 46–47, 113–120
porches 252–253, 300–301
Portola Valley Passive House, Portola Valley, California 54, 62–63
prefabricated components 34–35, 272–275
prefabricated houses 254–265
Prescott House, Kansas City, Kansas 72, 73, 242–253
Project Green Home, Palo Alto, California 73, 88–89
Pumpkin Ridge Passive House, North Plains, Oregon 20, 22–23, 73, 86–87, 115

quadruple-glazed windows 142–145

rainscreen cladding 98–99, 142–143, 288–289
Rantis, Daryl (architect) 123
Red Company (builders) 88
retaining walls 30–31, 216–219, 256–257
R&G Bilodeau Carpentry and Electrical 293
roofs 13, 71–73; Ankeny Row Net Zero Community 130–133; Cowhorn Vineyard House 140–141, 146–147; Earthship Farmstead 152–159; gable 78–79, 84–85; Hayfield House 182–183, 188–189; Hollis Montessori School 71, 76–77; Lone Fir Residence 72, 73, 82–83, 115; Louisiana Passive House 210–211; Midorihaus 71, 74–75; New York Street Passive House 72, 73, 78–79; Orchards at Orenco 234–235; Orchard Street House 73, 84–85; Prescott House 248–249; Project Green Home 73, 88–89; Pumpkin Ridge Passive House 73, 86–87, 115; San Juan Passive House 260–261; Saugerties Residence 274–275; shed dormers 88–89; skylights 88–89, 108–109; Viridescent Building 296–299; VOLKsHouse 1.0

72, 80–81, 115; Zero Cottage 73, 90–91; see also terraces

Saft, Corey (architect and builder) 205
San Juan Passive House, Shaw Island, Washington 115, 254–265
Santa Cruz Green Builders 46, 74
Saugerties Residence, Saugerties, New York 39, 54, 266–279
schools, Hollis Montessori School 71, 76–77
Scott | Edwards Architecture 22, 86
screens, door 110–111
Sebastian Tooker Construction 26, 106
shading 98–101, 132–133
SHED Architecture & Design 100, 215
SHGC (solar heat gain coefficient) 40, 76
Shick, Wayne 9
shutters 186–187
single-family housing see Arlington House; CH2 Passive House; Cowhorn Vineyard House; Earthship Farmstead; Hayfield House; Fineline House; Freeman House; Full Plane Residence; Jung Haus; Karuna House; Lone Fir Residence; Louisiana Passive House; Madrona Passive House; MARTak Rest/Work Space; Midorihaus; New York Street Passive House; Orchard Street House; Portola Valley Passive House; Prescott House; San Juan Passive House; Saugerties Residence; Skidmore House; Specht Residence; Tighthouse Brownstone; VOLKsHouse 1.0; Windy View Passive House
SIPs (structural insulated panels) 68–69
sites 7–8
Skidmore House, Portland, Oregon 38, 42–43, 53, 54, 56–57
skylights 88–89, 108–109
Soffits 284–285
solar gain 66–69, 110–111
Specht Residence, Thaxton, Virginia 21, 34–35
splayed windows 170–171
stairs 116–117
Stanford, Jonah (architect) 40
"State of the shelf" technologies 104–105
steel framing 48–49
Stellar Apartments, Eugene, Oregon 21, 28–29, 93, 96–97
Stern, Jeff (architect and builder) 42, 56
Straube, John 55
structural insulated panels (SIPs) 68–69
Structures Design/Build 34, 149
Studio 804 (architects and builders) 78, 243

STUDIO-E Architecture 50, 84
super-insulation 9–10, 62–63, 76–77

terraces 48–49, 172–175, 196–197; see also decks
thermal bridge analysis 15–16
Tighthouse Brownstone, Brooklyn, New York 95, 108–109
TMD Construction Services 76
triple-glazed windows 42–43, 58–59, 66–67, 98–99, 102–103, 108–109
trusses 76–77, 86–87, 260–261; Larsen 40–41, 66–67

Uptown Lofts on Fifth, Pittsburgh, Pennsylvania 21, 280–291

vapor retarder 16, 72, 79, 104, 105, 127, 139, 231, 235, 237, 239, 241
ventilation 6, 8, 13, 117–118, 154–155, 182–183, 256–257
Virginia see Arlington House, Arlington; Earthship Farmstead, Stuart; Specht Residence, Thaxton
Viridescent Building, Falmouth, Maine 20, 94, 115, 292–305
VOLKsHouse 1.0, Santa Fe, New Mexico 20, 24–25, 72, 80–81, 115

walls 12, 53–55; Ankeny Row Net Zero Community 126–127; Arlington House 54, 58–59; CH2 Passive House 54, 64–65; Cowhorn Vineyard House 146–147; curtain 60–61, 98–99, 304–305; double stud 58–59, 104–105; Freeman House 26–27; Full Plane Residence 60–61; Hayfield House 180–181; Louisiana Passive House 208–209; MARTak Rest/Work Space 66–67, 114; Orchards at Orenco 232–233; "perfect" 16, 55, 114–115; Portola Valley Passive House 54, 62–63; San Juan Passive House 258–259; Saugerties Residence 270–273; Skidmore House 53, 54, 56–57; Uptown Lofts on Fifth 284–287; Viridescent Building 302–305; Warren Woods Ecological Field Station 54, 68–69, 115; see also cladding; retaining walls
Walsh Construction Company 229
WAMO Studio (architects) 24, 80
Warren Woods Ecological Field Station, Berrien County, Michigan 54, 68–69, 95, 110–111, 115
Washington, D.C., Empowerhouse 39, 162–175

Washington State *see* Madrona Passive House, Seattle; San Juan Passive House, Shaw Island
water collection systems 60–61; *see also* planters
water resistive barrier (WRB) 17
windows 13–14, 92–95; Ankeny Row Net Zero Community 128–129; Bayside Anchor 54, 94, 104–105; casement 96–97; clerestory 90–91, 212–213; corner 106–107, 226–227; Cowhorn Vineyard House 142–143; Earthship Farmstead 150–153, 158–161; Empowerhouse 170–171; Freeman House 54, 94–95, 106–107; glazing 56–57, 60–63, 66–67; Jung Haus 94, 102–103; Karuna House 198–199, 202–203; Lone Fir Residence 94, 98–99; Louisiana Passive House 212–213; louvers 250–251; Madrona Passive House 94, 95, 100–101, 226–227; Orchards at Orenco 236–237; Prescott House 250–251; quadruple-glazed 142–145; San Juan Passive House 262–263; Saugerties Residence 276–277; shutters 186–187; skylights 88–89, 108–109; splayed 170–171; Stellar Apartments 93, 96–97; Tighthouse Brownstone 95, 108–109; triple-glazed 42–43, 58–59, 66–67, 98–99, 102–103, 108–109; Uptown Lofts on Fifth 288–291;

Warren Woods Ecological Field Station 95, 110–111
Windy Hill Associates (architects) 76
Windy View Passive House, Philomath, Oregon 38, 44–45, 115
WM Dorvillier & Co. (builders) 108
woodstoves 119
Wright, Frank Lloyd 8, 72, 73
Wright-Ryan Construction 104
WUFI®Passive (software) 14, 15, 17

Young, Justin (builder) 24, 80

Zero Cottage, San Francisco, California 73, 90–91